HOW GOD
WILL SAVE
THE WORLD

TODD DIXON MD

DIXON
PUBLISHING
COMPANY

How God Will Save the World

Todd Dixon MD

ISBN: 0963649515
ISBN 9780963649515
Library of Congress Control Number: 2017908437
Dixon Publishing Company, Albuquerque, NM

Printed in the United States of America

In memory of

My daughter Michelle
My brother Jerry, a true adventurer

TABLE OF CONTENTS

CHAPTER 1

THE GATHERING STORM

THERE IS A growing apprehension in the world and concern about how safe our world is. Our anxieties and fears are growing and making more people uneasy. Many are wondering what is making them nervous, but they cannot put their finger on it. People sense our world unraveling, coming apart, no longer working and it does not seem to make sense anymore.

I remember being seven years old and walking miles to school without a second thought of whether it was safe. I remember a world that was safer. People are sensing more places where it is not safe to go. School and public shootings are increasing. Newtown was a disturbing reminder of where we are going. Grade school children in the pristine, ideal suburb of Connecticut were gunned down in the beginning of their young lives. Many Americans believed it could not happen to them, but no matter how much money one has or how safe the neighborhood, there is no longer a safe haven.

Wars are a daily event, and ISIL (ISIS) and the terrorists are not going away. Prisoner beheadings and being burned alive is being shown on the nightly news. Christians are being taken prisoners for ransom, brutal murder and sex slavery. Terrorism has come to the American soil. The war in the Middle East is not over and is leading toward the next world war.

Why was there such an uproar in Ferguson, Missouri? A shooting of anyone's child is a tragedy and should be mourned. I don't want to see any parent bury their child, but much worse has happened. Great injustices by police and those in authority have happened before and will happen again. Why did Ferguson, Missouri erupt into protests across America? Ferguson is only a symptom of civil unrest.

There are more frequent and severe tornados and hurricanes. There are more earthquakes, volcanoes, floods, landslides, droughts and climate change. AIDS is a worldwide pandemic that affects every country and all mankind. The death toll of the AIDS pandemic stands at 78 million infected and 39 million deaths. Why did Ebola spark such fear? It is a virus for which there is no antibiotic to kill the virus.

The United States government knows much more about looming disasters than they are telling us. What is more important, we already know what is about to happen; it is written on our soul. There are some of us that are aware of what is coming and many that are becoming aware. There are disasters coming that are exactly what the prophets and enlightened ones have been telling us would happen. You are not going to have to ask your advisor, your psychiatrist, mother or father, state representative, bishop or priest; your soul knows what is about to happen.

What is taking place is the ultimate battle of good and evil, being played out on the world stage and in society. Just as there is a Christ ruling over the light, there is a dark Lord ruling over his kingdom of darkness. The ultimate battle is taking place.

DARK STORM

There is a growing mist that is hardly noticeable, hardly perceivable at first. It comes and grows so slowly, that we don't see how large it has become. Week by week, year by year the mist grows, and clouds grow darker. There are dark clouds gathering and a storm approaching. The meteorologists (many spiritual leaders and some scientists) have warned us that this terrible storm will eventually happen, not knowing the exact timing of its arrival. Not much heed is paid to the warnings of the meteorologists. Most believe the storm could not be that bad or dangerous. We have never had a storm in the history of the earth that is going to be this fierce, dangerous, destructive and will take so many lives. Never have we had a storm that could destroy all life and everything we know and love.

Most that are preparing for the storm do not really know how intense, ferocious and deadly the storm will be. It will grow in intensity and size and many will think it will subside, but it won't. People will try and find shelter, but can't. They will try and get accurate information where the storm will hit, where to evacuate to but will be confused, just as the reporters and those who are in authority are confused.

It is biblical prophecy that in the last days, mankind will be on the verge of total annihilation. Mankind and all life is teetering on the brink of disaster, where mankind and all life can end. The world is looking for a leader, group or nation that is going to save us. They are looking for something or someone who will right the world, restore order, rid us of evil and bring about peace and prosperity. Will it be the president of the United States, the western allies, Warren Buffet, the next Mother Theresa or Gandhi, or a brilliant invention? If there is not divine intervention, then all mankind and all life will soon end. Do not look for the president to save us, it will be God that saves the world.

This book is designed to help you understand what is about to happen and why. Those who understand and prepare will weather the storm, however, those who do not understand and do not prepare will not do well with the coming challenges.

CHAPTER 2

————— § —————

PROPHETS, SEERS, ORACLES, PROPHECY AND REVELATION

PROPHETS, SEERS, AND oracles have existed for a long, long time. Prophets, seers and those who are given the gift of prophecy and revelation exist today. There are many gifts of God, which are termed gifts of the Holy Ghost in Christian religions. Some of them are healing by the laying on of hands, tongues, prophecy, working of miracles, knowledge, wisdom, revelation and the ability to see past, present and future events. This list is by no means exclusive, for there are many gifts. The gifts of God are the powers of God.

PROPHECY

Prophecy is a future event that is meant to be and has God's power and will behind it to bring about this event. Stated another way, prophecy is truth about the future with God's will behind it. Examples of prophecy were the prophets foretelling the coming Messiah, the birth of the Christ, the signs of his birth and the fall of Babylon. There are prophecies about the latter days and some examples are earthquakes, fierce storms, volcanoes, wars, famine and plagues. A common misconception is that prophecy is fixed. Just as future events can be changed through our free will and our choices so can prophecy be changed. **Prophecy is not fixed.** There is one source of all truth, just as there is another source of all lies. **All truth and all true prophecy has one source and that is the one God.**

There is church prophecy and there is personal prophecy. Maybe you were meant to go into politics, and this is part of the divine plan. This will have God's will and power behind it, so going into politics will come true. This is an example of personal prophecy. Someone in your church could be given the gift of prophecy, and from time to time speak prophecy. Prophecy is a gift of God and although I love Christ and I am a follower of Christ, the gift of prophecy is not exclusive to those who are Jewish or Christian. It is a gift of God for anyone who is worthy and will use it to help their fellow man. There have been many cultures and people who have had those in their society who had been given the gift of prophecy and used it wisely to serve their fellow man

REVELATION

Revelation is a revealing of God's word, knowledge, divine truth and His kingdom. There is another common misbelief that revelation may have existed back in the days of the Old and New Testaments but it does not exist today. God is a God of revelation; past, present and future. Prophets can have revelation, but so can you. Revelation is for any of God's children; it is your birthright! Everything that you need to know, God can show you and this is called personal revelation. Revelation was not meant for a few prophets, but for every one of us. God can reveal which direction you should go in life, who you should marry and which group of people you should go into business with. Lead you to friends that love you for who you are, and not because of what you own. Lead you to the one who will bring you happiness. Lead you to a vocation that will bring fulfillment in your life.

All the great, inspirational scientific breakthroughs came from God. They were a revelation given by the One who created us all and knows all. The great scientific breakthroughs of Sir Isaac Newton and Einstein were not a simple analytical deduction of their brain, but enlightened thoughts coming to their minds from the creator. For those of you who are technology savvy, this can be thought of as information downloaded from the master computer (God) to the individual computers (minds) of Sir Isaac Newton and Einstein. Every great truth and even the small ones come from one source and that is God. Thomas Edison called his work 1% inspiration and 99 % perspiration. True inspiration is revelation from God, for all great thoughts and inspiration come from the same source. Sir Isaac Newton's Law of Gravity, Einstein's Law of Relativity, the teachings of Christ and Buddha all come from the same source. True inspiration is revelation, for we are connected to all that is and God.

A classic example of scientific revelation was from a chemist who discovered the structure of cyclohexane. This chemist knew the number of carbon molecules in a molecule we now know as cyclohexane but was trying to visualize its shape. After days of thinking, pondering this chemist fell into a dream. In this dream, he saw a snake and to his amazement he saw the snake turn around and bite his own tail. The chemist woke up and eureka, he had scientific revelation. This scientist was shown the structure of the molecule we now know as cyclohexane. His statement to his scientific colleagues was "Let us learn to dream, my friends, in making our scientific discoveries." This implies, let us learn how God reveals His secrets of the universe.

SEERS
Seers are people who have been given a gift of God, which allows them to be able to see past, present and future events. Many of the prophets had this gift and could see future events before they happened. The most poignant example of a seer is Saint John the divine who saw these times that we live in and wrote what he saw. Some of his visions were literal, while some were symbolic.

One of the most famous seers is Nostradamus. Nostradamus was given this gift from God and used it wisely. He could see past, present and future events and recorded what he saw. If a seer sees something this does that mean it will come to pass. Mankind was given free will and because we have free will, the future is not fixed. Just because Nostradamus saw something in the future does not mean it will come true. Edgar Cayce was also a seer, although less well known than Nostradamus, and like Nostradamus used his gift wisely. Edgar Cayce and Nostradamus not only had the gift of being able to see past, present and future events but they had been given the gift of prophecy. It is unfortunate that these good men, who were given gifts of God, would be given a name that would mislead people. Both Nostradamus and Edgar Cayce have been called prophets by many who have read their writings. They were not prophets. I heard some call Nostradamus the greatest prophet ever. I believe Nostradamus was a humble, good physician and if he heard someone today call him the greatest prophet ever he would shudder and turn in his grave.

PROPHETS

A true prophet is a seer, communicates with God, is the mouthpiece of the Eternal Supreme Being, and has been given the gifts of prophecy and revelation. Even though someone in your church may be given the gift of prophecy, this does not make them a prophet. One of my favorite teachers had been given the gift of prophecy and would from time to time speak prophecy. Although he was given the gift of prophecy and would occasionally speak prophecy, he was not a prophet. Even if someone has been given the gift to see past, present and future events, this does not make them a prophet. A true prophet is called by God to do God's work; it is a rare and sacred calling and should be treated with the utmost love and respect. I will talk about true and false prophets later in this book.

There are some that teach that there were prophets of the Old Testament, but they believe that was only in the past and there are no more prophets. This is untrue. True prophets are on this earth at this very moment, for the two prophets prophesied in Revelation are currently in the Middle East.

ORACLE

One of the names used to describe a priest or priestess who could communicate with the higher power, speak prophecy and was given the gift of revelation was called an oracle. There are some famous oracles in ancient times who have been put into the history books. There are many more who could communicate with God and speak prophecy, called by other names in different cultures.

FALSE PRIESTS

I have written an entire chapter on false prophets, false Christs and false churches, but there are also false priests. Throughout time there have been people and cultures that have worshiped the one God and had true priests and who served God and the people. These priests could be given the gift of prophecy and other gifts of God. There have been many cultures and people who worshiped false Gods and idols and had false priests. These priests served themselves and those with political power and had the appearance of having the gift of prophecy but did not. Anyone who claims to be given God's authority, the gift of prophecy or any of the other gifts of God and does not have these gifts, is a false priest. There are even those true priests who had been given the gift of prophecy and other gifts of God, and ultimately abused these powers. These gifts of God are to be used to serve our fellow man and not to serve themselves or the few that have political power. To abuse the gifts of God carries a heavy penalty and debt. God will take away the gifts if they are abused.

CHAPTER 3

§

SIGNS OF THE TIMES

Luke 21:31- *So also, when you see these things taking place, you know that the kingdom of God is near.*

Matthew 16:1-3- *The Pharisees also with the Sadducees came, and tempting desired him that he would show them a sign from heaven. He answered and said unto them, When it is evening, ye say, It will be fair weather: for the sky is red. And in the morning, it will be foul weather today: for the sky is red and lowering, O ye hypocrites, ye can discern the face of the sky; but can ye not discern the signs of the times?*

Matthew 2:1-12- *After Jesus was born in Bethlehem in Judea, during the time of King Herod, Magi from the east came to Jerusalem and asked, "Where is the one who has been born king of the Jews? We saw his star in the east and have come to worship him." After they had heard the king, they went on their way, and the star they had seen in the east went ahead of them until it stopped over the place where the child was. When they saw the star, they were overjoyed.*

Doctrine and Covenants 45:37-38- *Ye look and behold the fig trees, and ye see them with your eyes, and ye say when they begin to shoot forth, and their leaves are yet tender, that summer is now nigh at hand; Even so it shall be in that day when they shall see all these things, then shall they know that the hour is nigh.*

A WELL-QUALIFIED PHYSICIAN will not wait until every sign and symptom of a disease is present to make a diagnosis and start treating the disease. The physician will hopefully make an early diagnosis of the disease so that treatment can be started early for a better prognosis for the patient. The same is true in looking for the signs for the end of the world as we know it and the Second Coming of Christ. Hopefully you will know early enough to know what is happening and why. This will help you take care of yourself and your family. This also means your extended family, for the brotherhood of man is all in the same boat.

In the same way, some of the signs have already started. There will be those scientists who say, "Don't worry about what is happening. This has all happened before. It is just a natural variation and cycle that happens in nature." Well, natural cycles do occur in nature. That is the way of the world and our environment, however, what is about to happen is not just another natural cycle but a prelude of what is to come.

There will be those who say the odd weather and storms will come but it will get better. There will be those that say the earthquakes can increase in size and frequency but then they will abate; unfortunately, the earth changes will not abate. They are being tempered for a while, and for a reason I will explain about in a later chapter, but the earth changes have begun. I am telling you this so you do not have to wait until near the end to understand what is taking place with the earth, mankind and our future.

How does a woman know that she is about to give birth? An obstetrician, a medical doctor that delivers babies, knows that there are certain signs that happen when a mother is about to be to deliver a baby. First, one can usually see by the size of her belly that it is time to get ready to have a child. Next, the pregnant mother will start to have contractions and the contractions will become more frequent. Next, the water will break, or the sac containing amniotic fluid that surrounds the baby will leak and there will be a flowing forth of amniotic fluid from the birth canal. Next, the mother to be will feel a lot of pressure in her lower pelvis as the child begins the descent down the birth canal. All these are signs that a pregnant mother is about to give birth to her child.

The birth of Jesus Christ was prophesied by the prophets. He would come from the line of Abraham, be a descendant of Isaac, from the tribe of Judah, born in Bethlehem and his mother would be a virgin. All these prophecies were fulfilled and there was a new star (Star of Bethlehem) that arose in the sky as a sign of the birth of Christ.

The Bible, New Testament and even the Christ himself gave signs to look for that we may be able to foretell the time of his Second Coming. The Hopi Indians, Native Americans, Mayans, Jewish religion, Muslims, Hindus, and Buddhists all have sacred scripture foretelling the end of the world as we know it. It is not just the Christians who are waiting for prophecy to be fulfilled. Many religions, cultures and people are seeing the fulfillment of prophecies. I will outline prophecies from different religions, cultures and enlightened ones that signal the end of the world as we know it.

What are these signs that we should be eagerly looking for and anticipating? There are many. Some have already occurred, some are currently being fulfilled and some have not yet happened. As each prophecy is fulfilled, it should become clearer to those that have faith, where we are in the history of mankind. It is important to be able to discern the signs of the times. Those who can discern the signs of the times and prepare shall fear less. It is not a time to be feared or dreaded, but a time of eager anticipation. It is a time for completion of the plan of free will, a time when the world shall be renewed into a paradisiacal glory and a time of celebration. We have waited for this, for a long, long time. It is time to go back home. Before we return home to a grand celebration, there are some challenges we need to walk through together. Here are the challenges that are called the signs of the times. Do not let your heart be heavy laden, but lift up your eyes and be happy that your inner most heart's desire is about to be fulfilled. I will do what I can to shed light on these signs.

THE SIGNS THAT HAVE OCCURED

CHAPTER 4

---- § ----

LITERAL RECREATION OF THE STATE OF ISRAEL

Ezekiel 22:19- Therefore thus says the Lord God: Because you have all become dross, therefore, behold, I will gather you into the midst of Jerusalem.

2 Nephi 30-7- And it shall come to pass that the Jews which are scattered also shall begin to believe in Christ; and shall begin to gather in upon the face of the land.

Koran 17:105- And after him We said to the Children of Israel, 'Dwell Ye in the promised land; and when the time of the promise of the Latter Days come, We shall bring you together out of various people.'

Edgar Cayce- In 1932, Cayce advised the Jews to regard the advent of Fascist anti-Semitism in Europe as the time to fulfill the biblical prophecy which foretold that the Jews would return to Israel.

Figure 1- The State of Israel is Born

PERSECUTION OF THE Jews in the late 1800's led to the Zionist movement, which is the returning of the Jewish people to their homeland. At the end of World War I, the British conquered Syria and controlled Palestine and adopted the Balfour Declaration, to establish a home for Jews in Palestine. The Mandate of Palestine allowed increased immigration of Jewish people into Israel and the League of Nations supported the State of Israel in 1922. These policies led to tension between the Arabs and the Jews, and Palestinian sentiment against the State of Israel. There was an illegal mass migration of Jews from various countries into Israel, which could not be controlled. The British Royal Commission recommended a partition in Palestine, and in 1947 the United Nations recommended the creation of two separate states, Palestine and Israel. This led to the Arab-Israeli War and on May 14, 1948, and Israel proclaimed itself an independent nation, recognized by President Harry Truman.

This is fulfillment of the prophecy of the recreation of the State of Israel. I have compassion for the Jewish people for I know the persecution they have endured. They are not alone, for it has been the history of man to persecute his brother because of their beliefs and way of life. The literal recreation of the state of Israel is another stone in the roadway paving the way for the rebirth of the hearts of all men and of our planet.

CHAPTER 5

———— § ————

FALL OF COMMUNISM

Mother Mary (Our Lady of Fatima) - *Spoken to three children July 1917- Russia will be converted, and a certain period of peace will be granted to the world.*

THE SOVIET UNION also known as the Union of Soviet Socialist Republics (USSR) was started in 1917. The USSR expanded to include 17 satellite nations. The fall of the communism was foretold by Mother Mary, our Lady of Fatima, who spoke to three children in July 1917.

The start of the fall of communisms started in Poland. The Poles wanted free trade and established Solidarity, the free trade movement. This was a democratic union for free trade, and eventually led to a democratic social movement. The Solidarity Union strikes made the government recognize its union and Solidarity became more popular in Poland. In 1985 Mikhail Gorbachev came to power and the Brezhnev Doctrine, to preserve the Soviet Union with military force, was abandoned. Mikhail Gorbachev encouraged the satellite block nations to win popular support for communism. In 1989, Poland held elections and Solidarity won a majority of the Senate seats and a non-communist Prime Minister. The Solidarity movement's Lech Walesa was elected president one year later; the first democratically elected president in the Soviet Bloc. This encouraged East Germans who also wanted political reforms, and soon the East and West Germans were allowed to cross their border. November 9, 1989 will be remembered in the history books with the fall of the Berlin Wall.

It was the Berlin Wall that was symbolic of the cold war and dividing the free world from the world of communism. One by one the Soviet Bloc nations fell and receded from the Soviet Union. The dissolution of the Soviet Union followed and fulfillment of Mother Mary's prophecy of the fall of communism.

Figure 2 - Germans celebrating the fall of the Berlin Wall on November 10, 1989. (Photo by Lear 21 wikipedia.org)

CHAPTER 6

—— § ——

WARS AND RUMORS OF WAR, BROTHER AGAINST BROTHER AND NATION AGAINST NATION

Matthew 24:6-7- *And ye shall hear of wars and rumors of wars: see that ye be not troubled: for all these things must come to pass, but the end is not yet. For nation shall rise against nation, and kingdom against kingdom:*

Luke 21:9-10- *But when ye shall hear of wars and commotions, be not terrified: for these things must first come to pass; but the end is not by and by. Then said he unto them, Nations shall rise against nation, and kingdom against kingdom:*

Doctrine and Covenants 1:35- *The hour is not yet, but is nigh at hand, when peace shall be taken from the earth, and the devil shall have power over his own dominion.*

Koran 80:34-36- *That Day shall a man flee from his own brother, and from his mother and his father, and from his wife and his children.*

Koran 43:67- *Friends on that Day will be foes, one to another - except the Righteous.*

Hopi- *The white man will battle against other people in other lands -- with those who possessed the first light of wisdom.*

Buddhism- *For many centuries, the mystical tradition of Agharti (or, Aghartha) and its ruler, the King of the World, has existed in Tibet and Mongolia. "Men will increasingly neglect their souls. The greatest corruption will reign on earth. Men will become like bloodthirsty animals, thirsting for the blood of their brothers. The crescent [Islam] will become obscured, and its followers will descend into lies and perpetual warfare. The crowns of kings will fall. There will be terrible war between all the earth's peoples; entire nations will die --- hunger, crimes unknown to law, formerly unthinkable to the world. The persecuted will demand the attention of the whole world. The ancient roads will be filled with multitudes going from one place to another. The greatest and most beautiful cities will perish by fire. Families will be dispersed; faith and love will disappear. The world will be emptied."*

Buddhism- *Prophecy of Shambala (Buddhist, BEF 700 CE): -The related prophecy of the idyllic hidden kingdom of Shambhala states that each of its 32 kings will rule for 100 years. "While they reign, conditions in the outside world will deteriorate. Men will fight more and more wars, seek power for its own sake, and materialism will reign. Drought, famine, disease and war will sweep the world... Nation will fight nations, and the larger will devour the smaller."*

Buddhism- *Digha Nikaya iii.71-72, Cakkavatti-Sihanada Suttanta- " keen ill will, keen animosity, passionate thoughts even of killing, in a mother toward her child, in a child toward its mother, in a father toward his child and a child toward its father, in brother to brother, in brother to sister, in sister to brother. Just as a sportsman feels toward game that he sees, so will they feel."*

Hindu- *In the summer of 1983, Guru Bhagwan Rajneesh Chandra broke a 3-1/2-year period of silence to announce the impending end of the* *world. "Man is now living in his most critical moment and it is a crisis of immense dimensions. Either he will die or a new man will be born... There will be wars which are bound to end in nuclear explosions... Tokyo, New York, San Francisco, Los Angeles, Bombay --- all these cities are going to disappear, and the holocaust is going to be global, so no escape is possible."*

PROPHESY FOUND IN the Bible, Koran, sacred texts, Hopi religion and spoken by enlightened ones from the world's religions foretell a time when there would be war and rumors of war, brother against brother and nation against nation. As you turn on the world news at night it has become very evident that this prophecy has been fulfilled. Throughout the world there is war. World governments try to contain the wars, but they cannot be contained. One fire is contained and another fire will break out; war is everywhere on our planet. Where there used to be a unity of a nation, there becomes fighting because of beliefs or history. Brother against brother leads to civil war and sometimes creation of new nations within that former nation. This sign has been fulfilled, but will continue.

What is the cause of wars, brother against brother and nation against nation? This is due to the unleashing of darkness that you are seeing the fruition of the plan of darkness; war and discord among the brotherhood of man. One of the greatest weapons available to darkness is deception and the wolf in sheep's clothing. It is the plan of darkness to divide and conquer. It is unleashed darkness in the hearts of men that stirs up anger and hatred, and causes them to see their fellow men as the enemy. Have mankind fight amongst themselves and they will destroy themselves. The great military minds know the strength of this plan and it has been used successfully throughout the history of mankind. If you want to conquer a nation, first divide and then conquer.

CHAPTER 7

---- § ----

GREAT POLLUTIONS UPON THE FACE OF THE EARTH

Mormon 8:26-41- Yea, it shall come in a day when there shall be great pollutions upon the face of the earth.

Koran 30:42-Corruption has spread on land and sea because of what men's hands have wrought.

Hopi- This is the Seventh Sign: You will hear of the sea turning black, and many living things dying because of it.

North American: Anishinaabe-Ojibwe- "The Seven Fires" -The Seventh Prophet was younger than the others who had come and there was a glowing light from his eyes. He said that there would come a time when the waters had been so poisoned that the animals and plants that lived there would fall sick and begin to die. Much of the forests and prairies would be gone so the air would begin to lose the power of life.

Figure 3- Pollution (Photo by Frank John Aleksandrowicz)

THE FOLLOWING FACTS ARE TAKEN FROM DO SOMETHING.ORG

- *40% of America's rivers and 46% of America's lakes are too polluted for fishing, swimming, or aquatic life.*
- *The Mississippi River, which drains the lands of nearly 40% of the continental United States, carries an estimated 1.5 million metric tons of nitrogen pollution into the Gulf of Mexico each year. The resulting dead zone in the Gulf each summer is about the size of Massachusetts.*
- *1.2 trillion gallons of untreated sewage, storm water, and industrial waste are discharged into U.S. waters annually.*
- *Polluted drinking waters are a problem for about half of the world's population. Each year there are about 250 million cases of water-based diseases, resulting in roughly 5 to 10 million deaths.*
- *Vehicle exhaust contributes roughly 60% of all carbon monoxide emissions nationwide, and up to 95% in cities.*
- *Large hog farms emit hydrogen sulfide, a gas that most often causes flu-like symptoms in humans, but at high concentrations can lead to brain damage.*
- *Each year, U.S. factories spew 3 million tons of toxic chemicals into the air, land, and water.*
- *In the U.S. 41% of all insecticides are used on corn. Of these, 80% are used to treat a pest that could be controlled simply by rotating a different crop for just one year.*
- *Every year, one American produces over 3,285 pounds of hazardous waste.*
- *Over 80% of items in landfills can be recycled, but they're not.*
- *Americans generate 30 billion foam cups, 220 million tires, and 1.8 billion disposable diapers every year.*

THE FOLLOWING FACTS ARE FROM CLEANAIRSYS.COM

- *During winter months, 49 percent of soot and other particle pollution in Sacramento is caused by burning wood in fireplaces and wood stoves.*
- *According to the World Health Organization, if you are one of the 18 million residents of Cairo, then breathing daily air pollution is like smoking 20 cigarettes a day, which is over 20 times the acceptable level of air pollution each day.*
- *The World Bank reported in 2002 that pollution causes 2.42 billion dollars of damage to the Egyptian environment annually, equaling about 5 percent of the country's annual gross domestic product.*
- *The risk of cancer from breathing diesel exhaust is about ten times more than ingesting all other toxic air pollutants combined, with diesel emissions contributing to over 70% of the cancer risk from air pollution in the USA. – reported by Environmental Defense*
- *According to the US-EPA, emissions from power plants contribute to over 2,800 lung cancer deaths and 38,200 heart attacks annually in the US.*

THE INDUSTRIAL REVOLUTION has brought many great inventions and advancements for all mankind, but it has come at a great cost. The price of progress can be measured not only by the products we produce but the quality of the environment that we live in. The facts about pollution that have been mentioned above, is but a drop in the bucket of the vast scope of pollution that we are producing.

Figure 4- Picture of Planet Earth (Image by NASA/MODIS/USGS)

One of our astronauts looked upon our earth from the distance of the moon, and finally he realized what a fragile precious planet we live on. God, not mankind, created this planet, and he charged us to take care and be good stewards of the earth. As much as I love science, inventions and even progress, man has not been a good steward of planet earth. The prophecy of great pollutions upon the face of the earth has been fulfilled.

CHAPTER 8

————— ◊ —————

PEOPLE SHALL GO TO AND FRO AND AN INCREASE IN KNOWLEDGE

Daniel 12:4- many shall run to and fro, and knowledge shall be increased.

Koran 81:5- And when the she-camels, ten months pregnant are abandoned.

Koran 16:9- And He has created horses and mules and asses that you may ride them, and as a source of beauty. And He will create what you do not yet know.

Koran 81:8- And when various people are brought together.

Koran 51:8- And by the heaven full of tracks.

TRAVEL

I REMEMBER MY medical training in New York City. In the morning, I could be in my New York City apartment in the heart of winter in the freezing, bitter cold month of January. Walking on the streets of New York City was at times harsh with the cold wind that seemed to pierce right through my winter clothing. I could walk a few blocks to catch a subway, fly directly to a beach in the Caribbean and be walking the beaches of a tropical island with white sands and balmy 80-degree weather that same day. I was amazed. These are the modern-day miracles prophesied in the Bible.

In the past, we were limited to walking, horses and boats as a means of travel. Today with the invention of the automobile, subways, trains, buses, ships, airplanes and jets, we can travel the world as we please. There are plans underway to make travel to earth's outer space affordable to the public. This is the time prophesied in Daniel, Timothy and the Koran with increase of travel.

> *2 Timothy 3:1-7- In the last days, said Paul, men shall be ever learning and never able to come to the knowledge of the truth.*

> *Koran 81:11- And when books are spread abroad.*

> *Hopi-This is the Fifth Sign: The land shall be crisscrossed by a giant spider's web.*

INCREASE IN KNOWLEDGE

Daniel prophesied about an increase in knowledge in the last days. I happen to love knowledge and learning. At times, I will go to a university and walk the campus simply because of the atmosphere of learning. I was fascinated in college to go to the library and see rows and rows of books, with many areas of books and many floors to the library. I would at times just sit in this building and feel the wondrous energy of knowledge and I became a lover of knowledge. I remember Oprah Winfrey talking about one of her most treasured possessions. It was not a mansion on the hill, a yacht in the Mediterranean Sea, a jet that travels the world nor even the most precious jewel; it was her library. What a sight to behold, for Oprah to have all her wondrous books in one room. This was one of her greatest treasures. There has been an explosion of knowledge, starting with the renaissance and the invention of the printing press.

With the invention of the computer and the internet, there has been again an explosion in knowledge. I use the internet often in emails, managing finances, research and to gain information. It is a wondrous tool that has been given us, and again there has been an explosion in knowledge.

This is fulfillment of prophecy of Daniel, Timothy and the Koran. The Hopi prophesied about "land being crisscrossed by a giant spider web," which was initially a web of telegraph and telephone wires and now the World Wide Web. There is a downside to this explosion of knowledge and Paul warned that men shall be ever learning never able to come to the knowledge of truth. Mankind in general is seeking knowledge to get what they want, rather than seeking truth and knowledge to benefit all. Knowledge is a double-edged sword. The correct use of knowledge can serve all mankind; the wrong use of knowledge cannot only hurt, but destroy all mankind. For mankind to progress, he needs to have wisdom. Knowledge is power and as with all power, there needs to be responsibility with the use of that power. The wrong use of power and knowledge has dire consequences. With the explosion of knowledge there has not been a proportionate increase wisdom. Man has the power of knowledge at his fingertips but lacks the wisdom in how to use it correctly.

Never has the information in how to build a nuclear bomb or to make a deadly microorganism that could potentially wipe out mankind existed on the internet, for all to access. This is the time when mankind is on the precipice of a cliff and the outcome is not yet known. Walk in one direction and it will lead to safety, walk in the other and it will be the end of all life and the great plan of free will.

CHAPTER 9

------ § ------

2012

Mayan Priests- *Anthropologists visit the temple sites and read the inscriptions and make up stories about the Maya, but they do not read the signs correctly. It's just their imagination. Other people write about prophecy in the name of the Maya. They say that the world will end in December 2012. The Mayan elders are angry with this. The world will not end. It will be transformed.*

We are no longer in the World of the Fourth Sun, but we are not yet in the World of the Fifth Sun. This is the time in-between, the time of transition. As we pass through transition there is a colossal, global convergence of environmental destruction, social chaos, war, and ongoing Earth Changes.

All was predicted by the mathematical cycles of the Mayan calendars. -- It will change --everything will change. Mayan Day keepers view the Dec. 21, 2012 date as a rebirth, the start of the World of the Fifth Sun. It will be the start of a new era resulting from and signified by the solar meridian crossing the galactic equator and the Earth aligning itself with the center of the galaxy.

AT SUNRISE ON December 21, 2012 for the first time in 26,000 years the sun rises to conjunct the intersection of the Milky Way and the plane of the ecliptic. This cosmic cross is an embodiment of the Sacred Tree, The Tree of Life, a tree remembered in all the world's spiritual traditions.

There have been thousands if not hundreds of thousands of people who have predicted the time of the end of the world or the exact time of the Second Coming of Christ and they have all been wrong. Some of these groups and predictions have been written about. A charismatic leader claims to know the date of the end of the world and gathers a large following. Many of these leaders claim if the followers come with them (the leader) they will be saved. Many have also claimed that as faithful followers they will be taken up into heaven and not have to face the trials and tribulations of the end times. The time they predicted came and went and there was no end of the world and no Second Coming of Christ. The leaders went back to the followers and said, "It was your faith that kept the world from ending." I tell you simply, that this leaders' belief of knowing the exact date of the end of the world was not of God, but of his own ego. Every one of these individuals who predicted the time of the end of the world has been wrong. So, the naysayers will come along, and say "These people have come forth to say the end of the world will occur on a certain day and they have all been wrong. There is no truth in Bible prophecy. The world goes on as it always has; so, eat, drink and be merry."

A change did occur December 2012 and yet there were very few sensitive enough to sense or feel the change that happened. The end of the Mayan calendar signified the end of the fourth world and the beginning of the fifth world as taught and prophesied by Quetzalcoatl. We have finished one chapter in the history of the world and started the next chapter.

We are now living in a transition period in the beginning of the fifth world. The world continues to change and we continue to wake up. The world seems the same and there was nothing dramatically different in November, 2012 compared to January, 2013. The prophecies and the timing of the prophecies are unfolding according to royal command. Even the great Jehovah (Jesus Christ) follows the timing and the authority of the one God.

THE MAYAN CALENDAR

The Mayan calendar is the most accurate calendar known to man. It is a combination of four different calendars. The first is the solar calendar and is like our yearly calendar. It has 365 days, with 18 months of 20 days and then an extra 5 days. The extra 5 days are unlucky ones. The second is a ceremonial calendar of 260 days, corresponding to 9 months of human pregnancy. It has "13 numbers with 20 day signs." This calendar was "intended to unite the heaven with earth and is correlated with astrological alignments." This calendar gives the best dates for marriage, ceremonies and important events. The third calendar was the calendar round and it was the combination of the solar and ceremonial calendars. It takes 52 years to complete a calendar round.

Figure 5- The Mayan Calendar (Photo by George and Audrey DeLange)

The fourth calendar of the Mayan calendar is the long count and it is based on precession, or wobble in the earth's axis. It takes the earth approximately 26,000 years to complete this wobble in the earth's axis.

PRECESSION

We have all been taught that the earth spins on its axis. It is this spin of the earth on its axis that gives us daytime and nighttime. We were typically not taught the earth spinning on its axis, is in a very, very slow wobble. This is easier to understand if you remember the spinning tops we played with as children. If you perfectly spin the top, then the top will be perfectly upright at a 90-degree angle from the floor. After a while the spinning top will develop a noticeable wobble, due to the earth's gravitational pull and slowing of the spin of the top. The axis of the top instead of being straight up and down will tilt and rotate in a circle. The scientific name for this wobble of the earth's axis is called **precession**.

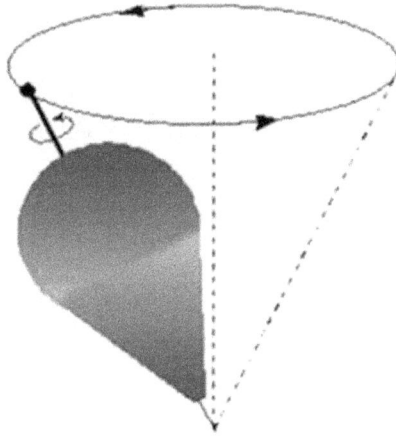

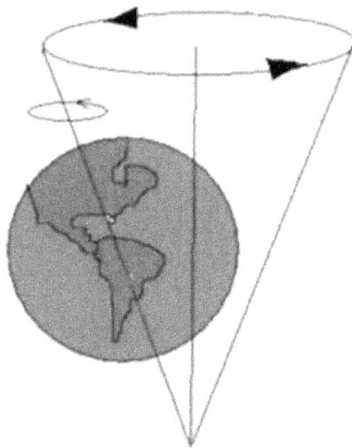

Figure 6- Top- Wobble of Spinning Top (from NASA.gov)

Figure 7- Bottom- Wobble of Spinning Earth

CAUSE OF THE EARTHS'S WOBBLE (PRECESSION)

As was stated before, it is the earth's gravitational pull on the spinning top that causes the top to move from a perfectly upright spinning position to a tilt of the axis of the top. So, it is for the wobble of the earth's axis. If the earth was a perfect sphere, then the spin of the earth on its axis would remain perfectly still and there would be no wobble. The earth is not a perfect sphere, but has a greater diameter from along the equator than it does from North to South Pole. This bulge of the earth at the equator is what causes the wobble, by the gravitational pull of the moon and the sun on the variation of mass distribution of our planet earth.

This wobble of the earth's axis was discovered by the Greek astronomer Hipparchus, by comparing observations made centuries apart. There are many who claim that the ancient Babylonians as well as the ancient Egyptians knew about the precession of the earth. The Mayans also knew about precession.

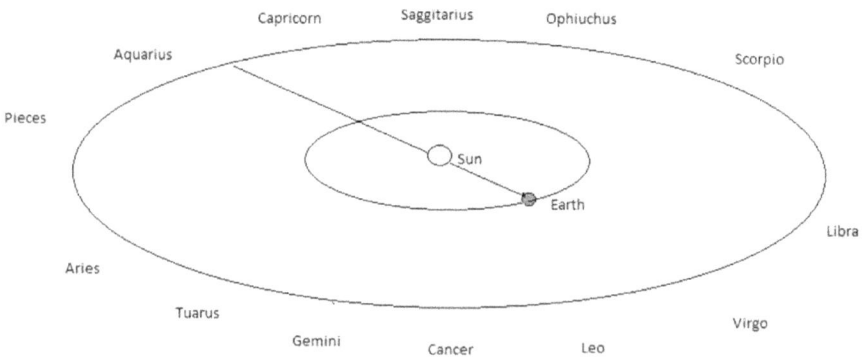

Figure 8- Precession – Earth's Precession Rotating Through Thirteen Constellations

The earth's wobble is so slow that it takes approximately 26,000 years for the earth to make a complete rotation on its axis. Let's see how this would look to the ancient people who looked to the night sky and considered the night sky (heavens) and the celestial bodies to have a major impact on their lives. The axis of the earth is slowly rotating in a 26,000-year wobble through the 13 constellations (see Figure 8). There is a 13th constellation that the earth's axis rotates through, besides the 12 well known constellations that are included in the Zodiac. The 13th constellation is Ophiuchus.

Another way to understand precession is by thinking about the North Star. Polaris is currently called the North Star. It is moderately bright and can be easily seen by the naked eye and it is within ½ degree of the direction of the North Pole as you look at the horizon. Because the earth's axis is in a wobble and very slowly rotating, in 13,000 years the North Star will be in the direction of the South Pole, then after completion of the 26,000-year cycle, the North Star, Polaris, will once again be in the direction of the North Pole. In other words, because of the wobble in the earth's axis, every thousand years we need to pick out a new North Star, that will point in the direction of the North Pole.

SOURCE OF MESSAGES FROM MOTHER MARY AND THIS BOOK

There are different ways for angels and spiritual beings (which I include in the term higher power) to communicate with us. I talk about communication with God in the last chapter of this book, Communication with God. I have not had a visitation, vision, nor apparition of Mother Mary, and the only thing that I have seen is what some would call a mini-vision of Mother Mary. Never the less, Mother Mary has communicated to me and I have clearly felt her presence in writing this book and received her messages. I have had many angels and spiritual beings assist in the writing of this book, and Mother Mary was one of them. The source of the quotes in this book were messages given to me by Mother Mary. There are a few messages in this book by Mother Mary given to Gianna Sullivan and three children in Fatima, Portugal, those messages have Gianna Sullivan's name and Our Lady of Fatima as the source of these messages.

> *Mother Mary- There are thirteen two thousand year periods making up a 26,000-year cycle. We are coming to the end of a 26,000-year cycle.*

> *Mother Mary- Every two thousand years, God sends a great teacher to the earth, Jesus was the last of the great teachers.*

Messages from Mother Mary, "There are 13 two thousand year periods making up a total of 26,000 years." and "Every two thousand years God will send a great teacher to the earth, Jesus was the last of the great teachers." We are coming to the end of a 26,000-year cycle, which coincides with the rebirth of our planet and the Second Coming of Christ.

There is a correlation between the precession of the earth's axis and what was stated by Mother Mary. There are 13 constellations (Figure 8) that the earth's axis will rotate through every 26,000 years. 26,000 years divided by 13 equals 2,000 years. This is God's way of giving us and our ancestors a heavenly marker to know where we are in the cosmic timeline.

THE SACRED CROSS

Figure 9 is a picture of our Milky Way Galaxy with a white haze of billions of stars and a dark band across the center of the galaxy. Figure 10 is a drawing of what we saw in the sky on December 21, 2012. The Milky Way Galaxy is stretching semi-vertical from the upper left to the lower right of figure 10. There is a line in the middle of our Milky Way Galaxy and this is the galactic equator. There is another horizontal dotted line, which is the plane of the path of the planets as they orbit around our sun in our solar and this is called the ecliptic. The X made by the crossing of these two lines, forms the sacred cross, which is symbolic of the tree of life, known in many cultures and religions. The tree

Figure 9- Picture of Our Milky Way Galaxy (Picture by Steve Jurvetson)

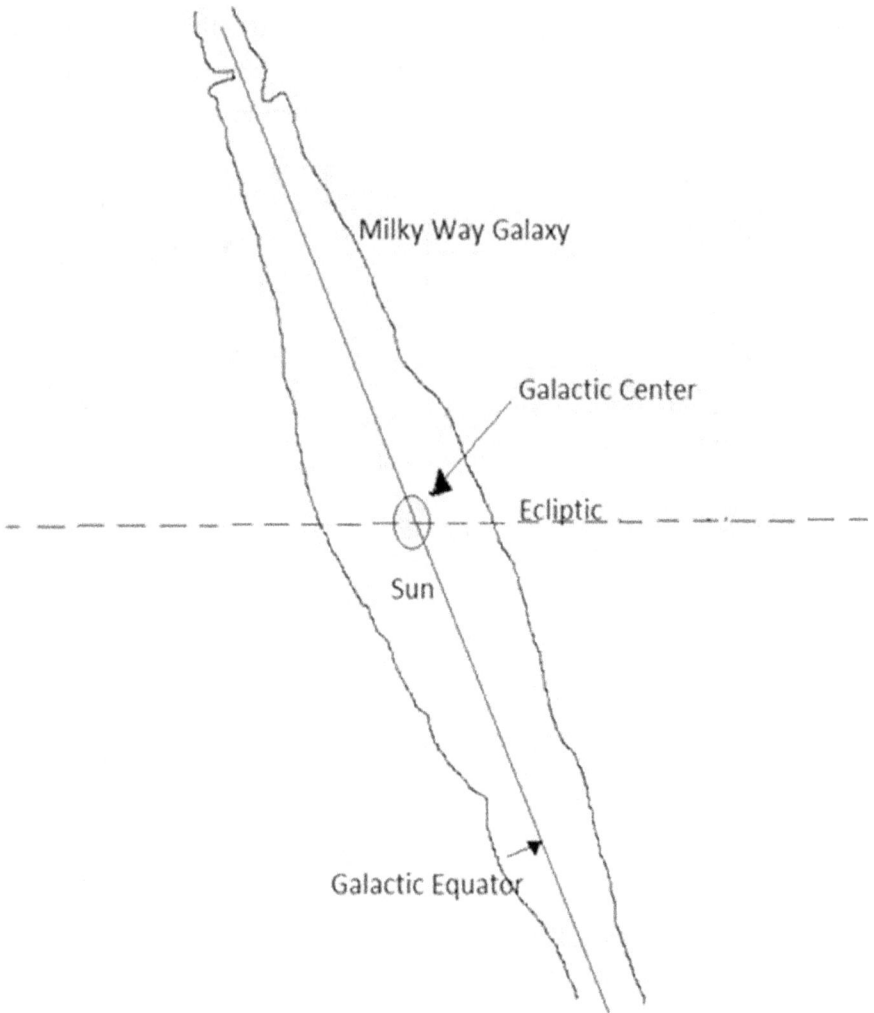

Figure 10- The Sacred Cross

of life is symbolic of God's love and is essential for the health and well-being of all living and non-living things in the universe. Our sun (see Figure 10) on December 21, 2012 was right at the intersection of the lines of the sacred cross.

The Mayan calendar ends on December 21, 2012. The Mayans believed that after 2012, mankind would enter a new age. Why was this date chosen, as the date the Mayans believe will be the end of the world as we know it and what happened on this day? There was a rare intergalactic alignment. On December 21, 2012, the center of the Milky Way Galaxy aligned with the sun and the earth. This is a cosmic heavenly clock which signifies the end of a 26,000-year cycle. What lies at the center of the Milky Way Galaxy is very important and overlooked? Scientists have discovered a super massive black hole in the center of our Milky Way Galaxy. On December 21, 2012, there was an intergalactic alignment between the earth, the sun and a super massive black hole at the center of our Milky Way Galaxy. It is the day of this intergalactic alignment that was, according to the Mayans, the last day of the world as we know it.

SUPERMASSIVE BLACK HOLE

It may surprise you to learn the immense size of our sun. The earth is massive to those who live on the earth, but on a universal scale it is small. Our sun is so large that 1,300,000 earths could fit inside our sun. What may also surprise you is the enormous amount of gravity found on the sun. Current physics states nothing in the known universe travels faster than light, which travels at 186,000 miles per second. How long do you think it would take light to travel from the center of the sun to the surface of the sun? Due to the enormous gravity of the sun it would take light 20,000 years to travel from the center to the surface of the sun. This exceptionally slow speed of light traveling within the sun is due to the sun's enormous gravitational pull.

What is a black hole? As stars (our sun is a star) orbit in the galaxy and the universe they are attracted to each other by their gravitational pull. Eventually they collide with each other to form a bigger star. They in turn attract other stars and plasma (stuff which make up stars). Eventually when they have collided with enough stars and attract enough plasma, their mass becomes so massive, that not even light can escape their immense gravitational field. The term black hole refers to the fact that for a considerable distance (millions of miles?) from the black hole all that can be seen will be darkness, since no light can escape its gravitational pull. Even though black holes have yet to be seen, scientists know they exist by their gravitational effects on nearby stars.

What is a super massive black hole? Black holes also can collide with each other as well as other stars and plasma. When enough black holes, stars and plasma collide and coalesce with each other, they become a super massive black hole. What is the size of a super massive black hole? It may take hundreds of our suns to have enough mass to create a black hole. It may take the mass of 10,000 or more suns to have enough mass to create a super massive black hole. The volume of a super massive black hole (10,000 suns) you would expect to be massive in size, right? Wrong! Once you have that much mass, the distance between protons, electrons and neutrons collapses. The atoms themselves collapse on each other forming an extraordinarily dense super massive black hole. No one knows the size of a super massive black hole, but let us say there is enormous mass in a relatively small space. It is this super massive black hole that is the future doorway for the rebirth mankind, all life and the world into a paradisiacal glory.

Why are black holes and super massive black holes important? There are many reasons why black holes are important but only one of the reasons is of importance to understand why this intergalactic alignment is of such importance to mankind. Scientists have theorized that wormholes exist and are shortcuts to different parts of our universe. According to the higher power, wormholes do exist and provide shortcuts across the universe. Black holes were theorized to exist, and now scientists have proven their existence. Black holes are the universal doorways to the higher dimensions. It is this intergalactic alignment between the earth, the sun and a super massive black hole at the center of our Milky Way Galaxy that is the doorway for mankind's rebirth and the rebirth of our planet into the fifth dimensional plane. Our earth will become a fifth dimensional planet and those of us who survive this adventure to the Second Coming of Christ will become fifth dimensional beings.

THE EGYPTIAN- MAYAN CONNECTION

It is interesting to note the similarities between the Mayans and the Egyptians. Both the Mayans and the Egyptians built pyramids and there is considerable evidence to show the pyramids of the Mayans and the Egyptians were built based on astronomical observations. For example, the correlation of the placement of the pyramids in Egypt correlates with the location of the stars on Orion's belt. Also interesting is that many of the ancient people of the world also saw time as cyclical. Most people and scientists have always thought as time as linear, drawn as a straight line with a beginning and an end. Look at the time line in any book and it will have a starting point and an ending point on a straight line and then all the time in between. The Egyptians, Mayans, and many Buddhists, Hindus and Native Americans would have drawn a circle in their time lines with the starting point and ending point being the same point. They saw history repeating itself and going in a circle and the Mayans believed there was a correlation to the cyclical history of man which was tied to the heavens (stars and celestial bodies).

MAYAN BALL GAME

This was a sacred game played next to the Mayan Temples. This game was played on a field similar to a soccer field. On either end of the field hung two hoops, like basketball hoops, but the hoops were placed so they were vertical and not horizontal. The game the Mayans played has both elements of modern day soccer and basketball. There were two teams and the ball weighed about 7 kg and made of rubber. The ball was to be kept in motion and the players could only use their hips and possibly elbows to keep the ball in motion. The object of the game was to put the ball through the hoop at either end. Depending on which hoop the ball went through, would declare the winning team. Once the ball went through the hoop the ball game was over. At the end of the game there is a ceremony and the heads of the losers were cut off, although some theorize that it was the head of the captain of the winning team whose head was decapitated. If it was the head of the captain of the winning team who was decapitated, this must have been an enormous honor for him and his team.

This was a sacred game of great religious significance to the Mayans for the ball game was full of symbolism. The hoop is symbolic of the center of the Milky Way Galaxy and the ball is symbolic of our sun. As the ball goes through the hoop, this is symbolic of the center of the Milky Way Galaxy aligning with the sun and our earth. As stated before, when the ball goes through the hoop, the ball game is over. This is symbolic of the grand plan of free will, for when there is perfect alignment of the earth, sun and the center of the Milky Way Galaxy, the game is over. All that we have worked so hard for will have come to a close. The alignment of the earth, sun and center of the Milky Way Galaxy was sacred knowledge given to the Mayan people by the great white God, Quetzalcoatl.

FEATHERED SERPENT

Figure 11 is the artwork of the Feathered Serpent who is Quetzalcoatl; Quetzalcoatl means feathered serpent. This is not what this great white God looked like and he did not dress up as a feathered serpent but this art is full of symbolism.

Feathers are worn by Native American Chiefs to symbolize the communication with the Great Spirit and are used in Native American healing to remove unclean spirit and bring in the healing spirit. The serpent is a powerful symbol used in many different cultures but primarily symbolic of rebirth, as the snake sheds its old skin.

Figure 11- Quetzalcoatl- The Feathered Serpent (image from wikipedia.com, Wikipedia Commons)

In the Middle East, the female serpent represents enlightenment and wisdom. Therein is the meaning behind the symbolism of Quetzalcoatl. He represents the bringing in of the spirit of God for the rebirth, spiritual ascension and enlightenment of man.

PAHANA

The Hopi legend of Pahana is the same legend as the Mayan legend of Quetzalcoatl. The Hopis call Pahana the true white brother and that someday in the future Pahana will return. As in Mayan legend he will bring the end of the fourth world and the beginning of the fifth world. He will come wearing red. At his coming the wicked will be destroyed and this will bring a new age of peace. He will not bring religion with him but will bring the power of God.

AWANYU

In the Hopi prophecy of Pahana is symbolized as the Horned Serpent (Figure 12 is petroglyph of Awanyu) and is the equivalent of the Mayan Feathered Serpent. The horns symbolizing the communication and bringing in the spirit of God and the serpent symbolizing the rebirth.

Figure 12- Petroglyph of the Awanyu which is symbolic of Pahana (image from wikipedia.org)

QUETZALCOATL

Quetzalcoatl was a bearded great white God that came from the sky. He appeared in the time period of 400 BC to 600 AD (about the time Christ was on this earth in Israel) and was born of a virgin goddess. The worship of this bearded great white God spread throughout Mesoamerica (central Mexico to Honduras and Nicaragua). He was the inventor of books, the Mayan calendar, giver of corn, arts, science and he was a wise legislator. He was the patron of priests and had the title of the Aztec high priest. He was the symbol of death and resurrection. Quetzalcoatl is the creator sky-god and "represented the forces of good and light pitted against those of evil and darkness." He "organized the original cosmos and participated in the creation and destruction of various world periods. He rules the fifth world and created the humans of that cycle. He went into the underworld and gathered the bones of human beings of previous epochs. Quetzalcoatl sprinkled his blood upon these bones and fashioned thus the humans of the new era, to imbue the bones new life." After giving of teachings, priesthood and sacred knowledge he left but stated he would return someday in the future.

The Mayans and those living on the American continent were taught by Quetzalcoatl that he would return. In 1519, Don Cortes and the Spanish conquistadors landed in Mexico. The Aztecs saw these white men and believed it was the return of the great white God Quetzalcoatl and other gods. The Spanish were treated as Gods and unfortunately the Mayans were conquered resulting in much of their culture and sacred writings being destroyed.

QUETZALCOATYL AND PAHANA

I have seen many shows, media, books, articles and writings all fixated on the date December 21, 2012, a date taken from the Mayan calendar. Most of the media and writings on this subject and this date are based in fear but have served their purpose and have brought awareness to this important date. I have seen an obsession with this date spreading fear to many, while others take this date as the great pearl, great knowledge that will somehow give them power. The date of December 21, 2012 is a sacred date taken from sacred knowledge, but it is a small pearl compared to the source from where this sacred date came. The source for the date December 21, 2012 is the pearl of great worth and value. The source of this sacred knowledge was Quetzalcoatl.

> *John 10:16- And I have other sheep that are not of this fold. I must bring them also, and they will listen to my voice. So there will be one flock, one shepherd.*

Jesus Christ taught that he had other sheep in his flock. He was telling his disciples that he would be leaving them to teach others in the world. Jesus Christ was crucified, but after three days resurrected and brought back to life. After spending time with his apostles, he ascended into heaven. Jesus Christ then descended onto the American continent where he taught, traveled and performed his ministry to those who lived upon the American continent, including the Mayans. He taught inhabitants of the American continent about precession and other sacred knowledge which the Mayans used to make the Mayan calendar. The Book of Mormon is a written record of one of the lost tribes of Israel who traveled to the American continent on a boat. It is a written record of Jesus Christ descending from heaven to the inhabitants of the America, his ministry and his teachings. Jesus Christ is the Mayan's bearded great white God Quetzalcoatl, Hopi's True White Brother Pahana and the Cherokee's Pale One. The sacred knowledge of the end of the Mayan calendar, which is December 21, 2012, comes from Jesus Christ.

THE SOURCE OF ALL TRUTH

Throughout the history of mankind there have come forth great truths. The great scientific truths of Sir Isaac Newton's law of gravity, Einstein's law of relativity and current string theory all come from one source. The great teachings of Jesus Christ and Buddha and even the small day to day truths in the world come from one source and that is God. All truth comes from one source. The source of the date December 21, 2012 came from the Mayan calendar. **This date and sacred knowledge used to make the Mayan calendar was given to the Mayans by Quetzalcoatl. Quetzalcoatl is the great teacher Jesus Christ, and the source of this sacred knowledge is God.**

CHAPTER 10

———— ◊ ————

SPIRIT OF GOD TO FLOOD FORTH

Joel 2:28-29- And it shall come to pass afterward, that I will pour out my spirit upon all flesh; and your sons and your daughters shall prophesy, your old men shall dream dreams, your young men shall see visions: And also upon the servants and upon the handmaids in those days will I pour out my spirit.

Doctrine and Covenants 45:28- *And when the times of the Gentiles is come in, a light shall break forth among them that sit in darkness, and it shall be the fullness of my gospel.*

Dogon tribe in western Africa- *The Return of the Original Visitors- "At this time, a sacred, purifying energy force described as a 'stream' or 'electric light' from Sirius, known as the 'Reorganizer of the World' will cascade down upon the Earth and bring about a new order in the world. For the sons and daughters of the Nommo who are harmoniously in tune with the heavens and earth, this energy will nourish their mind, body and spirit. However, the stream will wash away the corrupt order of Ogo, those who are not in tune with the divine order established by Amma. This cosmic radiation will be like brimstone and fire falling from the sky, burning up the wicked and unrighteous. There will be nowhere to run or hide."*

IT IS PART of the divine plan that the spirit of God shall flood forth in the last days. In order to complete the grand plan of free will there needs to be the ultimate choice. We will all soon need to make the ultimate choice of good or evil, light or darkness, love or fear, God or the world, love of your fellow man or love of the world. To make this final choice two things must happen. The light and spirit of God will need to flood the world and all flesh. Next, darkness will be unleashed. There will be a balance between the two and there will be the two opposing forces very clear for many of us to see. With the two forces at the opposite ends of the spectrum, we must make the biggest decision of our lives and for the grand plan of free will.

There are effects of the flooding forth of God's spirit. The gifts of God that many believe only existed in the days of old shall naturally occur. The gifts of the Holy Ghost are a natural by-product when the spirit of God floods forth and the mind, body, heart and spirit are purified. As the Joel states "your sons and daughters shall prophesy, your old men shall dream dreams, your young men shall see visions." This is not limited to what was written, for all manner of gifts shall come forth. There shall be revelation about God's kingdom, personal revelation, visions, dreams, healings, prophesy and miracles.

I have seen miracles first hand so I never again deny the existence of miracles or God's power. I have also heard of many miracles. If I have heard of miracles, then I know that I am not alone. The miracles are occurring all over the world, in every country, city, religion and culture. They are occurring as a natural by-product of the flooding forth of the spirit of God. As the spirit floods forth, faith will increase and the miracles are the natural by-product of faith.

What is a miracle? Miracles are the divine manifestation of God's love and power. They defy known laws of physics, although many scientists are beginning to understand a new world of physics and physical laws. There are many in a state of unbelief who say, "Maybe in the days of old, possibly Christ might have done something, but we will never know." Christ did perform miracles, but miracles are occurring now and they are a result of the flooding forth of God's spirit. They were not meant to be an extraordinary event, where suddenly the lame can walk when medical science said he would never walk again. Miracles were meant to be a natural event, a natural by-product of God's love. A miracle was not meant to be read about in days long ago for they were meant to be an everyday phenomenon. "See daddy, see Uncle Joe who could not walk and now he can. Do you see God's love in action?" "Susan can now see, when she was told she could never see again. Do you see how much God loves us?" "There was someone about to do great harm, and his heart was opened and he has had a change of heart. Do you see what God's love can do?" These are what we are supposed to be hearing every day. These phrases are being spoken and miracles are manifestations of God's love, light and power. Open your ears and your heart, you will hear of "miracles and rumors of miracles."

CHAPTER 11

MUCH TO BE REVEALED ABOUT GOD'S KINGDOM

IT HAS BEEN said, and taught that it is possible that revelation occurred in the days of old, but revelation is dead. This is not true. God is a God of revelation. There is much that shall be revealed about God's kingdom in the last days. This revelation will come in two forms, personal and for everyone.

Personal revelation was meant to be for everyone. Does a good Father say, "Look I am too busy today, come back and I will try and talk to you in a few years?" Does a good Father say, "How many times have I told you, that if you need to ask me a question, then ask so and so, who will relay the information to my favorite person, who will relay the information to this angel and then that angel and then maybe I will find time in my busy schedule to get back to you?" A good Father makes time for every one of His children; everyone! There is no problem that He does not want to hear about. There is nothing and no situation that He does not care about. It is not that He isn't listening; He is. Some say He doesn't exist, is too busy or the greatest fallacy of all, that He does not want a one on one relationship with each and every one of his children.

This doesn't mean that we are not a community, here to help each other; we are. It doesn't mean we can't counsel and help each other along the way; we should. It doesn't mean that we can't have physicians, financial advisors, friends and family to give us counsel along the way. It does mean that we should go to the One who cares for us above all others, first. It does mean we should trust in Him above all others in the counsel He gives us. God speaks and works through all of us. He has always been there, patiently waiting for us to return. He has always listened, while we were too busy or distracted to listen to Him. There has never been a time when we have needed Him more. There is no question that is beyond Him, is taboo or that He cannot answer. The more you call upon Him and listen, the more you will be amazed at what you will hear. Do not think it must come as a baritone, deep thundering voice. Do not constrain the way or the avenue that God chooses to answer your question and your prayers. It is a matter of putting your trust into the One who loves you more than you will know. The more you trust, the more it will happen. We are helping each other, but in the end, there is only One who has the ultimate knowledge and wisdom to see you through the challenging times ahead.

It means trusting in yourself and trusting in God. You may have a friend who is wise or some friend who you believe to be very spiritual. You might ask them who you should marry. You might ask them which job you should take. All these questions should be directed to the One God. The more you ask, the more you trust, the more you shall receive.

There is also revelation for church, for many or for everyone. This means that God may choose someone who is faithful to give revelation to a group of people or to all those who may benefit. At this very moment, God is sending forth revelation about His kingdom as prophesy is fulfilled. Keep your ears and eyes open.

Now comes one of the greatest attributes needed in the last days and that is discernment. There is a great deal of information coming forth at this very moment. What is the source of this new information? Is it of God, fantasy or of darkness? If you can call upon the God and will listen to what He has to say, He will not lead you astray. He will guide and counsel you at every turn and every decision. There are false priests and wolves in sheep's clothing, who have the appearance of speaking God's word but will lead many astray. One of the greatest weapons in the arsenal of darkness is deception. The ability to sound and look like light and then only to discover later it was darkness. It is your ability of discernment that God wants all His children to have that will help you make the right choice. It is your ability to call upon the Father who will give you any answer and all the discernment you need. Does this mean we should not seek counsel from our elders? No, we should seek counsel from our elders who have wisdom that benefits us all. It does mean trust in God and yourself above all.

Within each man and each woman there exists the Light of Christ. It does not matter of which religion you are, it does not matter if you have issues with God, or whether you are agnostic or atheist. The same light exists in every one of our hearts. This light can help you in discerning what is of God and what is of darkness.

I love my mind and all that education and knowledge has brought me. Be careful with the mind for it can trick you. Your heart is the key to discernment. The more you trust it, the more you purify it, the more you will be able to discern with clarity.

If you read a book or watch a program or hear someone speak and it has brought you to a state of fear, despair, confusion, knowing that all hope is lost and your faith diminished, then you will know the source from where it came. On the other hand, the opposite is also true. If you read a book or watch a media program and it brings peace, hope, understanding, clarity, and renews or strengthens your faith, then again you shall know the source from where it came.

CHAPTER 12

───────── § ─────────

GOD'S WORD TO BE TAUGHT TO ALL NATIONS

Matthew 28:19-20- Go therefore and make disciples of all nations, baptizing them in the name of the Father and of the Son and of the Holy Spirit, teaching them to observe all that I have commanded you. And behold, I am with you always, to the end of the age.

Doctrine and Covenants 1:23- That the fullness of my gospel might be proclaimed by the weak and the simple unto the ends of the world, and before kings and rulers.

IT IS ESSENTIAL that the word of God be taught to every soul on the planet before the Second Coming of Christ. Every soul must be offered the knowledge of God and the gospel, light, darkness, good and evil. If this was not the case how would we be able to make the ultimate choice, between good and evil? No one will be able to stand before the Christ and God and say, "I did not know the difference between good and evil." No one will be able to say at Judgment Day, "I am innocent, for I did not know."

CHAPTER 13

DARKNESS SHALL BE UNLEASHED

EVERYTHING IS PROGRESSING according to divine plan. It was divine plan that in the last day's darkness would be unleashed. Is it Lucifer, the Prince of Darkness that unleashes himself? It is not. Who is unleashing the power of darkness in the last days? It is the one God that is unleashing darkness and has ultimate power over all things. Why would God do this to us? Look around at all the terrible events in the world, war, famine, plagues, pestilence, brother against brother and nation against nation. There is so much anger and hatred in the world. Why would God unleash darkness if it would cause so much chaos and ill will in the world? It is divine plan. God is unleashing darkness so that every soul will be able to see clearly darkness and the light. With darkness unleashed and the light brought forward, there will be a balance between the dark and the light. Both will be in the world and have influence over their kingdoms. Every soul will have been offered the knowledge of good versus evil and every soul must make the ultimate choice. The unleashing of darkness is proceeding according to divine plan and we all knew in the preexistence that it would happen.

CHAPTER 14

———— § ————

INIQUITY SHALL ABOUND

Jude 1:4- ...For there are certain men crept in unawares, who were before of old ordained to this condemnation, ungodly men, turning the grace of our God into lasciviousness, and denying the only Lord God, and our Lord Jesus Christ.

2 Timothy 3:1-5- For men shall be lovers of their own selves, covetous, boasters, proud, blasphemers, disobedient to parents, unthankful, unholy, without natural affection, trucebreakers, false accusers, incontinent, fierce, despisers of those that are good. Traitors, heady, high-minded, lovers of pleasures more than lovers of God. Having the form of godliness, but denying the power thereof.

2 Timothy 4:3-4- The time will come when they will not endure sound doctrine; but after their own lusts shall they heap to themselves teachers, having itching ears; and they shall turn away their ears from the truth, and shall be turned unto fables

Matthew 24: 12- And because iniquity shall abound, the love of many shall wax cold.

Matthew 16:26- For what will it profit a man if he gains the whole world and forfeits his soul?

Ether 15:19- *The Spirit of the Lord had ceased striving with them, and Satan had full power over the hearts, and the blindness of the minds that they might be destroyed.*

Doctrine and Covenants 112:23- *Verily, verily, I say unto you, darkness covereth the earth, and gross darkness the minds of the people, and all flesh has become corrupt before my face.*

North American: Anishinaabe-Ojibwe- *"The Seven Fires"- The way of the mind brought to the red, black, and yellow nation by the white nation would bring danger to the whole earth.*

Buddhist- *The following are excerpts from a number of prophecies and scriptures about the era preceding the coming of Maitreya, characterized by a decline in morality, a lack of compassion and truth, an increase in ignorance and false teaching and the "Five Disappearances".*

Buddhist- *the Lotus Sutra 13- In the evil age to come, living beings will decrease in good qualities and increase in utter ignorance, coveting gain and honors, developing their evil qualities, and being far removed from deliverance.*

Buddhist- *Padmasambhbava -The signs of these times are new and fantastical modes of dressing - traditional styles forgotten. The arrogant elevate profanity. The proletariat rules the kingdom; kings become paupers; the butchers and murderers become leaders of men; unscrupulous self-seekers rise to high position.*

Buddhist- *Prophecy of Shambala (Buddhist, BEF 700 CE)-People will no longer have any religion to which they can turn for solace or liberation:*

the doctrines of materialism will overwhelm their minds and drive them to struggle for their own selfish ends. The lust for power and wealth will prevail over teachings of compassion and truth.

Buddhist-*Digha Nikaya iii.71-72, Cakkavatti-Sihanada Suttanta-There will come a time, brethren, when immoral courses of action will flourish excessively; there will be no word for moral among humans - far less any moral agent. Among such humans, homage and praise will be given to them who lack filial and religious piety, and show no respect to the head of the clan; just as today homage and praise are given to the filial minded, to the pious and to them who respect the heads of their clans.*

Among such humans, there will be no such thoughts of reverence as are a bar to intermarriage with mother, or mother's sister, or teacher's wife, of father's sister-in-law. The world will fall into promiscuity, like goats and sheep, fowls and swine, dogs and jackals.

Among such humans, keen mutual enmity will become the rule, keen ill will, keen animosity, passionate thoughts even of killing, in a mother toward her child, in a child toward its mother, in a father toward his child and a child toward its father, in brother to brother, in brother to sister, in sister to brother. Just as a sportsman feels toward game that he sees, so will they feel.

Hindu-*"The Coming of the Great Avatar and the Return of the Golden Age"- you want to forget God, then God will put you in such a condition that you can never understand what is God. That is demonic life. That time is also coming. At the present moment, still a few men are inter-ested, what is God. Arto. But time is coming ahead when there will be no sense to understand God. That is the last stage of Kali-yuga, and at that time Kalki avatara, Kalki avatara will come. At that time there is no preaching of God consciousness, simply killing, simply killing. Kalki* *avatara with His sword will simply massacre. Then again Satya-yuga will come. Again golden age will come.*

Kogi- South America- *The Earth is decaying and losing its strength because of your greed.*

THIS SIGN HAS been fulfilled. It is not just the terrible headlines in the daily news, it is the everyday acts of all of us that determines if our hearts are turned towards our fellow man or the vanity of the world, whether our hearts are upon all that is good or the ways of the world.

The love of self is not bad but is essential if you are to be happy and healthy. If you want to love others, it starts with the true love of self. It is pride that shuts out light and God's love. If you think yourself better than your fellow man, that is pride, which is the opposite of humbleness and humility. It is pride that sets our hearts upon the things of the world, while humbleness and humility sets our hearts upon the welfare of our fellow man and God.

Alma 38: 12- *see that ye bridle all your passions.*

Timothy states well about the pitfall of pleasures. Pleasures are not of themselves wrong and it is my firm belief that passion is of God and god-like. The problem is being lovers of pleasure more than lovers of God. Passion was meant to be bridled (Alma 38:12) for it is a wonderful servant, but terrible master.

CHAPTER 15

———— § ————

FALSE PROPHETS, CHRISTS AND CHURCHES

Matthew 24:5- For many will come in my name, saying, I am Christ, and will mislead many.

Matthew- 24:23-26- If any say unto you, Here is Christ, or there... He is in the secret chambers; believe it not. Then if anyone says to you, 'Behold, here is the Christ,' or 'There He is,' do not believe him. "For false Christs and false prophets will arise and will show great signs and wonders, so as to mislead, if possible, even the elect.

Matthew 24:11- And many false prophets shall rise, and shall deceive many.

Mormon 8:32- Yea, it shall come in a day when there shall be churches built up that say: Come unto me, and for your money you shall be forgiven of your sins.

Buddhist -Padmasambhbhava- Drunkards preach the path to Salvation... Guileful imposters claim psychic powers... False doctrines are devised from the Buddha's Word and the teachers' interpretations become self-vindications... Ideas are established contrary to traditions.

THE CHURCHES ARE not meant to have you pay them money, so you can make it back to God. We cannot "buy our way into the kingdom of heaven."

Churches are meant to teach us God's word to bring about lifestyle chang-es that will bring about our health, love and happiness. Churches are not put here to make us feel quilt. It is the same for doctors. So many patients want to smoke, drink, eat and do all manner of things excessively then go to their doctor to get a pill, for these lifestyles that are slowly destroying their health. The doctor should be actively involved in lifestyle changes to maintain health and happiness. The doctor who doesn't, is doing his patients a disservice. The churches who say, "Do whatever you want, pay me your money and you will be saved," are not telling the truth and doing their parishioners a great disservice.

This is the time of false prophets. I have seen many who have called themselves prophets and many who call their spiritual leader a prophet. A prophet is a calling of God that should not be taken lightly. A prophet of God is a great and important calling. Some may conclude that since this is the time of false prophets, that there will be no true prophets. This is also not true and soon will come into public awareness the two prophets prophesied in Revelation. These true prophets are in the Middle East at this very moment. It is also the history of mankind that whenever there is a real phenomenon there be many who will try and imitate the real thing. For every miracle worker, there will be those who say they produce miracles and can't. That is the way of the world, and will continue until the world is forever changed.

This is the time of false Christs and there are those professing they are the Christ. Keep your ears open and you will hear and see many who might be able to perform true miracles, for miracles were meant to be a natural phenomenon. Just because someone can produce a miracle does not make them the Christ. According to prophecy "There shall come forth false Christs and prophets, and shall show great signs and wonders… they shall deceive the very elect…" This prophecy of false churches, false prophets and false Christs has been fulfilled.

CHAPTER 16

───────§───────

THE LOVE OF MANY SHALL WAX COLD

Matthew 5:45- While one portion of the human race is judging and condemning the other without mercy, the Great Parent of the universe looks upon the whole of the human family with a fatherly care and paternal regard; he views them as his offspring, and without any of those contracted feelings that influence the children of men, causes his sun to rise on the evil and on the good, and sendeth rain on the just and on the unjust.

Matthew 24: 12- And because iniquity shall abound, the love of many shall wax cold.

Doctrine and Covenants 63:32- I, the Lord am angry with the wicked; I am holding my spirit from the inhabitants of the earth.

Doctrine and Covenants 29:15- There shall be weeping and wailing among the hosts of men.

Doctrine and Covenants 122:8- ... know thou, my son, that all these things shall give thee experience, and shall be for thy good.

GOD'S LOVE FALLS on the unjust and the just. God's love is unconditional and no matter what we do God loves us just the same. Does a good father love conditionally or say I will love you if you do this or do that? We came here to experience this beautiful world which has both light and darkness. We have all played in the garden, broke divine law at times and hopefully learned from these experiences. We have all fallen and made mistakes. It is not that we are innately bad or evil, for we were meant to be born into the world of good and evil and experience it. This experience is not bad but in an eternal sense all good. That was in the past and now it is time to go back home. God's love fell on all of us, no matter how much we strayed into darkness and no matter what we did. God knew that we came to this third dimensional school to experience both light and darkness. **God loves ALL his children unconditionally.** A wise good Father will not let His children keep going astray. Finally, the good Father will let the child know that there are consequences of their actions, so they can correct their behavior. When the spirit is withheld and the love of God waxes cold, then we shall know what it is to be without God's love. This is a necessary step in helping us with the ultimate decision of choosing light or darkness.

We have no idea how much God's love does for us every day. It is God's love that provides for us, keeps us healthy, brings peace, prosperity, harmony, happiness, purpose, and fulfillment and provides for our daily needs. It is God's love that gives us safety. We are all His children and He loves every one of us more than we know. We have no idea how much safety God provides us with. We assume that it is just the natural order of things, that our world is naturally safe. It is God's love that moderates severe weather, natural disasters and earthquakes. The reason that we do not see this is because you need to be without God's love to see the effects. Without God's love our health and happiness would deteriorate, our needs would not be provided for and this world would become very unsafe. It is God's love that has kept the rains falling, plant life growing, maintains our health and yet we have given Him little credit. God's love is a tremendous stabilizing force in the world and our lives. When God's love is withdrawn from those who are choosing darkness, they will see how much of a stabilizing and healing force God's love is.

Some of us are headed in the wrong direction and God will be cutting off His love to those going in the wrong direction as a type of biofeedback. Those who continue to choose darkness will have their love wax cold. When many feel the pain and suffering caused by the loss of God's love, it will help them choose light and God. It is all divine plan to help the ultimate decision.

Why are there are so many addictions in the world, and prescriptions for anti-anxiety pills, antidepressants, pain killers and sleeping pills? There is a big hole in us, causing pain, anxiety, fear, depression and insomnia. People are looking for a way to function and ultimately a way to stop the pain. Researchers, scientists, doctors have discovered pills to alter our neurochemistry to help sleep, stop anxiety and kill pain. In a crisis, in the hands of a wise physician these drugs can be a very helpful. In the long run our souls are not looking for a pill to temporarily help us function. We are looking for a cure. I am an anesthesiologist and work closely with powerful pain killers, and when used after a major operation they are of enormous benefit to the patient. Using pain killers for the long term to deaden the pain we feel from the lack of love, only makes the problem worse. All those who succumb to addictions are also trying to kill the pain, and the addictions will temporarily numb the pain. In the long run, the pain will return with a vengeance and more and more will be needed to stop the pain. Addictions are not the cure. We are all looking for the cure to our pain, anxiety, fears, sadness, depression, lack of sleep and addictions.

Our souls remember where we came from and our true nature. We are love and where we came from we were bathed, nurtured and saturated with love. It was what we knew, what we came from and where we long to return to. Our souls are not just looking for love but cannot exist without it. This is why God's love falls on all of us, the just and unjust. It is necessary for life, health and happiness. We have a hole in ourselves and nothing but God's love can fill the void. There is only one cure. It is what we are looking for and have been since we left our true home. This will be our ultimate choice to live our lives in love or fear.

To live without God's love and light is hell on earth. This world would be pure hell without His love and spirit. Soon some will know what it will be like to be without God's love. It will not be pleasant. I see this darkness every day and it saddens me, for the choice of darkness is causing great pain and suffering. I do not like to see anyone or anything suffer. If there was another way to complete the grand plan of free will without so much suffering I would ask that the suffering would stop. Most of this suffering is of our own free will and I do hope the suffering will not last long. This sign has been fulfilled but will become even clearer.

CHAPTER 17

─────── § ───────

THE PURIFICATION

Hopi- *"Overall, the theme of Hopi prophecy is that the Earth is going to soon go through a great purification and that humanity can make the decision as to how extreme this purification will be."*

IT WAS SIR Isaac Newton that stated after discovery of the physical laws of the universe, that man will deny the existence of the spirit of God in all things. Sir Isaac Newton states "Look at the way the universe behaves. The natural order of it, shows it is under the divine order of God." Sir Isaac Newton's statement was prophetic and this is exactly what is taking place. It is God that will turn desert into paradise and paradise into deserts, and create tempests, earthquakes, disasters, plaques and famines. These are not punishments but cleansing of the earth and God's hand is in all of it. There will be those that say that God is punishing us. The opposite is true. If he did not love us, the earth would not be purified, and we would destroy ourselves.

Revelation states there shall be seven seals opened that shall bring trials and tribulation to the earth. There are two reasons for the trials and tribulation. The first is purification and the second is for the hearts of all mankind. It may seem there are more compassionate ways to bring about purification then to release trials and tribulations upon the world. I cannot question God's plan or His wisdom for my wisdom and knowledge is small compared to His. This is all in the hands of the purest and the most compassionate. Purification is necessary if the world is to be saved and be reborn into paradise. The extent of the purification is up to us. There have been many, many prayers to end the greed, drugs, war, evil doing, misery, pain, disease and other hardships upon mankind. Those prayers have been heard and those prayers are being answered at this very moment. Purification is necessary and by the time we look back at what we have been through and having made it to a better place, we will say it was good and necessary. We will be grateful for God's wisdom and his plan.

The earthquakes, tidal waves, volcanoes, tempests (fierce storms), famine, plagues, fires, economic chaos and floods shall provide a purification of the land and peoples on those lands. The purification is like the microbiologist who burns his metallic instruments in a heated flame. The heated flame kills all the harmful bacteria and microbes on the instruments and then the instruments have been purified. The burning of our earth with fire destroys the impurities of the land and the people. The earth and mankind will return to their original state and a state where the love can dwell once again.

Mother Mary- *You will not be tested to the extent my son was tested.*

Message from Mother Mary was "You will not be tested to the extent my son was tested." Trials and tribulations, is a period of suffering for many, but should be thought of as a time of purification. It is a period of testing, and see what we are made of. We are made of the spirit of God, in his likeness and image, and this period of testing will be a purification.

These trials and tribulations can be a great blessing if you have the right attitude. In preparation for this purification, the earth was baptized by water with the great flood in the time of Noah. The earth will be purified by fire and the spirit of God. It is necessary for the earth to be purified and become paradise. For those of us that want paradise, it is necessary for us to be purified by the spirit of God. This is accelerated by trials and tribulation and facing our fears. We are going to have some tough challenges ahead and be tested, but this is a request of our souls saying we want paradise. We are about to face every one of our fears, individually and as collective human race. The reward at the end of our trials is paradise.

CHAPTER 18

———— § ————

FACING OUR FEARS

Psalms 23:4- Yea, though I walk through the valley of the shadow of death, I will fear no evil: for thou art with me;

WHAT IS FEAR?

DR. HERBERT BENSON, a Harvard Cardiologist and author has helped bring to light what fear is and how it affects our central nervous system. Fear is a very primitive basic emotion, located in our primitive brain. Fear has been helpful in the survival of mankind. If our early ancestors did not have fear, then we would have been eaten by animals or destroyed by natural elements. It is fear of the saber tooth tiger, carnivorous animals and natural forces that prompted the development of weapons and behaviors that allowed our early ancestors to survive. Without the fear response in our ancestors, they would not have survived to have babies and we would not be here.

Any perceived danger triggers our central nervous system and the flight or fight response. The hypothalamus triggers our fight or flight response and there is a release of the hormones epinephrine, norepinephrine and cortisol. Our mind becomes focused, heightened awareness, our heart beats faster and our rate of breathing increases. Our blood is diverted away from areas like our digestive tract and to our muscles that may need the extra flow of blood, oxygen and nutrients. Blood is also diverted away from the higher brain centers and more to the primitive brain, we develop tunnel vision and our thoughts become irrational. We perceive everything as a possible threat around us. Our thoughts become chaotic and a soup of thoughts trying to identify possible threats. As Dr. Benson puts it, "we see the world through the lens of fear."

This fight or flight mechanism is part of being in the human condition and part of our being human. It is part of our experience in this third dimensional school and from time to time helpful. This was very useful to our primitive ancestors but can be harmful in modern times. This fight or flight response can be counterproductive and many suffer from the over activation of the fight of flight response. If we are always on the state where we see danger all around us, then our body and central nervous system will eventually collapse from exhaustion.

What most scientists (there are some enlightened scientists and physicians) don't appreciate, is that our soul and spirit, mind, emotions and body are all interconnected. We are also connected to each other and the higher power. Fear is much more than the triggering of our fight or flight center of our brain. Fear is connected to our spirit and is a universal force. Just as love is a universal force and most powerful force in the universe and heavens, fear is also a universal force and has power.

Fear Shuts Out Our Light and Hides Our Soul

Fear directs the blood flow in the brain away from the higher centers which contain our rational mind and the parts of our brain that connect us to each other and the higher power. Fear directs blood flow away from the parts of our brain that maintains our happiness, love and centers of our brain important for enlightenment. Fear is a spiritual force and shuts out light and love. We are seeing a small portion of who we truly are and our potential. As we individually face our fears then more light will come in and more of our soul and spirit will begin to shine. As we face our fears collectively, then we will bring through more light to mankind as a whole.

There is an illustration that is used to illustrate fears and facing them. The sun represents our soul and spirit and potential for light, while the clouds represent our fears. The more fears we have then there will be more clouds and less of our light and soul is going to shine through. The bigger the fear, then the darker the cloud and even less of our light and soul will shine through. Every fear that we face gets rid a cloud. The bigger the fear, the darker the cloud that you get rid of, the more of you that shines through.

I was impressed by a woman in a public speaking class that I was helping teach. This woman had a deep fear of social groups and public speaking. It may be described as a terror. She had trouble talking in front of a few people, let alone a group. Social functions terrified her and I give her credit to face and confront one of her greatest fears. The person I saw at first was in deep fear of social situations and public speaking. It was such a deep-rooted fear that it affected her countenance, presence, facial expressions and her entire spiritual being. She was helped through her fear by gradual desensitization towards group situations and speaking. By the third night of the public speaking course she spoke in front of the whole class with poise and confidence. She had faced her fear, and I am not aware of anyone who had overcome their fear of public speaking and social anxiety as quickly as she did. The greatest point of this story is the change in her spiritual being and appearance. If you were to take a picture of her on her first night when she needed to say something in front of the whole class then compare it to a picture of her on her third night, you would swear it was not the same person. She had made a most miraculous transformation, and she was not the same person she was before. This may have been her deepest darkest fear and it ruled her life. By facing her fear and overcoming her fear, a part of her soul and spirit that was hiding came out for all the world to see.

TRIBAL CONSCIOUSNESS- CONSCIOUS VS UNCONSCIOUS

In the ultimate decision of choosing the light or the darkness, it ultimately boils down to becoming conscious beings or staying unconscious. In the past, tribal consciousness and tribal order were necessary for the tribe to survive. Fear played a role if the tribe was to survive. There was pressure to be part of the tribe, fit in and take on the tribal consciousness. Those who didn't fit in may be cast out of the tribe and then must fend for themselves. This was very risky proposition for our early ancestors. That same fear and tribal consciousness is with us today. Our tribes (family, social and work groups) tell us to fit in, be one of the tribe and take on the tribal consciousness. The risk of not taking on the tribal consciousness could be the loss of one's job or being ostracized from social groups. Fear controls the members of work or social network. The fear of not being able to put food on the table can be an intimidating force to be part of the tribal consciousness and remain unconscious.

Babies are fascinating and we have a spiritual attraction to them, for they have just come through the veil (that which separates us from God and the kingdom of heaven). They are still very much connected to the other side of the veil and where we all came from. Newborns have one foot on this side of the veil and one foot on the other side of the veil. I have seen babies, infants, toddlers and some young children who are communicating with angelic beings and at some point, learn fear and that it is not socially acceptable to communicate with the angels. They turn off what was very natural to them. The tribal consciousness tells these children to turn off their ability to see, hear and communicate with the angelic beings on the other side of the veil. "If you are to be one of the tribe and want us to take care of you, then turn off your communication with these angelic beings. Be one of us and part of the tribe, and we will take care of you." The young children turn off a part of themselves to become part of the tribe.

TWO GREAT FORCES IN THE WORLD

This beautiful world has both the light and darkness. It is divine plan that darkness and light shall be unleashed in the last days. There are also two great forces in the world: love and fear. It is these two great forces that have enormous impact on our everyday living. Every one of us must make the ultimate decision and choose the light or choose the darkness; choose love or choose the world. Surrender into love or succumb to fear. These two great forces rule our world and are in opposition to each other.

Consciousness is not just individual or group consciousness, but there is a collective consciousness of the world. We are coming to the completion of the grand plan of free will and God's promise to renew our planet into a paradisiacal glory. There is a force that wants the plan of free will to fail. Just as there is light and the Christ that holds the light, there is darkness and the antichrist that holds the darkness. These two forces are opposition in our planet earth and our third dimensional schooling. This third dimensional school was designed to have opposition in all things. They are both powerful forces in our world, and as Darth Vader in Star Wars eloquently stated, "Do not underestimate the power of the dark side of the force."

The antichrist and his group of angels want the world to stay unconscious and the grand plan of free will to fail. Christ, Buddha, Krishna, Mohammed, the enlightened masters, heavenly angels and the eternal God want the plan of free will to succeed. The outcome is up to us and our ultimate choice.

The world wants control and to control the masses and it is much easier to control others if they are in a state of fear. Fear is used by many in authority to control groups and the masses. Fear can and does shut down many of the higher centers of our brain and mind. One step at a time we are collectively making the choice to become conscious. No longer is it acceptable to live our lives in fear, we are choosing to live our lives in love.

Table 1 summarizes many of the key differences between love and fear and how these universal forces effect our bodies, mind and soul. We have been born into a world that has both darkness and light, two great kingdoms and two Lords that rule over each kingdom; the Christ and the anti-Christ. These kingdoms are pervasive throughout our world and part of our third dimensional schooling. The anti-Christ rules through fear while the Christ rules through love. The anti-Christ's goal is to keep us unconscious and live our lives in fear, while the Christ wants us to live in love and become conscious beings. The anti-Christ wants us to see our fellow man as our competitors and the enemy, while the Christ wants us to see our fellow man as our brothers and sisters. The anti-Christ wants to destroy our free agency and the plan of free will, while the Christ wants us to have our free will and choose God and love. One leads to bondage, pain and suffering while love leads to freedom, peace and happiness. Fear is a force that leads to hell, while love will take us to paradise.

THIRD DIMENSIONAL SCHOOL

Third dimensional school refers to our spiritual schooling here on earth. We came from God and a spiritual realm located in the higher dimensions. We came to earth for the great plan of free will, experience good and evil but also to experience a third dimensional realm of God's creation. This I refer to as our third dimensional school. We all made the choice to be born into this third dimensional school to learn, experience not only the light, fun and pleasant experiences, but darkness and some painful and challenging experiences. We were meant to learn about love, sharing and giving, but also fear, hardship and pain. You may look at this world as just good and evil and that evil should be destroyed and done away with. You may have said at some time "How could a loving God allow the evil to exist in our world?"

	FEAR	LOVE
AUTHORITY	Anti-Christ (Lucifer)	Christ
RULES OVER	Darkness	Light
RULES THROUGH	Fear	Love
INTENT OF AUTHORITY	Control	Cooperation; Harmony
CONSCIOUSNESS	Keep Mankind Unconscious	Enlightenment and Mankind becoming Conscious
FREE WILL	Destroy the plan of Free Will	Success of Plan of Free Will
MINDS	Narrow, focused, irrational, full of mind chatter. Perceives danger everywhere. Hyper vigilant.	Broad, calm, rational. Listens to inner voice, Perceives safety. Increased awareness.
AUTONOMIC RESPONSE	Activate hypothalamus release epi, norepi and cortisol. Increase HR and RR.	Decrease HR and RR.
BLOOD FLOW	Decreased to GI tract, higher centers of brain. Increased to lungs, heart, muscles, and primitive brain.	Increased flow to higher centers of the brain.
INTENT OF INDIVIDUAL	Survival.	Thrive, life, fulfillment love, happiness
SHORT TERM	Can help survival.	Beneficial.
LONG TERM, IF EXCESSIVE	Fatigue, collapse, anxiety, depression, sadness, fear, poor concentration, Insomnia weakens immune system, more susceptible to infection and disease.	Health, happiness, well-being, calm, better concentration and sleep, strengthens immune system, less susceptible to infection and disease.
RESULT	Shuts out our light and soul.	Brings forth our light and soul.

Table 1- Love vs. Fear Chart - Abbreviations for Love vs. Fear chart- epi- epinephrine, norepi- norepinephrine, HR- heart rate, RR- respiratory rate, GI tract- gastrointestinal tract.

Every one of us chose to come here, be born into this world and experience this world, the darkness and the light first hand. We did not want to be secluded in a fortress and look at the world through the looking glass. We chose to experience this world of good and evil and it is time to accept responsibility for being here and what we have created.

WE ALL HAVE OUR FEARS

We all have our fears; it is a matter of what our fears are and to what extent. Even those that say they have no fear, are about to have a rude awakening. It may surprise you to learn how much of our everyday living is out of fear. Much of our life is stemming out of fear. Fear of not enough food, shelter, health and other daily concerns have a large effect on our lives. Do you go to work every day, because you love your work and wouldn't be doing anything else in your life, or because the consequences of not having a job and providing for you and your family? Do you live your life out of love and passion or because you are afraid of the consequences of not having enough? I thought greed was an entity all to itself. I have learned that greed is fear of lack and not having enough. God is a God of abundance and can give you more than you can imagine, and most of us have great imaginations. The world says, "There is only so much, so take all you can because then it will be gone." Out of the fear of lack, people take more and more and more, never being satisfied.

> **Doctrine and Covenants 122:8-** *The son of Man hath descended below them all. Art thou greater than he?*

Buddha had to face fear when he fasted and meditated for forty days and nights under the Bodi tree. He faced his fears and found enlightenment. Christ had to face fear when he fasted and prayed for forty days and nights in the wilderness. I might add the more enlightened the spiritual being the greater will be the fear they must face. It was the Christ who descended into darkness, far below what we will descend as a part of our spiritual schooling to lead by example. He showed us that if he can descend into darkness and face his fears, to a much greater degree than we will, then we can face our fears as well. Christ leads by example and would not ask us to do anything that he has not done and to a far greater degree. There is not one of us that will suffer to the extent that he has suffered.

PRIMITIVE VS. ENLIGHTENED BRAIN

Our physical bodies and brains have evolved and are still evolving. The primitive part of our brain is important for our survival. Fear will trigger our flight or fight response and if our ancestors didn't have it and their sex drive, we wouldn't be here today.

The PET scanner can see parts of our primitive brain and the hypothalamus light up when we are in fear. Researchers have discovered the part of our brain that is connected to love. Researchers studied couples that are in love and discovered that the part of their brain called the anterior ventricular system lights up. Many couples fall out of love, and they are always trying to find ways to activate this part of their brain. After years of marriage or relationship, some couples stay in love and the PET scanner shows this area of the brain continues to light up.

What most scientists and medical doctors do not understand, yet, is that our brains work better when this part of our brain is activated. Physicians and scientists know that our brains work better when we are happy, but do not realize our brains work better when the love center is on.

In the past, medical doctors and scientists learned about our brain by patients who had tumors or destructive lesions in their brains and then doing a neurologic exam. If the lesion or tumor was in a certain area of the brain and the patient could no longer move their arm, then the doctors and scientists knew this area of the brain had to do with movement of the arm. The doctors and scientists found areas of the brain that when destroyed by lesions, they could not see much physically wrong with the patient. The physician and scientists concluded that these were unimportant areas of the brain that don't do much. WRONG! Every part of our brain has a purpose. Our brain is continually evolving as man is evolving. As mankind becomes enlightened so will our brains change and become enlightened.

Just as there is an area of our brain connected to our love, there are areas of the brain connected to our spirituality and enlightenment. Living your life in fear will shunt blood away from the higher centers of the brain and toward the primitive areas of the brain. The brain goes away from our connection to spirit, our soul, the higher power, and into survival mode.

INFLUENCE OF THE MEDIA

Look at our media and news and you would be led to believe that the world is full of fear, and love hardly exists at all. Our news and media are driven by economics and unfortunately "Bad news sells." Love does not get the media coverage because it is fear, scandal and bad press that sells.

In doing research for this book I had to read and watch a lot of different material from various sources. I must say it was rewarding but very difficult at the same time. Most of the material I read on the events that are about to happen are full of fear. Even though I learned a lot, it was very difficult for me to read material that was coming from a standpoint of fear. I remember a show in the 1970's that reviewed movies with the critics Siskel and Ebert. Roger Ebert stated how difficult it was to watch these horror films and watching them had a negative and unhealthy effect on him. I was counseled many, many years ago, by the higher power not to watch horror movies. We are what we eat, and whatever we fill our minds, body and spirit with we will eventually become. If your eyes are fixed on love, peace and hope you will become love, peace, hope and love will pervade your life. If you fill your mind, body and spirit with fear then you will become fear and be ruled by fear.

Our media has enormous power to influence our lives, to bring us to a better place or keep us in fear. This is where discernment is important. If a program, book or article is based in fear then put it down and move on. If a program, book or article is based on hope, optimism, courage, understanding, love or facing and overcoming your fears, then enjoy and savor it. Programs, books and articles that help our awareness and help us face our fears are much different than those based in fear. This chapter is about facing our fears, and those who take it to heart will benefit from it.

CHAPTER 19

———— ◊ ————

PLAGUES AND PESTILENCE

Luke 21:11- ...*and famine, and pestilences*

Matthew 24:7- ...*and there shall be famines, pestilences*

Doctrine and Covenants 45:31- And there shall be men standing in that generation, that shall not pass until they shall see an overflowing scourge; for a desolation sickness shall cover the land.

Hopi- Only those which come will cause disease and a great dying.

Buddhist- Padmasambhava- Famine, frost and hail govern many unproductive years... release[ing] diseases, horrible epidemics and plagues which spread like wildfire, striking men and cattle.

IT IS GOOD to start with some definitions. Plague refers to any disease with a high death rate. There have been plagues sent by God such as invasion of locusts. Many of the plagues coming will be infectious disease. Pestilence is more of the same and is a contagious or infectious epidemic disease that is virulent and devastating. There will be widespread infectious diseases with a high number of deaths.

The smallest living organisms on the planet can be the demise of all mankind. These viruses, bacteria and microorganisms can be benign and not hurt man, they can help protect us from other deadly microorganisms. It is beneficial to have healthy friendly bacteria in our mouth, stomach and intestines. These friendly bacteria make it much harder for unfriendly and potentially deadly bacteria and microorganisms to cause a serious infection or even death.

Infectious epidemics have been with us through the ages. The bacteria, viruses and other microorganisms that caused epidemics and pandemics and death have always been with man. Mankind has forgotten the plagues of the past and has a false sense of security with modern medicine and antibiotics. The plagues that have afflicted mankind in the past will come again.

THE BLACK PLAGUE
The Black Plague, which is also referred to as the Black Death, started in China and central Asian and then spread to Europe and other countries. From the shipping trade routes, it reached Italy in 1348. The plague would present as swellings or buboes in the lymph nodes. These swellings or tumors would appear in the groin and armpits and then spread all over the body. They could swell to the size of a baseball. Those infected also had fever, headaches, nausea and vomiting, painful joints and in general did not feel well. Soon, black and purple spots on the body appeared which signified impending death. The experience was painful and led to death usually within a week. This was referred to as the bubonic plague killing 30-75% of those infected, but there was also pneumonic plague affecting the lungs and respiratory tract that killed 95% of those infected and septicemic plague (infecting the blood) which killed close to 100% of those infected.

People believed that if they avoided those who were sick and their property, that they would be safe. The sick were left to care for themselves, except from brave family or friends. The stench of death and rotting bodies was everywhere. Many only knew the plight of their neighbor by smell of their decaying bodies coming from their home. The dead bodies filled the streets and every corner. The dead bodies were brought to the church for burial, but soon the amount of dead bodies became overwhelming and the priority became to get rid of the decaying bodies. Individual graves were abandoned and mass graves became a necessity. Huge trenches were dug and bodies buried by the hundreds, then covered in dirt. Getting rid of the dead decaying bodies became a daily routine. The cause of the death was a bacterium called Yesinia Pestis, which was spread by fleas that lived on the back of rats.

The total number of deaths worldwide is estimated to be 75 million people and killing 25-50 million people in Europe. In Europe, it is believed that 30-60% of the population died, while in Southern France and Spain 75%-80% of the population died.

The Black Plague epidemics continued to recur throughout the world. In the first half of the 17th century, the plague killed 1,730,000 in Italy (14% of the population), and the 17th century the plague killed 1,250,000 in Spain. In the Thirty Years War, 1618-1648, 8 million Germans died of the plague and typhus fever. The plague killed one third of the population in the region of the Great Northern War (Russia vs. Sweden) in 1700-1721. In 1710, it killed two thirds of those living in Helsinki, Finland. In, 1710-1711 one third of the population of Stockholm died. The Black Death did similar outbreaks in the Middle East and the Islamic nations up to the 19th century. In the 19th century 10 million people died in India. The plague bacteria and the plague disease are still with us today, with 362 cases of the plague reported in 1944 to 1993.

1918 INFLUENZA PANDEMIC OR SPANISH FLU

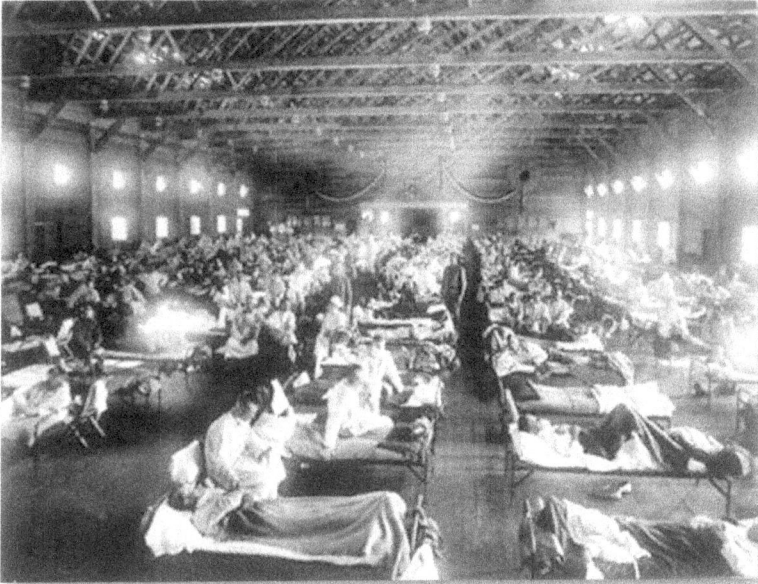

Figure 13- 1918 Influenza Pandemic (Historical photo of the 1918 Spanish influenza ward at Camp Funston, Kansas, showing the many patients ill with the flu. Image from wikipedia.org)

In 1918 at the end of World War I, people throughout the world began having symptoms similar to the common cold. Those infected developed fever, chills, cough, sore throat and muscle aches but then the illness progressed rapidly to pneumonia. One physician wrote his patients "died struggling to clear their airways of a blood-tinged froth that sometimes gushed from their nose and mouth," another physician wrote patients would rapidly "develop the most viscous type of pneumonia that has ever been seen," "it is simply a struggle for air until they suffocate." The virus caused bleeding in their lungs and the victims drown in their own blood and bodily fluids. There were no drugs to combat the illness and little that physicians could do. The disease progressed rapidly with often bringing death within hours of first signs of infection. There was one report of one man catching a cough on the way to work and within a couple of hours dying. Another report of four women playing bridge and within hours three of them were dead. Caskets of the dead were lined up in the streets. One report had little caskets for little babies stretched for 4 to 5 blocks.

The influenza virus is particularly dangerous because it is so contagious and spreads so rapidly from person to person. One infected person can enter a crowded room and infect everyone in the room. This influenza virus had unusual characteristics. This viral infection infected mostly the young healthy adults, instead of the babies, the elderly and those with weakened immune systems. The influenza pandemic quickly spread and was highly contagious. Soon, people throughout the world were infected and panic and chaos ensued. In the end, the pandemic had taken the lives of 675,000 Americans and has been called the worst pandemic ever in American history. Worldwide, between 30-40,000,000 people died.

MODERN DAY PLAGUES

BIRD FLU

This influenza bird virus has health professionals in charge of public health very nervous. Why are they so nervous? Take one more look at the 1918 Spanish Flu Epidemic and see how devastating a worldwide Influenza Pandemic can be. The mortality rate (percentage of people who died once infected) was 2.5% for the Spanish Flu. The H5N1 Influenza some have estimated may be 50% fatal for those who become infected, while other sources have stated the mortality rate may be as low as 20%. If there was a H5N1 Influenza pandemic the number of deaths would be 10 times higher. Looking at what happened in 1918 and making that disaster ten times worse, it is understandable why health officials are nervous about this form of influenza.

The influenza virus is carried in the intestines of wild birds and it does not usually infect these birds. One of the two forms of the influenza virus is highly contagious among birds and domestic poultry (chickens, ducks and turkeys) can become infected. 90-100% of these birds die in 48 hours. Eventually, these bird viruses mutate and these influenza viruses that normally only infect birds, can become viruses that can be spread person to person. So far, the H5N1 bird flu has not mutated to the point where it can infect person to person. If it does, then the concerns of the public health officials will be validated.

Public Health experts have said there have been 10 pandemics over the past 300 hundred years and we are overdue for the next for the next one. It is just the matter of time.

MALARIA

Malaria is an infectious disease caused by parasites and transferred by mosquitoes. It occurs in the tropical and subtropical areas of the Americas, Asia and Africa. Those infected develop fever, chills, and flu-like symptoms. If untreated, patients develop severe complications and can die. Malaria infects 350-500 million people each year, and over one million die. Most of those who die are young children in sub-Saharan Africa.

AIDS

I remember my medical training in the inner-city hospitals of New York City. One of my patients had contracted an illness that was rare and relatively new to medical science and we diagnosed him with AIDS. He developed pneumonia and became very ill. He eventually needed a breathing tube put down his throat to give him more oxygen, assist his breathing and save his life. After two months of intensive care he survived. He was one of the lucky ones for most who were diagnosed with this mysterious illness did not survive. I remember him wasting away before my very eyes and despite our good nutritional efforts. In one of the hospitals I rotated through in my medical training I remember wards of patients that were solely patients who had AIDS. As I walked down the halls with rooms full of AIDS patients, I had the sense and inner awareness that I was witnessing a modern-day plague.

AIDS is a worldwide pandemic that effects every country and all mankind. The death toll of the AIDS pandemic stands at 78 million infected and 39 million deaths. Approximately, every 12 seconds someone becomes infected with the AIDS virus, and every 15 seconds someone 15-24 is infected. 5,700 people die every day from AIDS and one child dies every minute. 15 million children have been orphaned, by one or both parents dying of the disease. In the United States, approximately one million people are infected with the AIDS virus and 524,000 have died of AIDS.

TUBERCULOSIS

Those who have seen the famous movies of Shootout at the OK Corral or other movies about Doc Holladay and Wyatt Earp know that Doc Holladay had a chronic cough and coughed up blood. He was sick and had what some call TB and others know as tuberculosis. Tuberculosis is caused by bacteria that infects the lungs but can infect any part of the body. It is spread through the air, person to person. Some people carry the bug and never get sick, while others do get sick and can spread the disease. One third of everyone in the world is infected with the bacteria, but only 10% will develop tuberculosis and become ill. Each year 8.8 million people will be diagnosed with tuberculosis and 1.6 million will die. A drug resistant form of tuberculosis is now worldwide, has no cure and has potential to cause many deaths.

EBOLA

December, 2013 a two-year-old boy in small village in Guinea, Africa became ill. He developed a fever, vomiting and black stools. The illness was painful and this two-year-old boy died December 6, 2013. The boy's mother, three-year-old sister and grandmother became ill with the same illness and all three died. This small village where the family lived is close to the borders of Sierra Leone and Liberia. People who attended the funeral of the grandmother spread the infection to other areas outside the village. The Ebola virus is spread by contact with bodily fluids (blood, diarrhea, urine, regurgitated stomach contents and saliva) when the person has a fever.

The infection is called hemorrhagic fever, because in addition to the fever, the person develops bleeding. The virus has tiny spikes which attach to the blood vessel walls. The blood vessel walls eventually break down and bleeds as a result. There are typically black stools (blood in stools) and other sites of bleeding.

The World Health Organization, Center for Disease Control and health officials know how potentially serious an Ebola outbreak can be. There is an international coalition to send supplies and workers to contain the outbreak, and treat those infected with the Ebola virus. Heroic health professionals and other workers have volunteered to help those infected and try to prevent a world-wide pandemic.

MAN-MADE KILLERS- BIOLOGICAL WARFARE

Biological warfare has existed for centuries. In the 13th century Mongolian armies catapulted corpses infected with plague over the walls of their enemies. The British gave blankets infected with small pox to the Native American Indians.

I remember reading in a national magazine in the 1970's, a victory of modern medicine and the world health organizations. A scourge of all mankind, smallpox, had been wiped off the face of the planet; or so we thought. One of my professors told me, that it is a sure bet that governments of the world took samples of small pox into the laboratories not only for study, but for biological warfare. Biological warfare has been with us for centuries or maybe longer and will continue until the rebirth of our planet.

All technology is a double-edged sword. Unraveling the secrets of DNA and microbiology has benefited all mankind and has led to the cure of many diseases. With the discovery of DNA and microbiology mankind took a giant leap forward in science and technology which benefits all. This knowledge is one of the secrets of life and should be held as sacred knowledge given to us by the One who created us all.

After unraveling the knowledge of DNA and microbiology, governments of the world put money into the development of biological warfare. Scientists were sent into the labs to make some very deadly microorganisms with the potential to possibly wipe out mankind. These deadly bugs exist and can be unleashed at the will of those who possess them.

ONE BAD BUG COULD DECIMATE THE WORLD'S POPULATION

According to Benu, a modern-day psychic, a plague that we fear in our subconscious will come out of Africa. This microorganism will be contagious and will spread around the world and one fourth of mankind will die from this plague. Like the dreaded Spanish Flu Pandemic of 1918, modern medicine will not have any antibiotics to fight this deadly killer.

CHAPTER 20

———— § ————

WAR AGAINST ISRAEL

Zechariah 12:1-3 *- The burden of the word of the LORD against Israel. Thus says the LORD, who stretches out the heavens, lays the foundation of the earth, and forms the spirit of man within him: Behold, I will make Jerusalem a cup of drunkenness to all the surrounding peoples, when they lay siege against Judah and Jerusalem. And it shall happen in that day that I will make Jerusalem a very heavy stone for all peoples; all who would heave it away will surely be cut in pieces, though all nations of the earth are gathered against it.*

Islam- *Book 37, Number 4281-Narrated Mu'adh ibn Jabal: (Translation of Sunan Abu-Dawud) - The Prophet said: The flourishing state of Jerusalem will be when Yathrib is in ruins, the ruined state of Yathrib will be when the great war comes, the outbreak of the great war (i.e., the battle of Armageddon).*

Buddhism- *For many centuries, the mystical tradition of Agharti (or, Aghartha) and its ruler, the King of the World, has existed in Tibet and Mongolia. "Men will increasingly neglect their souls. The greatest corruption will reign on earth. Men will become like bloodthirsty animals, thirsting for the blood of their brothers. The crescent [Islam] will become obscured, and its followers will descend into lies and perpetual warfare. The crowns of kings will fall."*

Hopi- "The Great Purification and the Third Great Shaking" In 1986 at the Continental Indigenous Council in Fairbanks, Alaska, Hopi Lee Brown delivered a message on behalf of his People in which he pronounced the components of the Ancient Prophecies relating to the Great Shaking. The Hopi believe that there will be a Third 'Great Shaking' of the World. Given that the First and Second Great Shakings referred to the First and Second World Wars, many believe that this symbolizes the future possibility of a Third World War.

THE LITERAL RECREATION of the state of Israel was prophecy and has been fulfilled. The prophecy of the final war against Israel is currently being fulfilled. The following is from the Associated Press. August 3, 2006 Iranian President Mahmoud Ahmadinejad said, "the solution to the Middle East crisis is to destroy Israel... elimination of the Zionist regime...the middle east would be better off without the existence of this Zionist regime...He has called for Israel to be wiped off the map."

I have friends who lived in Palestine before the war and the recreation of the state of Israel. I could see the heartache in their faces and in their story as they told me about the war and the Jewish people taking over their homeland. I have compassion for anyone who has lost their home land in war. War is not a shining star in the history of mankind and yet it continues. A burning question in their minds as they told me their story was "Why did we have to lose our home land?" I answered as honestly as I could and I did not ease their pain or sadness. "It was prophecy and it was meant to be." This sounds very unsympathetic, unfeeling and un-compassionate on my part, but I was being honest. One of my friends said in return, "Yes I know, we are living the lives of the unchosen people." I look at my friends and do have compassion for them and their people. I do know the history of the Jewish people and I do have compassion for them also. I do not pretend to know the mind and will of God. I do not pretend to know or totally understand the plan of God although I do have a little understanding of prophecy and God's will. The literal recreation of the state of Israel was fulfilling of prophecy.

There are Muslim extremists who have a great deal of anger and hard feelings against the state of Israel, the United States and the Jewish people. The final war against Israel is taking place and fulfilling prophecy. Iranian President Mahmoud Ahmadinejad is one of the Muslim extremists who stated "the solution to the Middle East crisis is to destroy Israel. "He is one of the few Muslims, being the president of Iran, who has the belief that Israel should be destroyed and the political power necessary for war against Israel.

It is prophecy that "all nations will go to war" against Israel. Israel will do what any sovereign nation would do and defend itself. The United States being Israel's strong ally will come to the defense of the state of Israel, while some Arab nations and people will support their Muslim brothers. Herein lies World War III, which will be the war to end all wars. There will not only be conventional weapons, but the unconventional as well. The weapons and plagues in Pandora's Box that the world hoped would stay hidden shall be unleashed. The world and the United Nations shall be greatly concerned for they know that World War III could escalate to the point where all mankind and all life on the planet could end. This is a point in the history of man where everything could end and all life ceases to exist. An anti-Christ will want the destruction of the state of Israel.

WORLD WAR THREE

Pope Francis- November 2015, Pope calls the Paris massacre part of "piecemeal Third World War."

The Pope Francis of the Catholic Church is an enlightened soul, with insight into the mysteries of God and current affairs. Pope Francis has stated that World War III, which is the war to end all wars, has already started. World War III and the war against Israel is fulfillment of biblical prophecy. **Prophecy is not fixed**, but watch for ISIS, radical Islamic groups, Vladimir Putin and North Korea aggression.

CHAPTER 21

―――――― § ――――――

ANTICHRIST

IT IS PROPHESY that in the last days, the antichrist would be born into the world. He will be charismatic, a religious and political leader, and bring havoc upon the western nations. He will initially be heralded as a savior to the world to bring peace into the world. He will ultimately be a wolf in sheep's clothing causing war, much bloodshed and destruction. It was also prophesied that he would come from Rome.

Let me first clarify the meaning of the word antichrist. In the pre-existence, Lucifer and Christ came up with two plans for us, the spirit children, to enter this world and to return to God. Christ's plan to give us free will was chosen and there was what was described as a war in heaven, whereby Christ and his angels prevailed. Lucifer was cast down out of heaven and became the antichrist, Satan or the Prince of Darkness. The antichrist, Lucifer, is very real and reigning over the darkness on this planet, as Christ reigns over the light; both have dominion over their kingdoms.

It is a common misconception that Lucifer will be born into the world to fulfill Bible prophecy. Although Lucifer is also called the antichrist, the revelation prophesy about the antichrist is not talking about Lucifer. The antichrist referred to in the revelation is one of the children of God, one of our brothers, and not Lucifer. An antichrist is anyone who is in opposition to Christ and Christ's teachings.

***1 John 2:22**- Who is a liar but he that denieth that Jesus is the Christ? He is an antichrist that denieth the Father and the Son.*

***2 John** 7- Many deceivers are entered into the world, who confess not that Jesus Christ is come in the flesh. This is a deceiver and an antichrist.*

There have been many antichrists in the past and there are many living today. There are many alive now who preach against Christ and his teachings; they are antichrists. There is a difference, however, between these antichrists and the antichrist who is written about in Revelation. The difference between latter day antichrists is their ability to influence others through their power. Those who have great financial, political or religious influence and preach and stand against Christ and his teachings are great antichrists. The antichrist talked about in Revelation is a powerful antichrist who will be given power, shall deceive many and cause much bloodshed and death.

It was prophesied that the antichrist would come from Rome. There is a popular theory that the Pope of the Catholic Church is the antichrist. One of my good friends at work, told me of this theory and that Pope John Paul was the antichrist. Could my friend not look at Pope John Paul for herself and see the light coming from his eyes and radiating from his spirit? Could she not hear what he had to say and not hear God and Christ in his speech? It was very clear to me, that Pope John Paul was a man of God and not the antichrist.

What is the meaning of this prophecy that the antichrist would come from Rome? The answer comes in what we think of Rome. Today one mentions Rome and what comes to mind is the city of Rome, which was once the capital of the Roman Empire. The coliseum and the ruins of old Rome in the city of modern day Rome is a center for tourism. Saint John and the people of his time did not think of Rome as a 20th century city but as the Roman Empire. The Roman Empire expanded and contracted, but at one time included countries of Europe, the Middle East and Northern Africa (see figure 14).

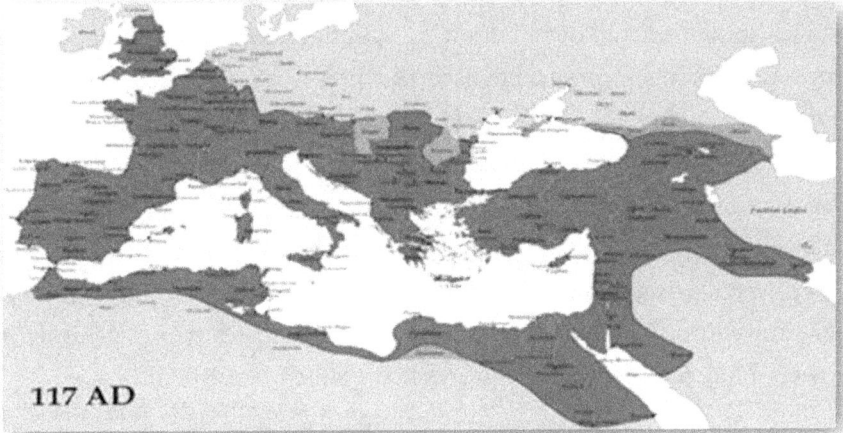

*Figure 14- Map showing extent of the Roman Empire (red)
during reign of emperor Trajan (map from Tataryn)*

*Figure 15- Colonel Kaddafi- A Great Antichrist (U.S. Navy photo
by Mass Communication Specialist 2nd Class Jesse B.)*

Colonel Kaddafi and Osama Bin Laden were both great antichrists and they have both been assassinated. A close friend of Colonel Kaddafi gives an account of Colonel Kaddafi over the number of years that she knew him. He started out a man who was charismatic, charming, with political and financial power. He used this power to terrorize, bully, murder and deceive many. Kaddafi's friend noted the change that took place with Kaddafi over the years and in the end, she noted his eyes. The eyes are the windows of the soul and in the end, there was a void; a dark abyss, a deep darkness when she looked into his eyes.

There are many antichrists in the world at this time, and there will be many more. There will be other great antichrists who will come into power. They will deceive many and bring much bloodshed.

CHAPTER 22

—— ◊ ——

THE NEW JERUSALEM

3 Nephi 20:22- And behold, this people will I establish in this land, unto the fulfilling of the covenant which I made with your father Jacob; and it shall be a New Jerusalem. And the powers of heaven shall be in the midst of this people; yea, even I will be in the midst of you.

Doctrine and Covenants 42:9- Until the time shall come when it shall be revealed unto you from on high, when the city of the New Jerusalem shall be prepared, that ye may be gathered in one, that ye may be my people and I will be your God.

NEW JERUSALEM LOCATION

Doctrine and Covenants 49:24-25- Before the great day of the Lord shall come, Jacob shall flourish in the wilderness, and the Lamanites shall blossom as the rose. Zion shall flourish upon the mountains, and shall be assembled together unto the place which I have appointed.

Doctrine and Covenants 28:9- And now, behold, I say unto you that it is not revealed, and no man knoweth where the city Zion shall be built, but it shall be given hereafter. Behold, I say unto you that it shall be on the borders by the Lamanites.

THERE ARE CLUES as to the location of the New Jerusalem. Prophecy states it will "flourish upon the mountains," "on the borders by the Lamanites."

THE LAMANITES

In a nutshell, the Lamanites are the some of the Native Americans tribes, who are descendants of one of the lost tribes of Israel. I will express my feelings towards the Lamanites (Native Americans). I met my greatest earth teacher in New Mexico who was a Native American medicine man, Christian minister and a man of God. He is my role model of everything that I know to be good and right. He has taken me into his family (tribe), of which to me is a great honor. I have come to love the Native Americans as I love my greatest teacher on earth, my friend Bearheart.

A map of the Native American Indian reservations (see figure 16) in the United States sheds light on the location of the New Jerusalem. The largest collection of Indian reservations is in Arizona and New Mexico right next to the Rocky Mountains.

LAND HAS ENERGY

Land has energy, just as we do. Robert Redford was attracted to Sundance in Utah as much for its energy as for its beauty. He can feel the energy of the land and that is a big part of why he bought the land. Have you ever seen the Grand Canyon, one of the seven great natural wonders of the world? What a spectacular sight to see. It is not just the view that is spectacular, it is the energy. The energy of the Grand Canyon is amazing, and I might add very spiritual. The land of the New Jerusalem is also blessed, for the spirit of God lives there.

Indian Reservations in the Continental United States

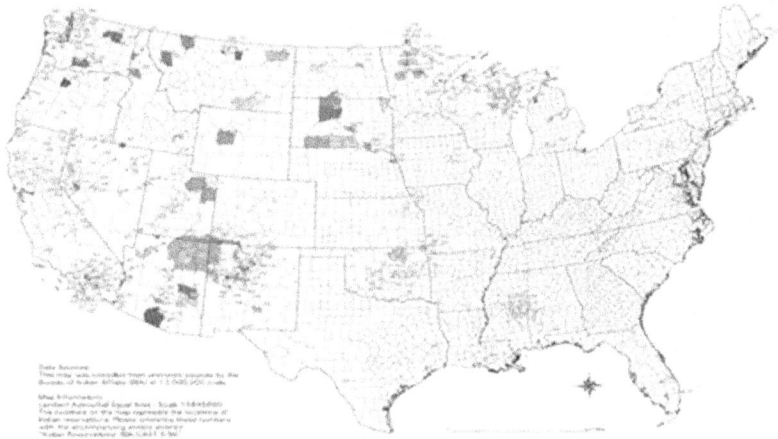

*Figure 16- Map of Native American Indian Reservations
in the United States (map from wikimedia.org)*

As a child, about 9 years old, I had a dream unlike any other dream before. The quality, vividness and spiritual feeling of the dream was exciting, eye opening and revealing. The quality of the dream was like seeing a movie with a blue ray DVD and plasma screen when you are used to seeing television on a 1950's television screen. The quality and feeling of this dream let me know this was not an ordinary dream. Some of the dream I cannot remember, but the important part of the dream, I vividly remember to this very day.

In this dream, I was looking towards the four corners area, where Colorado, Utah, Arizona and New Mexico meet. As I looked in this direction I saw a brilliant light coming from the land. It was a spiritual light and brightness; the kind I had not seen before. I woke up from this dream with eye opening, excitement and anticipation. My thought was that of a nine-year-old boy, "WOW!" I did not know the meaning or implications of this dream, but the quality and the memory of this dream is with me to this very day.

Mother Mary- The New Jerusalem will be built in northern New Mexico and southern Colorado.

I finished my medical training in New York City, and received a clear message of where I was to spend the rest of my life, in New Mexico. On the move from New York City to New Mexico, I received another message and an inner knowing, "I am going home." Message from Mother Mary is "The New Jerusalem will be built in northern New Mexico and southern Colorado." With this message from Mother Mary I finally understood the meaning of my dream when I was nine years old. I have been to this land, felt the spirit of this land and know the message from Mother Mary to be true. This is also fulfillment of prophecies that the New Jerusalem will flourish upon the mountains (Rocky Mountains), on the borders (border of Colorado and New Mexico) by the Lamanites (Native Americans living in New Mexico, Arizona and Utah).

THE GATHERING HAS ALREADY STARTED

The gathering has already started and continues at this very moment. I have seen and met people from all religions who were called by the spirit of this land and by the higher power. They have never read the scriptures of the New Jerusalem, but know they are being called. As the trials and tribulations of the world increase, the migration to the New Jerusalem will continue.

THE NEW JERUSALEM IS A CITY OF REFUGE

Doctrine and Covenants 63-75- Ye hear of wars in foreign lands; but, behold, I say unto you, they are nigh, even at your own doors, and not many years hence ye shall hear of wars in your own lands. Wherefore I, the Lord, have said, gather ye out from the eastern lands, assemble ye yourselves together ye elders of my church; go ye forth into the western countries, call upon the inhabitants to repent, build up churches unto me. And with one heart and with one mind, gather up your riches that ye may purchase an inheritance which shall hereafter be appointed unto you. And it shall be called the New Jerusalem, a land of peace, a city of refuge, a place of safety for the saints of the Most High God. And the glory of the Lord shall be there, and the terror of the Lord also shall be there, insomuch that the wicked will not come unto it, and it shall be called Zion. And it shall come to pass among the wicked, that every man that will not take his sword against his neighbor must needs flee unto Zion for safety. And there shall be gathered unto it out of every nation under heaven; and it shall be the only people that shall not be at war one with another.

People of the Jewish faith escaped from all over the world to Israel and America, because of persecution. The Jewish people will now flee to the New Jerusalem in the last days. It is not only the Jewish people that shall flee to the New Jerusalem but people of all faiths. It will be all those who choose to live God's covenants that move to this land of safety.

THE SPIRITUAL NEW JERUSALEM

John 14-2- In My Father's house are many dwelling places; if it were not so, I would have told you; for I go to prepare a place for you.

Rev 11:15- The kingdoms of this world are become the kingdoms of our Lord, and of his Christ; and he shall reign forever and ever.

To say that we go to heaven or hell at judgment day is an oversimplification. There are many dwelling places in the Father's house, many kingdoms. These kingdoms of heaven are bound by laws and if someone wants to live in that kingdom then they must abide by those laws.

God and Lucifer are building their kingdoms here on earth at this very time. I see the kingdom of heaven on this earth being built and I also see a kingdom Lucifer is building, which is spiritual Babylon (See destruction of Babylon). I see these kingdoms being built, growing and establishing themselves. I see people choosing which of these kingdoms they want to go. There will be saints from all over the world who are part of the New Jerusalem and dwell within this spiritual holy city, but live in another country. In the spirit realm, these kingdoms are outside of space and time and do not have a physical location. In the third dimensional world (planet earth) the physical location of the New Jerusalem will be in northern New Mexico and southern Colorado.

THE SIGNS THAT ARE OCCURING

Earth Changes

THE NEXT FOURTEEN chapters are a of group of signs which collectively are called the earth changes. These earth changes are earthquakes, tsunamis, volcanos, weather changes, fire and smoke in different lands, crop failure and famine, sun to become hot, falling stars, creatures in the sea dying, shift of the earth's axis, floods and the waterways to become unsafe. Part of these earth changes are a natural cycle in the history of planet earth. Part of these earth changes are directed and guided by a higher power. The size and extent of these earth changes is not fixed. There are some earth changes that will occur no matter what our best intents are. There are other earth changes that can be changed as we can change our future and our destiny.

CHAPTER 23

EARTHQUAKES

Isaiah 40:4- *Every valley shall be exalted, and every mountain and hill shall be made low: and the crooked shall be made straight, and the rough places plain:*

Ezekiel 38:20- *So that the fishes of the sea, and the fowls of the heaven, and beasts of the field, and all creeping things, and that creep upon the earth, and all the men that are upon the face of the earth, shall shake at my presence, and the mountains shall be thrown down, and the steep places shall fall, and every wall shall fall to the ground.*

Luke 21:11- *And great earthquakes shall be in divers places,*

Matthew 24:7- *and earthquakes, in divers places.*

Doctrine and Covenants 45:33- *when there shall be the testimony of earthquakes, that shall cause groaning in the midst of her (the earth), and men shall fall upon the ground and shall not be able to stand.*

Doctrine and Covenants 45:48- *...and the earth shall tremble, and reel to and fro, and the heavens also shall shake.*

Koran- 99:1-2- *When the earth is shaken with its earthquake. And the earth discharges its burdens.*

Koran- 89-21- *When the earth has been leveled - pounded and crushed*

Koran- 81-3- *And when the mountains are removed*

Edgar Cayce- *If there are greater activities in [the volcanoes] Vesuvius or Pelee, then the southern coast of California and the areas between Salt Lake and the southern portions of Nevada, we may expect, within the three months following same, inundation by the earthquakes. But these are to be more in the Southern than the Northern Hemisphere.*

Edgar Cayce- *earthquake in southern California*

Edgar Cayce- *The widespread destruction in Los Angeles and San Francisco as well as in many portions of the west coast will occur. Earth changes will occur in the central portion of the United States as well.*

Edgar Cayce- *The Earth will be broken up in the western portion of America.*

Edgar Cayce- *Canada; while the western land -- much of that is to be disturbed as, of course much in other lands.*

Hopi – *Earthquakes*

Buddhist- *Padmasambhbava- Earthquakes bring sudden floods*

Hindu-In the summer of 1983, Guru Bhagwan Rajneesh Chandra-
"... earthquakes, volcanic eruptions, and everything else that is possible
through nature."

Australian Aborigine- "The End of the 40,000-year Dreamtime" -
We're going to have tidal waves. We're going to have earthquakes.

THE EARTH AND THE HEAVENS SHALL SHAKE

AN INTERESTING PHENOMENON occurs during an earthquake and shaking
of the earth. Not only is there shaking of the earth, but there is shaking
of the heavens. As the earth shakes, the stars also appear to shake. They
are not really moving and shaking but the shaking of the observer who is
standing on the shaking earth sees the stars shaking (heavens shake).

TECTONIC PLATES

The earthquakes are an important and unmistakable sign that will occur before the end of the world as we know it and the Second Coming of
Christ. Divers in the Bible means diverse and it implies that earthquake activity will occur all over the world, on the land and ocean floor. The earthquakes, volcanoes, tsunamis and other earth changes will be generated by
the movement of tectonic plates. The tectonic plates (see Figure 17) are
sections of our earth's crust which approximates 50 miles in thickness. As
these plates of the earth's crust move past each other they occasionally get
stuck and when they get unstuck they generate earthquakes and tsunamis.

  The movement of these tectonic plates can create mountains, valleys,
deep ocean trenches, cause new land to appear and other land to disappear,
can make mountains low and valleys high.

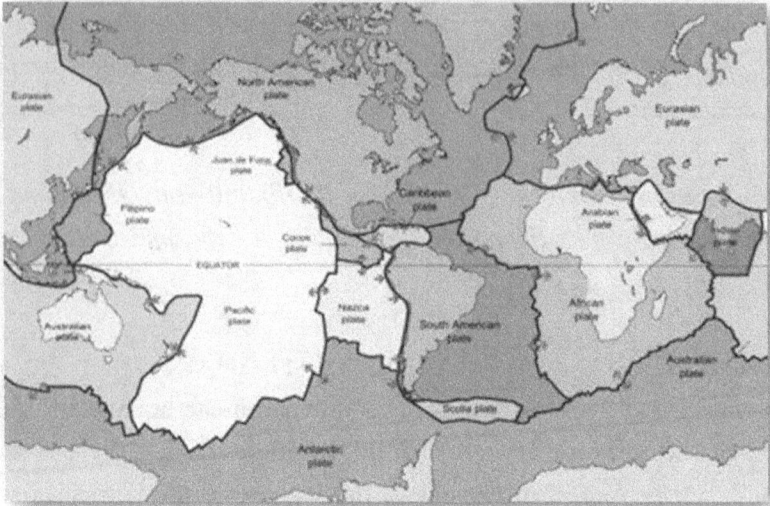

Figure 17- Tectonic Plates (Map from USGS.GOV)

The theory of plate tectonics was started in 1912 by a scientist Alfred Wegener who noticed something on the world map. He noticed that the two continents of North and South America seemed to fit quite well with the continents of Africa and Europe like a jumbled jigsaw puzzle. He thought it possible that these continents may have been one giant land mass and then they drifted apart. He called this theory continental drift, and it was met with an enormous amount of criticism in a skeptical scientific community.

Scientists studied earthquake and volcanic activity, and in the 1960's they discovered most of the earthquake and volcanic activity occurred along certain lines on the earth's surface. (See figure 17) They made a breakthrough discovery. They believed that the earth's crust was not just dirt on the surface of the earth, but rigid plates of the earth's crust. These plates are actively moving and as these plates of the earth's crust move past each other they can generate earthquakes, volcanoes and tsunamis. This groundbreaking theory became known as plate tectonics and was a revolutionary quantum leap forward in the study of earthquakes, volcanoes, tsunamis and continental drift. Plate tectonics confirmed the outrageous theory of Alfred Wegener that all the continents of the earth were once one land mass.

It is still a popular belief among seismologists and geologists that dramatic earthquakes predicted in the Bible are myth and nothing to be concerned about. The increase in earthquake activity around the world has already started and most scientists state this is nothing more than the natural variation in cycles in the history of the earth. It is normal for these tectonic plates to travel past each other a few inches each year. What scientists do not appreciate yet, is the rate that these tectonic plates move past each other is going to increase in divine order and according to divine plan. As the speed that these tectonic plates move past each other increases, there will be more frequent and greater intensity earthquakes, volcanoes and tsunamis. I have looked at the seismic data charts from around the world and my conclusion is that this sign has not **yet** been fulfilled, conclusively. I know that the earth changes and accompanying earthquakes have already begun. The seismologists and geologists will say the increase in earthquake activity is a normal variation and nothing to worry about, and certainly not of biblical significance. Their opinions will change as we are now seeing just the tip of the iceberg. As we get closer it will become clear that the amount of earthquake activity is not a normal variation, and is another sign of the end of the world as we know it and the Second Coming of Christ is at hand.

FAULT LINES

The tectonic plates (see Figure 17) showing the edge of the tectonic plates are not the only areas where there will be earthquakes and volcanic activity. There are many other faults in the earth's crust and many other places that earthquakes and volcanic activity will occur. Figure 18 (Major Faults of California) shows the major faults in the state of California. A noteworthy example of an area in the United States that is not near the edge of the North American plate is the Mississippi Valley. On December 16, 1811, New Madrid, Missouri had three powerful earthquakes (magnitude 8 on the Richter scale) and thousands of aftershocks. There were reports of cracks in the land, ground undulating like waves on the ocean, and large pieces of land rising or sinking. Damage from the earthquake occurred in Washington, DC and Charleston, South Carolina. Scientists have confirmed that earthquakes in the Mississippi Valley have occurred repeatedly in the past. The Mississippi Valley has more earthquakes than any other area in the United States east of the Mississippi.

Historical world earthquakes are the Shaanxi (Shensi,) China earthquake in 1556 was a magnitude 8 earthquake and killed 830,000 people. The Tangshan, China earthquake in 1976 was a magnitude 7.5 and killed 255,000 people. The Sumatra, Indonesia earthquake in 2004 was a magnitude 9.1 and killed 230,000 – 300,000 people.

In Utah, the Wasatch Fault runs along the west side of the Wasatch mountain range from the town of Nephi in the south to the Utah-Idaho border in the north. This is a major fault and based on history of earthquakes from the Wasatch Fault there is a 25% probability of a major earthquake occurring every 50 years.

California is one of the most beautiful parts of the United States and in the world. I fell in love with California as I would spend summer months on the beaches of the southern California coast. Geological forces played a creative roll in making California such a magnificent, diverse place to live and visit. California is also earthquake country. Figure 18 shows the major faults in the state of California and does not include the minor faults. It is not hard to see that when the earthquakes happen in diverse places throughout the world, that the state of California will have more than its fair share. I do not write this lightly, or without a pain in my heart, for it will be.

San Francisco had a major earthquake and is referred to as the 1906 Great San Francisco Earthquake (Figure 19). On April 18, 1906 at 5:12 am, a minor earthquake shook the San Francisco area. 25 seconds later the Great San Francisco Earthquake hit with major shocks for 45 to 60 seconds, as 296 miles of the San Andreas Fault moved. The quake was felt from southern Oregon to central Nevada to Los Angeles. The earthquake and the subsequent fires reportedly caused 700 deaths, although today it is believed that 2-3,000 may have died.

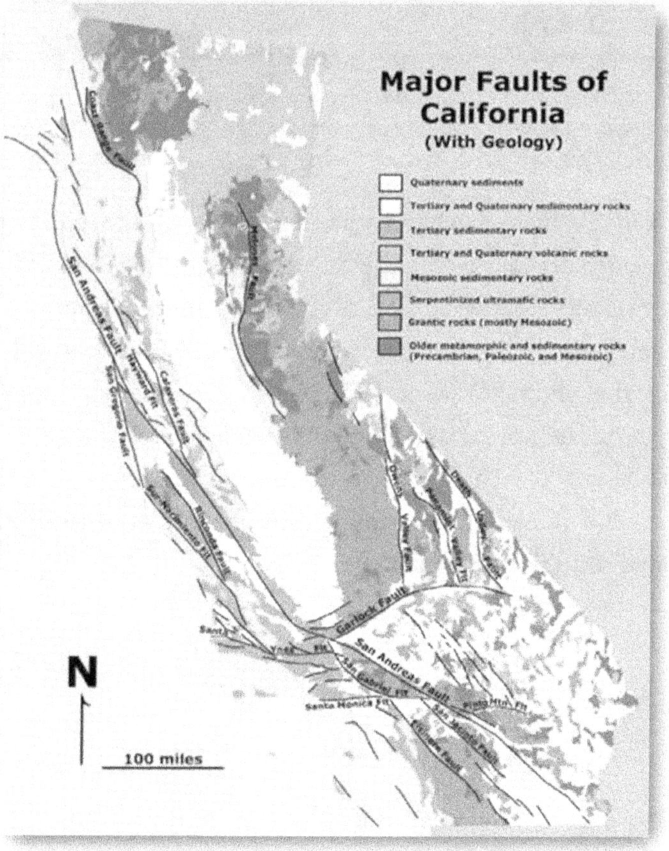

Figure 18- Major Faults of California (Geologic Map of California *by Jenning, C.W., 1997, California Dept. of Mines and Geology; geologycafe.com*)

Figure 19- San Francisco Earthquake- This photograph by Arnold Genthe shows Sacramento Street and approaching fire. (From Steinbrugge Collection of the UC Berkeley Earthquake Engineering Research Center)

A Native American shaman had a vision years ago, and in the vision he saw a major earthquake hit the San Francisco Bay area. Within minutes the city of San Francisco had disappeared into the ocean. This Native American shaman drew a picture of the vision that he saw. Figure 20 is a drawing that shows what the shaman saw. Looking northward into Marin county only the northern part of the Golden Gate bridge remained. The rest of the city of San Francisco had disappeared into the Pacific Ocean. The reason I include this vision of this shaman is because Mother Mary has stated something similar.

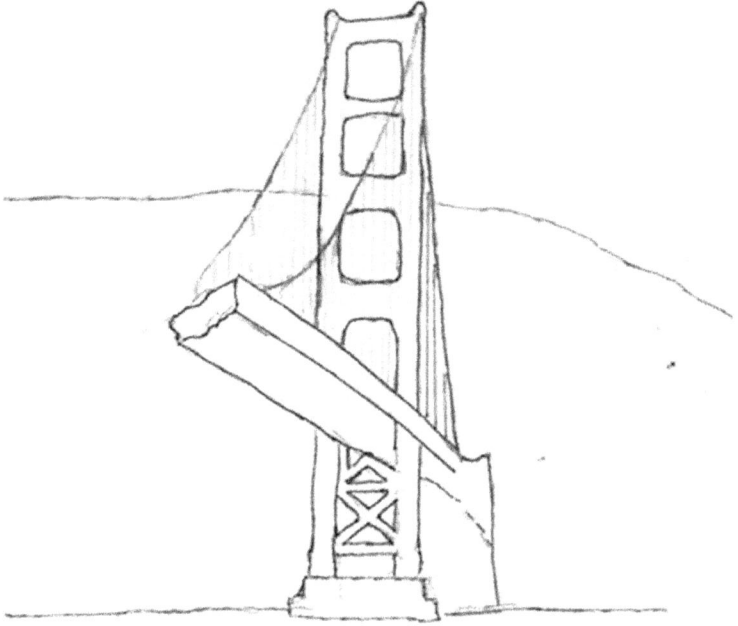

Figure 20- Shaman Vision of the Remaining Golden Gate Bridge after San Francisco Sinks into the Ocean from a Major Earthquake

115

Mother Mary- *If one person clears, San Francisco can be saved.*

Mother Mary states "If one person clears, San Francisco can be saved." This message implies that San Francisco could potentially have a disastrous end if nothing prevents it. What is the meaning of the statement by Mother Mary "If one person clears?" Mother Mary is referring to a stage of enlightenment. Depending on which tradition you train in, there are different types and number of stages of enlightenment. There are basically seven stages of enlightenment, with clearing being a final stage of enlightenment. Christians can refer to these stages of enlightenment as different stages of righteousness, for the prophets and saints of the Bible were called righteous but they were also enlightened. Who was more enlightened than Christ?

I know there will be some who do not like this writing on a potential disaster for one of the most picturesque and beautiful cities in the world. The message to me from Mother Mary was not of doom and gloom but of hope. One person could give of himself or herself in a lifelong pursuit of enlightenment to help others. This seemingly insignificant act of spiritual discipline and compassion by someone unknown can spare such a beautiful city and millions of lives. If one person attains this final state of enlightenment, then San Francisco and those that live in this beautiful city can be saved.

ALASKA EARTHQUAKES

Alaska has about 50-100 earthquakes per day; more and greater magnitude than all the earthquakes in all other states combined. Three of the six greatest earthquakes ever recorded were in Alaska. In 1964, the second largest quake ever recorded (magnitude 9.2) had an epicenter 120 kilometers southeast of Anchorage. There was a secondary tsunami along the Alaska, Canadian and western United States coast and Hawaii and the tsunami was 67 meters (200 feet) high in the Valdez inlet.

CHAPTER 24

———— § ————

TSUNAMIS

Doctrine and Covenants 88:90- *...and the voice of the waves of the sea heaving themselves beyond their bounds.*

Australian Aborigine- *The End of the 40,000-year Dreamtime"- We're going to have tidal waves. We're going to have earthquakes.*

DOCTRINE AND COVENANTS informs us that the seas shall heave themselves beyond their boundaries. This means tsunamis. A popular name for tsunamis is tidal waves but this termed is discouraged since tidal waves are not caused by the tides. A tsunami is the waves generated by the rapid displacement of a body of water. They can be caused by earthquakes, large asteroids or comets, volcanic eruptions, explosions (can be nuclear) and landslides.

Tsunamis most often occur when the tectonic plates converge and there is a sudden vertical displacement of water along the tectonic plate boundaries. Although the vertical displacement may only be one foot high in the open ocean, when it reaches shore it generates waves tens of meters high (20 to 90 feet high).

An earthquake near the Aleutian Islands, Alaska in 1946 was magnitude 7.8 on the Richter scale. It produced a tsunami of 14 meter (46 feet) high surge devastating Hilo on the island of Hawaii. The Great Chilean Earthquake of 1960 is the most powerful earthquake in recorded history with a magnitude of 9.5 on the Richter scale. Tsunamis were generated that caused waves on the Chilean coast of 25 meters (82 feet). Again Hilo, Hawaii had waves 11 meters (35 feet) high. Estimates for loss of life range from 2-6,000.

THE SUMATRA TSUNAMI

Probably the most famous tsunami was the December 26, 2004 Sumatra Tsunami. This was caused by a 9.3 magnitude earthquake off the coast of the Sumatra, Indonesia. This resulted from the Indian Tectonic Plate passing under the Eurasian Tectonic Plate causing a vertical displacement (pushing up) of the water overlying the tectonic plate boundary. There were waves as high as 25 meters (80 feet) and the tsunami killed 230,000 to 300,000 people.

THE CASCADIA SUBDUCTION ZONE

The Cascadia Subduction Zone (Figure 21) extends from Vancouver Island, Canada to northern California. This is where the Juan de Fuca Plate is sliding under the North American Plate. The last great earthquake occurred in January 26, 1700 and was a 9.0 on the Richter scale. A powerful earthquake lasted several minutes, and then the coast of Washington sank into the Pacific Ocean 1.5 meters (4.5 feet). Scientists know that the Cascadia Subduction Zone has great earthquake every 400-600 years with the last one occurring 300 years ago. They also know that this subduction zone has been storing up pressure from the plates sticking to each other as they slide past each other. This is creating stored up energy for another potential great earthquake and tsunami to hit the Pacific Northwest.

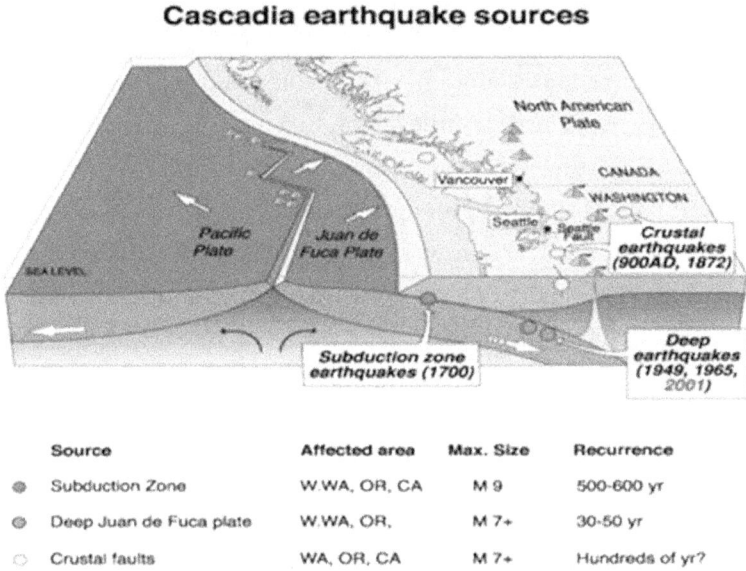

Figure 21- Cascadia Subduction Zone (Illustration
from wrgis.wr.usgs.gov and wikipedia.org)

MEGA TSUNAMI

Revelation 8:8- *And the second angel sounded, and as it were a great
mountain burning with fire was cast into the sea;*

There have been mega tsunamis in the past and will be mega tsunamis
soon. They can be up to 300 meters high (about 900 feet tall), travel as fast
as a jet, and flood 12 miles in past the coast line. Scientists have uncovered
a potential mega tsunami that could hit the east coast of the United States,
European and African coastlines. The Canary Islands lie off the northwest
coast of Africa which has an active volcano called Cumbre Vieja. A future

eruption could cause a landslide or a breaking of part of the volcano in a similar event of the Mount St. Helens volcanic eruption. This landslide would send an enormous amount of the volcano (rock) at speeds of up to 350 kilometers per hour (217 miles per hour) into the Atlantic Ocean. The mega tsunami wave is expected to reach a height of 100 meters (492 feet) on the west Sahara shore, 40 meters (131 feet) on the north coast of Brazil while Florida and the Caribbean would expect waves being 50 meters (164 feet) high. Florida is particularly vulnerable, since Florida is flat and low-lying. The tsunami would also affect the east coast of the United States.

CHAPTER 25

———— ❦ ————

VOLCANOES

Revelation 8:8- And the second angel sounded, and as it were a great mountain burning with fire was cast into the sea: and the third part of the sea became as blood;

Koran 70-8- The Day that the sky will be like molten brass

Hindu- In the summer of 1983, Guru Bhagwan Rajneesh Chandra "Man is now living in his most critical moment and it is a crisis of immense dimensions. Earthquakes, volcanic eruptions, and everything else that is possible through nature.

Edgar Cayce- After activities by Mt. Vesuvius, Mt. Pelee, the southern coast of California, the areas between Great Salt Lake and the southern portions of Nevada, we may expect, within the three months following, inundation by earthquakes, more in the Southern than the Northern Hemisphere.

THESE SCRIPTURES ARE referring to volcanoes. As the rate which tectonic plates move past each other speeds up there will be an increase in earthquakes, tsunamis and volcanic activity in frequency and size. It is one of the signs foreshadowing the end of the world as we know it and the Second Coming of Christ.

I am totally fascinated and mesmerized by Mother Nature and the force of nature. As I watch films on volcanoes and lava flows I am watching the primal force of creation as God and mother earth continue in the never ceasing path of creation. I can watch film footage of volcanoes showering forth jets of hot magma into the air for hours and be mesmerized. I see lava flowing down the mountainside of volcanoes and wish I was there to witness this act of creation firsthand. The red-hot magma exudes primal force but also beauty as if viewing the Mona Lisa. I am humbled by the sheer force and power of nature and how insignificant I might seem in comparison. With all the beauty, magnificence and power of one of God's greatest creations, this beauty not only has the power to create but also destroy.

Destruction has taken on a very negative connotation in the world today. God views destruction in a very different light. He views destruction and creation as different sides of the same coin and it is impossible to have one without the other. Destruction is part of creation. It is the divine order of the universe and all things. Before God can create a masterpiece, He must first clean the workspace. Only with the workspace clean and unspoiled is He free to create a beautiful and magnificent work.

God is about to create a world of unimaginable beauty, peace and abundance. Many of us can imagine quite a bit about paradise and it is still beyond our imagination. Before He can create and give us paradise, the world and all in the world must be purified. If we want paradise are we willing to pay the price? When we are standing in a world of unspeakable beauty, love and harmony we will look back and say it was a small price to pay for paradise. What a gift we shall give to our children, their children and their children. They will be born into paradise and will remember the sacrifices we made to give them such a gift.

There are steps or events that need to happen before we can enjoy and partake of paradise. The great flood at the time of Noah was necessary for the world to be reborn into a paradisiacal glory. This event was baptism by water of planet earth and a necessary step of purification. The second step in the purification of mother earth is about to happen. It is purification by fire and the Holy Spirit of God. Only after this second purification will our earth be ready for rebirth into a paradisiacal glory. This purification is third dimensional and spiritual. The spiritual is purification by the spirit of God. The third dimensional purification is by fire. This will be in two ways. First, is by volcanoes and their fire from deep beneath the earth's crust. Second, there will be by fire caused by weather changes, now referred to as climate change. Purification by volcanoes and wild fires will complete the process, and the earth we love will be ready to be reborn into a paradisiacal glory.

Volcanologists state Mt. Vesuvius (Figure 22) is ready to erupt again, and that "it is due for another cataclysmic eruption." The problem currently is so many Italians living near Mt. Vesuvius, because the land is so fertile. 550,000 people live in the "red zone" (close to Mt Vesuvius and in greatest danger in a volcanic eruption), and unless you have a boat, there are limited highways to escape the next eruption.

Mount St. Helens had a significant impact on people living in the Northwest. May 18, 1980 at 8:32 am Mount St. Helens in Southwest Washington State erupted (see figure 24). There was a 5.1 magnitude earthquake as ash and volcanic debris blew thousands of feet into the air. The north side of Mount St. Helens collapsed creating a massive landslide of rock and dirt. The largest landslide in recorded history at a speed of up to 150 miles per hour covered areas with debris 150 feet high. The force of the volcanic blast of 300 miles per hour leveled trees for 17 miles. The volcanic eruption lasted 9 hours. The pyroclastic flow covered 6 square miles with temperatures of 1,300 degrees. 57 people died, and the eruption destroyed 27 bridges, 200 homes, 185 miles of roadway and 15 miles of railway. Loss to animal life was large.

Figure 22-Top- Mt. Vesuvius Eruption 1944 (The March 1944 eruption of Vesuvius, by Jack Reinhardt, B-24 tailgunner, USAAF during World War II

Figure 23- Bottom- Plaster casts of Victims of 79 AD Vesuvius Eruption (Photo by LancevorPompeii Garden of the Fugitives, wikipedia.org)

Figure 24- Mount St. Helens Before and After Eruption 1980
Eruption (Photos courtesy USGS)

Revelation 6:12- *And I beheld when he had opened the sixth seal, and, lo, there was a great earthquake; and the sun became black as sackcloth of hair, and the moon became as blood;*

Koran- 75:7-8- *At length, when the sight is dazed, and the moon is buried in darkness.*

Koran 81:1-2- *When the sun (with its spacious light) is folded up; When the stars fall, losing their lustre;*

Something else happened with the eruption of Mount St. Helens; there was fulfillment of one of the signs in the last days talked about in the Bible. The ash blown into the atmosphere began to block out sunlight. The sun and moon initially turned red, then as more ash was blown into the atmosphere the sun and moon darkened and then eventually lost their light. This was fulfillment of the sign in Revelation of the moon turning to blood (red) and the sun darkened, turning as black as sackcloth and then eventually not giving any light at all. This is also fulfilling of prophecies in the Koran the sun, moon and stars becoming dim, and eventually losing their light. Just because this sign has been fulfilled does not mean that it won't happen again. It will and with greater size so this sign will become clear for all in the world to see.

CURRENT VOLCANIC ACTIVITY

The volcanic activity is increasing, according to some volcanologists. As of 2014, volcanoes are erupting in Iceland, Indonesia, Mexico, Hawaii, Ecuador, and recently in New Guinea, Italy, Columbia and the Philippines.

THUNDERINGS AND LIGHTNINGS

Revelation 16:18- And there were voices, and thundering, and lightnings

The eruption of Mount St. Helens caused fulfillment of another sign. The cover of ash causes lightning and thunder. There will be a new cause of thunder and lightning that is unique to volcanoes and it is called volcanic lightning. The ash cloud created by volcanoes has been termed "dirty thunderstorms." As the ash particles collide they create friction and static electricity. Volcanoes will be erupting all over the world there will be an ash cloud of enormous size. This ash cloud will cause static electricity and there will be thunder and lightning all over the world and fulfillment of another sign of the last days.

CHAPTER 26

─────────── § ───────────

WEATHER CHANGES

Revelation 16:12- And the sixth angel poured out his vial upon the great river Euphrates; and the water thereof was dried up, that the way of the kings of the east might be prepared.

Jeremiah 23:19-20- Behold, the storm of the LORD has gone forth in wrath, Even a whirling tempest; It will swirl down on the head of the wicked. The anger of the LORD will not turn back Until He has performed and carried out the purposes of His heart; in the last days you will clearly understand it....

Doctrine and Covenants 88:89-90- In our day there are to be dust storm, whirlwinds, tornados, floods, and a great hail storm sent to destroy the crops of the earth. --

Mormon 8:29- Yea, it shall come in a day when there shall be heard of fires, and tempests,

Hopi- The sun shall become hot.

Buddhist- Padmasambhava -No rain falls in season, but out of season; the valleys are flooded... while fire storms and tornadoes destroy temples, stupas and cities in an instant.

Iroquois- The Great Wind will cleanse the Earth and return it to its original state.

CLIMATE CHANGE

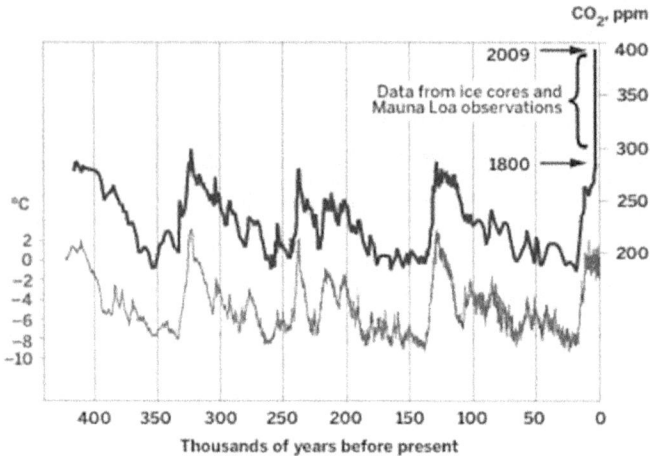

Figure 25 Data from the Vostok ice core in Antarctica, from 410,000 years ago to the present. The top curve (blue) shows CO2 (in parts per million) from air bubbles in the ice core. The bottom curve (brown) shows the temperature in the Antarctic region. Note that over the past 100 years the CO2 concentration has dramatically risen, while the temperature has not yet risen proportionally. (Credit: Michael Ernst/Woods Hole Research Center)

FIGURE 25 SHOWS that there is a direct correlation between the level of CO2 levels in the atmosphere and the earth's temperature. Over hundreds of thousands of years when the CO2 levels have increased so has the earth's temperature. We have had an increase in CO2 levels in our atmosphere and the current level of CO2 on figure 25 is near 400 PPM and climbing. The principal cause of the elevation of CO2 levels is the man's burning of fossil fuels (oil, coal and others).

Climate change does not mean that the whole world is becoming warmer. Climate change is just what its name implies, climate change. Some places will become warmer while others will become cooler. Some places will become dry and arid while others become wet and have flooding. Most climatologists agree that climate change is real and happening at this very moment. Al Gore did mankind and our earth a great service to bring climate change to public awareness. Greenhouse gases are a real threat to all life. Although the term climate change is more appropriate, accurate and descriptive, the term of global warming is becoming revitalized.

Leading scientists are concerned about the greenhouse gases, climate change and global warming. Scientists are aware that climate change or global warming has positive feedback loops. The warmer the atmosphere and oceans become, the more CO_2 and other greenhouse gases produced and then the atmosphere and oceans become even warmer. There are many positive feedback loops that scientists are just now becoming aware of. With the positive feedback loops, global warming can become a runaway train, impossible to correct past a certain point. This is a ticking time bomb waiting to explode.

As the oceans warm, they will continue to release more CO_2 into the atmosphere. As the Arctic, Antarctic and Greenland Ice Sheets melt the sunlight that was reflected by the white snow, will be absorbed by the earth. The more sunlight is absorbed and the warmer the earth and atmosphere become.

The Amazon rainforest is an enormous absorber of CO_2 in our atmosphere and has been described as the "lungs of the earth." The Amazon rainforest absorbs CO_2 in our atmosphere and gives us oxygen to breathe. The rain forest is a vital part of world ecosystem and is roughly the size of the continental United States. Some scientists have stated more than "half of the Amazon rainforest will be damaged or destroyed within 20 years if deforestation, forest fires, and climate trends continue" at present pace. Some of these effects could be irreversible.

With continued climate change, droughts are going to become more common. A big concern to planet earth is drought in the Amazon rainforest. A drought in the Amazon rainforest could kill trees and plants which would become rich fuel for forest fires. There was an extreme drought in the Amazon in 2005 and there will be more droughts in the Amazon rainforest and around the world in the future. The reason this is so harmful is there is not only loss of the ability to absorb CO_2 and produce necessary oxygen, but the burning of the forests produces CO_2. This will have a doubly devastating effect on global warming.

A major concern to scientists is permafrost, which is the plant life that froze and remained frozen for about 40,000 years with the onset of the ice age. The permafrost contains vast stores of CO_2 and methane, and methane is 22 times more powerful than CO_2 in greenhouse effect. As permafrost melts, bacteria in the soil start a decaying of this once frozen organic material. This decaying process releases CO_2 and methane. This also has a positive feedback loop and becomes a vicious cycle. The warmer the climate gets, the more permafrost melts and the more CO_2 and methane are released into the atmosphere. The more CO_2 and methane released into the atmosphere, the more sunlight trapped and the warmer the climate. The world has vast stores of permafrost and vast stores of CO_2 and methane within the permafrost. The release of these gases would have a profound effect on greenhouse gases and atmospheric temperatures.

Let's look at the results of climate change so far. Global land temperature is 1.26 degrees Fahrenheit warmer for June 2009 than the 20th century average and sixth warmest on record. The average surface ocean temperature is 1.12 degrees Fahrenheit above the 20th century average, and June 2009 and second warmest on record. This elevation of CO_2 levels is causing earth's temperatures to rise and the result is climate change.

"The average temperatures have climbed 1.4 degrees Fahrenheit around the world since 1880 and the rate of warming is increasing. Arctic ice is rapidly disappearing, as glaciers and mountain snows are rapidly melting. The hottest year ever was 2014, with 14 out of 15 of the hottest years occurring since the year 2000. The average arctic winter temperature has already increased by 11 degrees Fahrenheit. The northern polar ice cap has decreased in thickness by 40% and its size has decreased by 6% over the past 40 years. Coastal glaciers in Greenland are undergoing rapid thinning by as much as 3 feet per year. Reductions in crop yields are anticipated for many regions, especially in later decades as temperatures rise. Recent studies have shown that for rice, the world's most significant grain crop, yields fall by 10% for each degree of warming." "An upsurge in the amount of extreme weather events, such as wildfires, heat waves, and strong tropical storms, is also attributed in part to climate change by some experts."

TEMPESTS

The prophecy of tempests, literally means fierce storms. There will be increased number and intensity of tornados and hurricanes. The intensity of hurricanes (Atlantic) and cyclones (Pacific) is directly linked to the surface temperature of the oceans. Scientific data shows an increase in ocean surface temperatures. I have heard climatologists say there has been a double in the number of category 4 and 5 hurricanes. Experts think hurricanes will increase in intensity and number with increase rainfall, over the next century.

CLIMATE CHANGE AND TEMPESTS ARE FULFILLING OF PROPHECY

There are scientists who state these variations in our weather are just natural variations, although their numbers have been steadily shrinking. Most scientists will say the increase in the number of earthquakes, volcanoes, tsunamis and other disastrous events are just natural variations and are nothing to worry about. Even the hardline scientists will have their eyes open as events of the last days unfold. These events are fulfillment of biblical prophecy.

Climate change will have an enormous impact on our environment. Warmer oceans are fuel for developing storms and hurricanes (cyclones). These warmer waters will increase the number and intensity of hurricanes and storms that we will see over the coming years. It is climate change that will cause increase rains and flooding in areas not used to increase rain. Where once there was rich plant life, there will be dry conditions leading to loss of crops and contributing to famine. It is climate change that will lead to fulfillment of prophecy "In our day there are to be dust storms, whirlwinds, tornados, floods, and a great hail storm sent to destroy the crops of the earth." Another important sign given in Revelation is the Euphrates River will dry up, again the result of climate change.

Mother Mary- I shall turn deserts into paradise and paradise into deserts.

Message from Mother Mary is "I shall turn deserts into paradise and paradise into deserts." It may surprise you to hear what is true about climate change. The events of the world are influenced by our free will but there is only one in control at this very moment and that is the Most High God. God is the primal force behind climate change and the moving force behind the disasters that are to come. The climate change and resulting severe weather is part of the purification that will be occurring in the years to come. It is fulfilling of prophecy.

It would be wrong to say, "Well if God is the primary force behind these disasters then why should we interfere. Let the disasters run their course if that is what God wants." That would be a wrong conclusion. Everything we do to open our hearts to our fellow man is a step in the right direction. Every step we take to take care of God's creatures (animals) who are dependent on us and to be stewards of this planet is a step in the right direction. Every step we take to take care of the planet; a precious jewel of God's creation is a step in the right direction. Look at the baby in her mother's arms, looking into her mother's eyes or the child who looks into her father's eyes. Our babies and children are dependent on us to take care of them and are relying on us to see them through. All life and all animals are looking to us as the stewards of the earth. We are charged with their care and the care of the world.

It is true that we often do not appreciate what we have until it is gone. No one knows this better than the higher power. He will be taking us precariously close to losing all that we love. Look at the wondrous sights and beautiful places throughout the world, for we are coming close to losing them forever. Only when they are about to be taken away forever do we really appreciate them. Turning our hearts towards our fellow man is sine qua non; without which all will be lost. Almost important is the turning our hearts to one of God's jewels. Our planet that has kept us safe in a violent, inhospitable solar system, has provided water, food, shelter for man and all of God's creatures and a place of breathtaking beauty. God gave us stewardship over the earth, all plants and animals and we have not done a great job with our stewardship. When we are about to lose all that we love, our hearts will also be turned towards mother earth. Every step we make to help save our planet and the environment is a necessary step towards saving ourselves. We will become good stewards again.

Mother Mary- message to Gianna Sullivan - Children, for the last 20 years I have oftentimes spoken of "change." I have told you that there is no time for fear; there is only time for change. You must know by now that I have recently spoken of an arising of "two suns." When you see the two suns on the horizon, you must know that this is a time of change, a time of this new beginning about which I have spoken to you before.

After you see the two suns, there is only a short time before you will see a tremendous change in weather. After this, as you know, there are more changes to come.

The message from Mother Mary is there will appear two suns on the horizon which will be another sign to look for (see chapter on Falling Stars). Mother Mary further states that shortly after the prophecy of the two suns is fulfilled, we will see a "tremendous change in the weather."

CHAPTER 27

FIRE AND SMOKE IN DISTANT LANDS

Revelation 8:6-7- Hail and fire mingled with blood. A third part of the trees burned up. All green grass burned up.

Mormon 8:29- Yea, it shall come in a day when there shall be heard of fires, and tempests, and vapors of smoke in foreign lands;

Hopi- There will be many columns of smoke and fire such as White Feather has seen the white man make in the deserts not far from here.

THE FIRE AND smoke will come from different sources. The weather changes will bring drought and heat that will cause the lush forests and grasslands to become dry. The dry forests and grasslands become fuel for fire and will be set ablaze and burn. Lightning is another important source of fires. Volcanic ash clouds are a rich source of volcanic thunder storms and lightning from these thunder storms will cause many fires.

THE SIGNS YET TO COME

CHAPTER 28

---- § ----

Terrible Hail Storm, Crops Fail and Famine

Revelation16:21- And there fell upon men a great hail out of heaven, every stone bout the weight of a talent; and men blasphemed God because of the plague of the hail; for the plague thereof was exceedingly great.

Luke 21:11 -And great earthquakes shall be in divers places, and famines, and pestilences.

Doctrine and Covenants 88:89-90- In our day there are to be dust storm, whirlwinds, tornados, floods, and a great hail storm sent to destroy the crops of the earth.

Buddhist- Padmasamhbhava- Famine, frost and hail govern many unproductive years... release[ing] diseases, horrible epidemics and plagues which spread like wildfire, striking men and cattle.

THE COMET-ASTEROID THAT hits northern Europe will send dust into the atmosphere, which will block out sunlight and cool the earth's atmosphere. Volcanoes will be erupting all over the world. Volcanic ash will pour into the atmosphere and produce acid rain and leachates (minerals in high concentration, organic material and other contaminants making for difficult conditions for plants to grow. As volcanic ash fills our atmosphere there will be less sunlight that penetrates the volcanic ash cloud and then there will be another change in the climate. A great ash cloud (from volcanoes) and dust cloud (from the asteroid comet striking northern Europe) will result in much less light penetrating the atmosphere. There will be a drop in the earth's atmospheric temperature giving us cold, long winters and short summers. There will be less sunlight, a very short growing season and a great hail storm, leading crop failure causing famine. Those who have heeded the warnings and prepared, will weather the storm. Those who did not prepare will face famine and starvation. Food is a very powerful force necessary for life and famine is a major contributor to wars and civil unrest.

CHAPTER 29

—— § ——

SUN TO BECOME HOT

Hopi- *The sun shall become hot.*

METHANE HYDRATE IS (also referred to as methane clathrate or methane ice) is ice that contains a large amount of methane. There are enormous stores of methane in the sediments of the ocean and permafrost. Methane is 22 times more powerful a greenhouse gas than CO2, and the methane reserve is twice that, by volume of the world's fossil fuels reserves. Scientists are concerned about the vast storehouse of methane hydrate release would have on the environment.

Scientists are now saying that over the next one hundred years that the earth could have the temperature increase several degrees. We are not going to have to wait one hundred years to see fulfilling of prophecy and the temperature increasing several degrees. What can cause the earth's atmosphere and oceans to heat so dramatically, so quickly. The answer may come from the solving the mystery of the Permian mass extinction. This mass extinction baffled scientists for decades and no one could give clear understanding of why 95% of life became extinct 200 million years ago, during the end of the Permian period of the earth. Finally, the puzzle was solved by the combination of two naturally occurring disasters. First, was the massive eruption of the Siberian Traps volcano. Once the dust settled from the volcanic eruption there was a rise in atmospheric temperature of 5 degrees Celsius (9 degrees Fahrenheit) from the amount of CO2 put into the atmosphere. The next clue came from Permian rocks in Greenland.

Studying the rocks scientists found an enormous amount of carbon 12, which can come from the gas methane. Methane hydrate stores are found in our oceans all over the world and when the oceans temperatures rise enough these stores of methane are released into the atmosphere. Methane is a greenhouse gas, twenty-two times stronger than CO_2. This release of methane increased the temperature another 5 degrees Celsius (9 degrees Fahrenheit). The combined temperature elevation of the atmosphere was now 10 degrees Celsius (18 degrees Fahrenheit) higher, leading to 95% mass extinction and paving the way for the age of the dinosaurs.

Methane hydrate is precariously unstable, and needs low temperatures or a combination of high pressure and low temperatures to remain stable. If the temperature increases or pressure decreases, then the methane hydrate destabilizes and methane is released. There is another way that methane can be released and that is submarine landslides.

BIGGEST WILDCARD OF ALL

Scientists do not understand or appreciate the biggest wildcard of them all. Biggest wildcard is the coming earth changes. Let us see the effect the coming earth changes will have on climate change and global warming.

Volcanoes produce large amounts of CO_2 which will enter our atmosphere. With the coming droughts, large amounts of vegetation and forests will die off. The coming fires will burn the forests that we depend on to absorb CO_2. The fires also produce CO_2 as they burn the dying vegetation. This is doubly catastrophic with less vegetation and forests to absorb CO_2 and more CO_2 put into the atmosphere from burning vegetation.

The most threatening of all is methane hydrate. Earthquakes and volcanic activity will increase and the earthquakes will create slope failure and result in underwater landslides. The landslides will release the methane into the ocean which will rise into the atmosphere.

Prophecy of mountains made low and valleys made high, does not just apply to land but the oceans as well. As parts of the land sink into the ocean, parts of the ocean will rise and become land. As the ocean floor rises, the methane hydrate will be exposed to warmer waters and lower water pressures and the methane will be released. The methane released will dramatically increase the air and water temperatures.

Hopi prophecy also foretells "the sun shall become hot." The atmosphere and oceans are already warming but soon there will be a greater rise in the temperature of atmosphere and oceans.

CHAPTER 30

———— ◊ ————

SUPER VOLCANO

Figure 26- Yellowstone Caldera-
A Super Volcano (Image courtesy US Geological Survey)

SUPERVOLCANO

WE KNOW THAT volcanoes exist and we know their effects. We have seen the aftermath of the eruption of Mount Saint Helens. What is less well known is that here in the United States lies a super volcano that is active. This super volcano lies mostly in Yellowstone National Park and it is enormous. Figure 26 above shows a caldera in Yellowstone National Park. The magna chamber is 30 miles wide and 50 miles long. This super volcano erupted 640,000 years ago, and buried the land in one half mile deep pyroclastic flow with the equivalent size of "New York City and large portions of Long Island, New Jersey and Connecticut." The pyroclastic flow is the "heavy stuff that collapses out of an ash cloud and can travel up to 60 miles away at speeds up to 100 yards per second. No living beings caught in the pyroclastic flow can survive." "The ash you breathe is full of tiny bits of glass causing the blood vessels in your lung to rupture. Water in your lungs combines with this volcanic ash, and essentially you drown in a kind of soup or cement of wet volcanic ash." "A super eruption would smother many millions of square miles under an inch or more of ash. Less than an inch can disrupt most forms of agriculture, so a single super eruption could lead to the starvation of millions of people. (Wildlife and natural inhabitants would suffer just as grievously.) Ash would collapse roofs, poison water supplies, and clog machinery such as vehicle and aircraft engines, causing transportation to grind to a halt." "Probably something like a third of the United States would be uninhabitable maybe for a few months, even a year or two."

Yellowstone is super eruption that is likely to happen as a prelude and purification of mother earth. This is not the only super volcano. There are similar calderas under Hawaii, Indonesia, Japan and in New Zealand. It will not be one volcano erupting, but many volcanoes all over the world that will be fulfillment of prophecy.

CHAPTER 31

—— ◊ ——

FALLING STARS

Revelation 8:10-12- *And the third angel sounded, and there fell a great star from heaven, burning as it were a lamp, and it fell upon the third part of the rivers, and upon the fountains of waters; And the name of the star is called wormwood: and the third part of the waters became wormwood; and many men died of the waters, because they were made bitter. And the fourth angel sounded, and the third part of the sun was smitten, and a third part of the moon, and a third part of the stars; so as the third part of them was darkened, and the day shone not for a third part of it, and the night likewise.*

Doctrine and Covenants 29-14- *stars shall fall from heaven*

Koran- 81-2-And when the stars fall, dispersing

Mother Mary- message to Gianna Sullivan - Children, for the last 20 years I have oftentimes spoken of "change." I have told you that there is no time for fear; there is only time for change. You must know by now that I have recently spoken of an arising of "two suns." When you see the two suns on the horizon, you must know that this is a time of change, a time of this new beginning about which I have spoken to you before. After you see the two suns, there is only a short time before you will see a tremendous change in weather. After this, as you know, there are more changes to come.

After a while, you will see a time when there is another body in orbit around your solar system, coming between Earth and the Sun and leading to tremendous devastation. Approximately 60-70% of the world's population, as you know it, will cease. Of those who survive, 60% of them could die of disease and starvation.

Nostradamus *Century 1, Number 69.*
A mile-wide mountain strikes earth
after there is peace, war, famine, and floods,
the asteroid strike causes widespread flooding of nations,
some of which are ancient.

Nostradamus *Quatrain 2.41*
The great star for seven days will burn,
The cloud will make two suns appear:
The great mastiff will be all night howling,
When the great pontiff changes his land.

Edgar Cayce- *The upper portion of Europe will be changed as in the twinkling of an eye.*

Benu- *An asteroid (or comet) will hit northern Europe.*

Hopi- *And this is the Ninth and Last Sign: You will hear of a dwelling-place in the heavens, above the earth, that shall fall with a great crash. It will appear as a blue star. Very soon after this, the ceremonies of my people will cease.*

Hopi- *When the Purifier comes, We shall see him as a little star, which will approach very close and sit in out heavens, watching us. The Purifier will show us many wonderful signs in our heavens.*

Dogon people in western Africa: *"The Return of the Original Visitors" a new star, "the star of the tenth moon", will appear in the sky.*

I WOULD LIKE to start with a brief overview of smaller bodies orbiting our sun. We are aware of the major planets and minor planet (Pluto) and moons that orbit the planets in our solar system. There are also smaller bodies circling the sun. These have been categorized into three major groups: comets, asteroids and meteoroids.

COMETS

Comets have a visible coma or tail due to the ice in their outer core which is vaporizing by solar radiation. They originate in the Kuiper Belt (Figure 27) which lies beyond the orbit of Neptune and some originate from an even greater distance from the sun in the Oort Cloud. Some comets have become famous and well known, such as Haley's comet. Comets have been called dirty snowballs because of their composition of rock, dust, ice and frozen gases. They range from 100 meters to 40 + kilometers in diameter (328 feet to 25miles+). Comets do enter the inner solar system and do cross earth's orbital path.

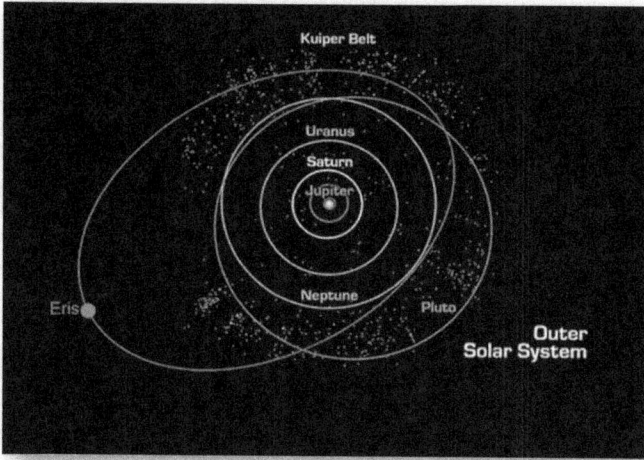

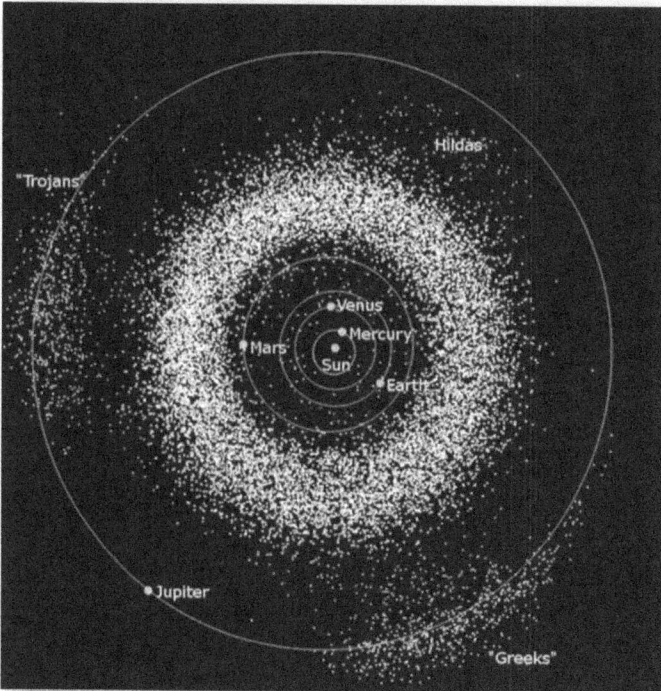

Figure 27- Top- The Kuiper Belt (from NASA.gov)

Figure 28- Bottom- The Asteroid Belt (from wikipedia.org)

ASTEROIDS

Asteroids originate in the Asteroid Belt (Figure 28) and vary in composition but appear to be more rock and less ice when compared to comets. They are greater than 10 meters (30 feet) in diameter and they originate mainly in the asteroid belt. One asteroid, Ceres, is 600 hundred miles in diameter. Occasionally asteroids collide, jettisoning an asteroid into earth's orbit.

METEROIDS

Meteoroids are asteroids but are less than 10 meters (30 feet) in diameter, and originate mainly in the asteroid belt.

FALLING STARS

Falling stars or shooting stars are a spectacle to see in the night sky. As small bits of rock, meteoroids, enter the earth's atmosphere they burn up leaving a trail of light. Like the rainbow, they are one of God's most beautiful creations and He wants us to watch and enjoy.

Figure 29- The Moon Showing Craters Created by Asteroid and Comet Impacts (Photo by Gregory H. Revera, wikipedia.org)

Mankind has long believed that our solar system was stable and safe, especially since we have a protective atmosphere. Take a close look at the moon and you will see that our solar system is a violent neighborhood. The moon is teaming with tens of thousands of craters, some gigantic in size. Our earth is larger than our moon and has been hit by asteroids and comets more than the moon. There have been many that have hit the earth and it is scientific consensus that a 6-mile-wide asteroid hit the Yucatan peninsula which wiped out the dinosaurs.

How does an asteroid or comet that is relatively small in size compared to our earth do such enormous damage? It causes such enormous damage by its tremendous speed. The comet or asteroid travels at 26,000 miles per hour or 13 miles per second, 60 times faster than a bullet (1,000 feet per second). As the asteroid or comet hits the solid earth all that kinetic energy (the mass of the rock times velocity) creates energy to be released. Scientists equate the energy released by an asteroid or comet hitting the earth to tons of exploding dynamite (TNT). This is how scientists equate the power of an exploding hydrogen bomb.

Figure 30- Meteor Crater in Northern Arizona (Photo by Churnett, wikipedia.org)

Every day we are hit by 25 tons of meteoric material. Once per year an asteroid the size of a car hits our atmosphere, creating a blazing fireball but burning up before it touches ground. Every thousand years an asteroid the size of the statue of liberty hits earth, which is about twice the size the asteroid which created the Arizona's crater. Every million years, one the size of a mountain hits earth, and threatens all life.

It was once believed that craters, like Meteor Crater in northern Arizona (Figure 30), were from extinct volcanoes. Scientists are now able to analyze the soil surrounding the crater to determine if the crater is the remains of an extinct volcano or an asteroid or comet hitting the earth. An asteroid 150 feet in diameter created crater one mile in diameter called the Meteor Crater. It pulverized 175 million tons of earth, flinging it tens of thousands of feet into the atmosphere. This asteroid released the equivalent of 10-20 megatons of TNT.

Scientists have concluded that every 100,000 years everything more than 50 lbs. dies from an asteroid or comet striking the earth. One wiped out the dinosaurs only 6 miles in diameter when it hit the northern border of the Yucatan peninsula, 200 miles west of Cancun 65 million years ago. It was 200 times bigger than the rock that hit in Arizona and released 100 million megatons of energy. The shock wave created earthquakes and massive tsunamis around the world. A global firestorm was started by red hot cinders and rock flung from the asteroid impact. Next, nitrogen oxides and sulfur dioxide combine with water to form acid rain. The dust in the air blocked out sunlight cooling the atmosphere and stopping plant growth. Global warming came from CO_2 created by the forest and grassland fires, and methane gas released from ocean sediments. The atmosphere could have reached temperatures of 1,000 degrees sparking fires all over the world. This combination of events was the ultimate demise of the dinosaurs and 50% of the species on the face of the earth.

Asteroids and comets do not have to hit the earth's surface in order to cause damage. Asteroids and comets can explode in the atmosphere. The asteroid or comet can hit the earth's atmosphere with such tremendous speed that it is like hitting a wall of cement, causing a release of all the kinetic energy in the atmosphere. On January 18, 2000, an asteroid in Western Canada appeared as bright as the sun. It crossed the morning sky and then exploded in the atmosphere with the force of 5-10 thousand tons of TNT (equivalent to a nuclear bomb) over Tagish Lake, Canada. It was a spectacle to behold, and was monitored on defense satellites and seismic monitoring stations. The asteroid was estimated to be 7 meters across and weigh 200 to 250 tons. In 2001, an asteroid hit and exploded above the Pacific Ocean releasing the equivalent power of 10 Hiroshima bombs. In 2002, another asteroid exploded over the Mediterranean Sea.

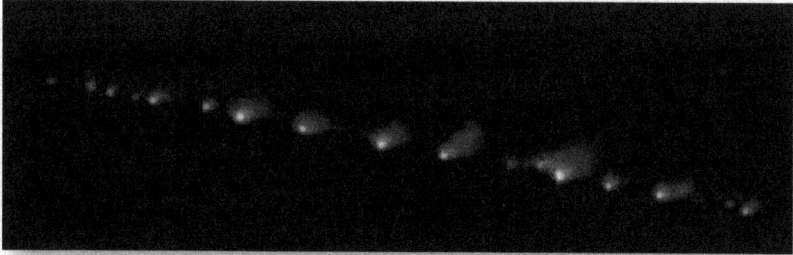

Figure 31- Top- Comet Schumacher Levy 9 Breaks into 20 Fragments (from wikipedia.org)

Figure 32- Bottom- Comet Schumacher Levy 9 Collides with Jupiter (Image ifa.hawaii.edu)

In July 1994, the comet Schumacher Levy 9 broke into 20 fragments (Figure 31). The twenty fragments of the comet then collided with Jupiter (Figure 32) and surprised and opened the minds of scientists and astronomers, because of the amazing destructive power released when these heavenly bodies strike a planet. The blast of the cloud was as big as planet earth and was the most destructive event ever witnessed in our solar system. Scientists received a rude awakening as to how vulnerable earth was to strikes from asteroids and comets. After this dramatic event finding asteroids and comets that could hit earth became top government priority. NASA, other organizations and individuals are now searching for what they call NEOs or near earth objects. NASA has found many NEOs and there are 850 NEOs orbiting near earth. One of the NEOs discovered is 1950, DA, is the "most dangerous known rock in space." It is scheduled to collide with earth in 2880 with energy release of 100,000 megatons of energy. Scientists have discovered many NEOs but estimate that there could be 600 more undiscovered NEOs and one that could hit earth. Scientists have mapped and named 100,000 asteroids. One is named Apophis and will dip below our earth's satellites on Friday the 13th, 2029. When it returns in 2036 it could collide with earth.

What is not well known and understood is that it is God and God's love that has kept our earth relatively safe from asteroids and comets. It is God's love that has kept comets from plummeting earth, kept the rains falling, plant life growing, maintains our health and yet we have given Him little credit. All that is about to change as prophecy is about to be fulfilled. After ages of time that God and God's love has protected man and our earth from asteroids and comets, God will allow the earth to hit by a comet.

God has used natural events in creating signs for those who have faith. Comets are one of those naturally occurring phenomenon that God will use to herald a significant event to happen. A great American writer, Mark

Twain, was born on the appearance of Haley's comet, and passed away with the return of Haley's comet. The coming of this comet heralds a time of change before the Second Coming of Christ.

According to Nostradamus, this comet will be seen for seven days. According to Mother Mary and Nostradamus this comet will look like a sun, thereby appearing that we have two suns in our sky on the horizon. After seven days of seeing this comet, the comet will hit northern Europe. Just as the comet Shoemaker-Levy broke into twenty pieces before striking Jupiter, this comet has the potential of breaking into several parts before striking earth. The majority of the comet will strike northern Europe, and as Edgar Cayce foresaw, "Europe changing in the twinkling of an eye."

According to Nostradamus, this comet or asteroid will be one mile in diameter. Let's see what would happen if an asteroid one half mile in diameter traveling at the velocity of 6 miles per second would do. There would first be a blinding flash in the sky and then a shock wave of air 9,000 miles per hour. Within five seconds, the asteroid would hit earth and the energy released would be 20 times all the earth's nuclear weapons exploding at one time. Next, an earthquake of magnitude 9.7 and a wave of superheated rock and debris, and everything within 200 miles incinerated. There will be fires started by heated rocks and debris blasted out from the impact. Next, the atmosphere will be full of dust particles that shall encircle the globe.

According to Mother Mary, "60-70% of the world's population will cease. Of those who survive, 60% could die of disease and starvation." This would mean 85% of the world's population would die, as a result of the comet, plagues, famine and war. I will say that **prophecy is not fixed** and even the prophecy of Mother Mary stating how many will die from this comet is not fixed. The power of our prayers is a very powerful force here on earth, and can attenuate the coming trials and tribulations. God is working to attenuate these trials and tribulations. There might only be a small part of this comet-asteroid that will hit the earth. There is even a possibility of this comet-asteroid coming close to the earth and missing earth, as an act of God's love, compassion and the power of our prayers. This comet and the sign of the two suns will be fulfilling of prophecy of falling stars, and a sign of "more changes to come."

STAR OF BETHLEHEM

Matthew 2:1-2- Now when Jesus was born in Bethlehem of Judea in the days of Herod the king, behold, there came wise men from the east to Jerusalem. Saying, "Where is he that is born King of the Jews? For we have seen his star in the east, and are come to worship him."

Matthew 2:9-10- When they had heard the king, they departed; and, lo, the star, which they saw in the east, went before them, till it came and stood over where the young child was. When they saw the star, they rejoiced with exceeding great joy.

Helamen 14:3-5- And behold, this will I give unto you for a sign at the time of his coming; for behold, there shall be great lights in heaven, insomuch that in the night before he cometh there shall be no darkness, insomuch that it shall appear unto man as if it was day. Therefore, there shall be one day and a night and a day, as if it were one day and there were no night; and this shall be unto you for a sign; for ye shall know of the rising of the sun and also of its setting; therefore they shall know of a surety that there shall be two days and a night; nevertheless the night shall not be darkened; and it shall be the night before he is born. And behold, there shall a new star arise, such a one as ye never have beheld; and this also shall be a sign unto you.

Figure 33- Adoration of the Magi by Florentine painter Giotto Bondone (1267–1337). The Star of Bethlehem is shown as comet above the child.

There has been much speculation as to the true nature of the star of Bethlehem. The different theories have been a supernova (a brilliant exploding star), a comet, aligning planets giving forth a brighter light and even a mystical creation of a bright star. God can create anything He chooses, but the signs He gives us are almost invariably natural phenomenon.

The wise men reported that the new star that appeared in the sky moved. This is the description of a comet. There is nothing else that I am aware of that will appear as a new star in the night sky that can move.

It is only the when the signs of his birth from the Bible and the Book of Mormon are put together do we get a clearer understanding of what the Star of Bethlehem was. The answer comes from solving the mystery of the Tunguska blast in Siberia, Russia.

THE TUNGUSKA MYSTERY

In 1908, in central Siberia near the Tunguska River there was an approximately 25 mega-ton blast. This was 1,000 times more power than the atom bomb which was dropped on Hiroshima. If the explosion occurred over a major metropolitan area, it would destroy the city. It leveled and destroyed 80 million trees. Over hundreds of miles away, it broke windows and men were thrown to the ground by the blast. This 25 mega-ton blast became the Tunguska mystery and top scientists around the world worked on solving the mystery. After years of research and study scientists solved the Tunguska Mystery. The explosion was caused by an asteroid exploding in the earth's atmosphere. Both asteroids and comets can penetrate the earth's atmosphere and hit the ground, but they can also explode in the earth's atmosphere.

Europeans had archaic seismographs that registered the Tunguska blast, and fluctuations in air density (air pressure) registered in Europe and England. The most interesting phenomenon was what some term "bright lights" that occurred after the blast. The explosion in Siberia sent dust into the high atmosphere. The reflection of sunlight upon this dust in the high atmosphere caused the atmosphere to glow possibly for days. People in Europe could read at night by the glow of the bright lights.

Star of Bethlehem appeared as a new star in the Middle East but also in America. The Nephite people, descendants of one of the lost tribes of Israel, living on the American continent had an additional sign the Christ had been born. They were told through prophecy that there would be a day, a night and a day, without a night. This prophecy is saying that there would be one night that would bright as daytime. The explosion of this comet or asteroid sent ice crystals and dust into the atmosphere. The reflection of sunlight off the dust and ice crystals brought light into the night sky, fulfilling prophecy of the night that was like daytime in the Americas. Solving the Tunguska Blast has solved the mystery of the Star of Bethlehem. The Star of Bethlehem was a comet.

CHAPTER 32

——— § ———

EARTH'S POPULATION DECLINES

Matthew 24:40-41- Then shall two be in the field; the one shall be taken, and the other left. Two women shall be grinding at the mill; the one shall be taken, and the other left.

AIDS, ANTIBIOTIC RESISTANT tuberculosis and Ebola are three of the plagues foretold in the Bible that would occur in the last days. AIDS has infected one out of every four people on the continent of Africa. AIDS is a worldwide pandemic that effects every country and all mankind. The death toll of the AIDS pandemic stands at 78 million infected and 39 million deaths. Figure 34 shows the graph of the world's population for 1950 to 2050. Despite the plagues, wars, earthquakes, tornados, hurricanes, tsunamis and other disasters, figure 34 below shows the earth's population has remained relatively smooth and steadily increasing. This graph and the projected world's population will significantly decrease. This will be fulfillment of biblical prophecy that there "shall be two in the field; the one shall be taken and the other left."

World Population: 1950-2050

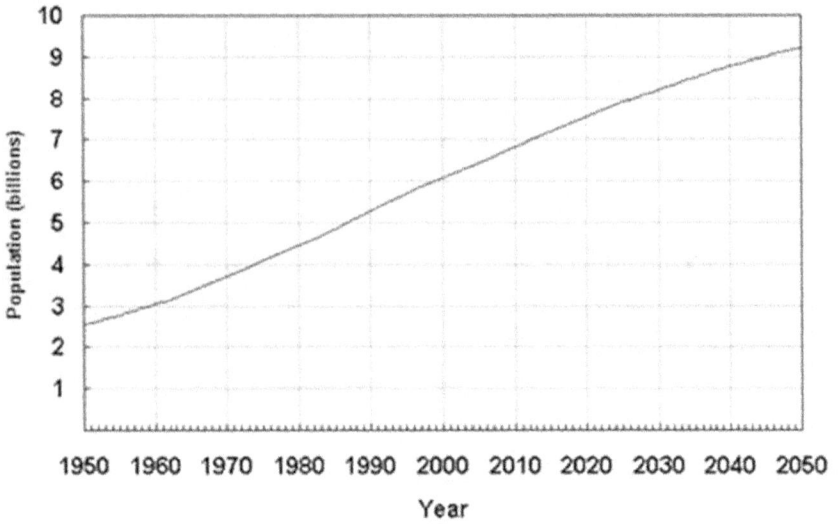

Source: U.S. Census Bureau, International Data Base, April 2005 version.

Figure 34- World Population Graph 1950 to 2050

CHAPTER 33

---- § ----

ONE THIRD OF THE CREATURES IN THE SEA DIE

Revelation 8:9- *And the third part of the creatures which were in the sea, and had life, died; and the third part of the ships were destroyed*

Revelation16: 3- *And the second angel poured out his vial upon the sea; and it became as the blood of a dead man: and every living soul died in the sea.*

Revelation16:4- *And the third angel poured out his vial upon the rivers and fountains of waters; and they became blood.*

Revelation 8:10-11- *And the third angel sounded, and there fell a great star from heaven, burning as it were a lamp, and it fell upon the third part of the rivers, and upon the fountains of waters; And the name of the star is called wormwood: and the third part of the waters became wormwood; and many men died of the waters, because they were made bitter.*

Mother Mary- *The dolphins will begin to die off; they have served their purpose.*

REVELATION STATES THAT the moon will turn to blood and this is not to be interpreted literally. Revelation means that the moon will turn the color red. The meaning of the scripture that the sea (waters of the world) shall turn red is a symbol for poisoning, death or dying. The interpretation of the scripture is that one third of the seas shall become poisoned. One third of the world's waters will become polluted with a poison and one third of the animal life in the seas and oceans and bodies of water shall die.

The increase carbon dioxide in our atmosphere not only providing a greenhouse effect and changing our weather, it is changing our seas and our oceans. Scientists have known for quite a while that the increased carbon dioxide in our atmosphere is being absorbed into our oceans. Carbon dioxide combines with water to form carbonic acid, which increases the acidity (decrease pH) of our oceans and seas. The increased acidity of our oceans and seas causes another chemical reaction. Carbon dioxide, combines with water and the carbonate ions to form bicarbonate ions. This makes carbonate unavailable for marine life who need calcium and carbonate to make their shells.

Scientists and others are studying the effects of increased acidity of our oceans. An ocean farmer discovered that the oysters he was harvesting from the ocean were dying. Their shells of the baby oysters were discovered to be malformed, and the baby oysters were dying. They eventually discovered it was the acidity of the ocean that was causing the abnormal development of the oysters' shells. Once the acidity was corrected, the baby oysters could form normal shells and they survived.

Scientists have studied the coral reefs in areas where there is increased acidity caused by carbon dioxide rising into the oceans from volcanic activity under the ocean floor. The coral reefs in these areas of increased acidity need carbonate to form their exoskeleton. With less carbonate available, these coral reefs are dying. The marine life that depends on a healthy coral reef for their survival are also dying.

Pteropods are small shell creatures in our oceans. The pteropods have been studied for decades and scientists have discovered that their shells are decreasing and becoming malformed. Many animals consume pteropods as a portion of their diet. Marine life depends on small organisms in our oceans and seas as a source of their diet. If the small organisms die off, so will the marine life in our oceans and seas. Scientists and researchers have reached a startling conclusion, because of the increased carbon dioxide from burning fossil fuels being absorbed into our oceans, **mankind is poisoning the oceans and seas**.

A comet will hit earth (see chapter on Falling Stars) and cause a tremendous explosion. There will follow a firestorm and will be dust blown into the earth's atmosphere. The firestorm will send toxins onto the land and rivers, lakes, seas and oceans poisoning the water. As the dust from the explosion settles on land and the waters, it will send heavy metals into the water, giving the waters a bitter taste. The water will become even more acidic resulting in poisoning of the waters of the planet.

252 million years ago, a catastrophic event happened. Massive volcanic eruptions in Siberia produced massive amounts of sulfur dioxide and carbon dioxide in the atmosphere. The sulfur dioxide combined with water in the atmosphere and became sulfuric acid, which caused acid rain. The combination of acid rain into our oceans and carbon dioxide absorbed into our oceans and seas caused a dramatic increased acidity of our oceans and seas. There was increase temperature and lack of oxygen in our oceans and seas. Thus, 95% of the species of the earth perished in the Permian Mass Extinction, which some refer to as the "Great Dying."

There will be increased volcanic activity all over the world (see chapter on Volcanoes). As the ash falls onto the waters of the earth. Ions and heavy metals brought by the ash, will make the water taste unpleasant and bitter, and make the waters even more acidic. Acid rain from the volcanoes will further acidify the waters, and vast amounts of carbon dioxide poured into the atmosphere by volcanoes and absorbed by the waters will dramatically acidify our waters. The result of acidity from greenhouse gases, dust and toxins from a comet striking northern Europe and volcanic activity will be poisoning of our rivers, lakes, seas and oceans. This will be fulfillment of prophecy of "One third the creatures in the sea shall die."

I love all animals, but some animals I have a stronger affinity to. I have always loved the playful, fun-spirited dolphins. They appear to have a smile on their face, as they play together with their families and friends. According to Mother Mary dolphins have served their purpose, which was to hold a high vibrational energy (spirit) for mankind and the earth. Now that earth is being reborn, the earth and mankind will be able to hold this spirit. What was asked of the dolphins has been completed, a job well done. I will miss these dear friends, one of God's most playful, fun-loving and spiritual creations.

CHAPTER 34

—— § ——

SHIFTING OF THE EARTH'S AXIS

SHIFTING OF THE EARTH'S MAGNETIC FIELD

THE GENERATION OF the earth's magnetic field baffled scientists for a long time. Even though there are many details of how the earth's magnetic field is generated that is still unknown, much is now understood. Current understanding states that the earth has an inner core of solid iron alloy (this solid core includes other elements as well). This inner core is surrounded by an outer core of molten (liquid earth) iron alloy. The liquid outer core, which contains iron, moves in currents in a similar fashion to the way water moves in currents in our oceans. The flow of this molten outer core of iron over the solid inner core of iron will generate a magnetic field.

There is a popular misconception that the earth's Geographical North Pole, which is the northern point of the axis upon which our earth spins is the same as our Magnetic North Pole. They are different (see figure 35). The axis upon which our earth spins (our Geographical North Pole) is about 11.5 degrees different from the axis of our Magnetic North Pole.

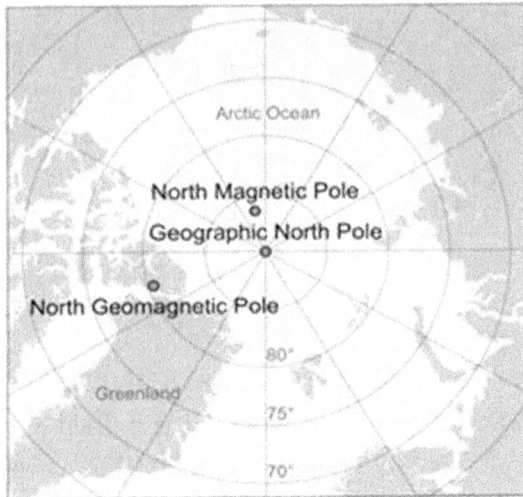

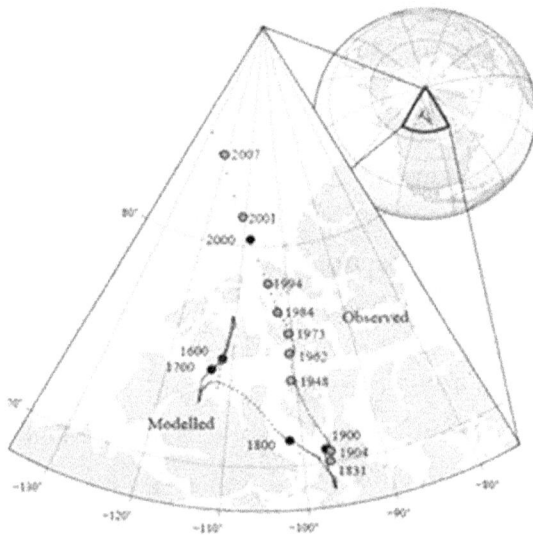

Figure 35- Top- Geographic vs. Magnetic North Poles (Image from Cavit, Wikipedia.org)

Figure 36- Bottom- Map of Drifting Magnetic North Pole (Image from Cavit, wikipedia.com)

The map in figure 36 shows our drifting Magnetic North Pole, which is drifting as the currents of iron alloy in the earth's molten outer core change. The map shows the position of the earth's Magnetic North Pole over the last century and its movement is speeding up. The Magnetic North Pole is currently moving at 40 miles per year. Although it is currently in Canada, it is heading for Russia.

Our earth's magnetic field runs from south to north. Scientists have studied the lava flows in Hawaii and made amazing discoveries. The lava as it comes from the earth's molten core contains magnetite, which is like a microscopic magnet. As long as the lava is hot and fluid, the magnetite will align with the earth's magnetic field. As the lava cools the magnetite will remain aligned with the earth's magnetic field and show the direction of the earth's magnetic field at the time the lava cooled.

A scientist has studied the lava flows of Hawaii going back hundreds of thousands of years and made a startling discovery. The scientist took lava samples and found that 780,000 years ago, the magnetite was aligned to the South Pole, yet ever since then the magnetite has been aligned to the North Pole. There was a shift in the earth's magnetic field 780,000 years ago. Further studies of magnetite in lava samples going back hundreds of thousands of years shows that the earth's magnetic field shifts on average every two hundred thousand years. This makes us overdue for the next shift in the earth's magnetic field.

Physicist Gary Glatzmaier of University of California Santa Cruz put every known equation on the movement of earth's molten outer core, which produces our magnetic field into the world's fastest supercomputers. All the equations describing the earth's molten core's viscosity, temperature, buoyancy, dimensions, which included dozens of equations, were fed into supercomputers. Gary Glatzmaier let the computers run, to "see what would happen to the earth's molten core over hundreds of thousands of years of simulated time." Dr. Glatzmaier ran these equations every day for four years. After four years of running his equations and mathematical models on the world's fastest supercomputers, suddenly there was reverse polarity of the earth's magnetic field. Via these mathematical models, every one hundred thousand years the earth's magnetic field shifts.

WEAKENING OF THE EARTH'S MAGNETIC FIELD

Interesting to note there was a prelude to the shift of the earth's magnetic field. Every time the earth's magnetic field was about to shift there was a weakening of the earth's magnetic field. The earth's magnetic field kept weakening until there was a shift in the earth's magnetic field. Today we are seeing a weakening of our earth's magnetic field.

There is a reason for the weakening of the earth's magnetic field before there is a shift in the earth's magnetic field. Figures 37 shows the magnetic field at the earth's surface and figure 38 shows the magnetic field at the surface of the earth's molten outer core. Light grey represents inward flow of the earth's magnetic field and dark grey outward flow of the magnetic field. Right before there is to be a shift of the earth's magnetic field, there begins to appear anomalies. There are areas in the northern hemisphere where there is outward flow of the magnetic field, these are dark grey islands in the sea of light grey. This is opposite flow of the rest of the magnetic flow in the northern hemisphere. The same thing same thing occurs in the southern hemisphere and appear as light grey islands in the dark gray sea. With time, there are more and more anomalies. As the anomalies become bigger and more numerous the earth's magnetic field weakens. Finally, there are anomalies everywhere and a very weak earth's magnetic field and then the earth's magnetic field shifts. The flow of the magnetic field is now in the opposite direction.

Over the past 300 years the earth's magnetic field has been growing weaker, and a reversal is close. The log books of Her Majesty's Navy have documented thousands of magnetic measurements over the past three hundred years. In the South Atlantic Ocean, these magnetic anomalies exist and are growing. This is called the South Atlantic Anomaly, where the earth's magnetic field is about 30% weaker. This anomaly has grown substantially in the past one hundred years. When will the earth's magnetic field shift? It may take about one thousand years from the time the magnetic field starts to weaken before there is a shift in the earth's magnetic field, but we are long overdue and the shift can happen at any time.

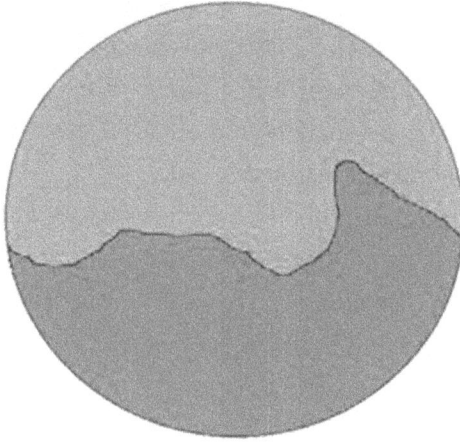

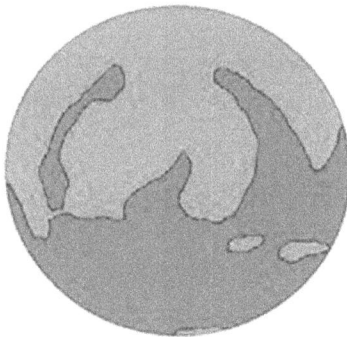

Figure 37- Top- Earth's Surface Magnetic Field

Figure 38- Bottom- Earth's Core Magnetic Field

Geologist Rob Kow has studied the immense lava flows of Steen's Mountain in Oregon. For 25 years, he has taken samples of the lava flows to see what happens during a shift of the magnetic poles. The earth's magnetic field weakens and then begins to behave erratically. The earth's magnetic field could weaken ten to a hundred times, before there is a shift of the magnetic field.

Our earth's magnetic field is an invisible deflector shield to cosmic radiation (charged particles) from our sun and other stars. This deflects cosmic radiation towards the North and South Poles and away from us. Without this protection, we would all be exposed to hazardous levels of radiation. Some estimate there would 100,000 more deaths from cancer each year with a very weak magnetic field.

There is a lighter, brighter side to the shift of the earth's magnetic field. One of God's greatest creations, the aurora, will be seen at lower latitudes as there is weakening of the earth's magnetic field. An amazing visual spectacle of dancing lights in the night's sky will put on a show for millions if not billions of people to enjoy.

SHIFTING OF THE EARTH'S AXIS

Doctrine and Covenants 88:87- For not many days hence and the earth shall tremble and reel to and fro as a drunken man;

Hopi- The earth shall rock to and fro.

Hopi- Turtle Island (USA) could turn over two or three times.

Edgar Cayce- There will be the upheavals in the Arctic and in the Antarctic that will make for the eruption of volcanoes in the torrid areas, and there will be the shifting then of the poles -- so that where there has been those of a frigid or the semi-tropical will become the more tropical, and moss and fern will grow.

Ruth Montgomery- Predicted the shift of the earth's axis around the turn of the millennium.

Much has been foretold about the shifting of the earth's axis by modern day psychics including Edgar Cayce and Ruth Montgomery and referred to in other prophecies. When I first read about the shifting of the earth's axis I was captivated and believed that such a dramatic event would happen to our earth. They are not talking about a shift in the magnetic poles but a shift in the earth's axis, although both can occur. Scientists have evidence that there has been a shift of the earth's axis in the past.

Although there has been shifting of the earth's magnetic poles in the past and the shift in the magnetic poles will occur, it is not the shift of the magnetic poles that is the event prophesied in Doctrine and Covenants, Hopi prophecy and modern psychics. Doctrine and Covenants tells us that "the earth shall reel to and fro as a drunken man." There is one event that can cause the fulfillment of this prophesy and that is shifting of the earth's axis. Shifting of the earth's axis implies that the North and South Poles will move from their current locations and be relocated to the earth's equator. Countries located near the equator would become our new North Pole and South Pole. It has been foretold that Japan will become our new North Pole.

There is a belief among those who believe in prophesy of the shift of the earth's axis, that the shifting of the earth's magnetic field will be the cause of the shift in the earth's axis. The shift of the earth's magnetic field is a contributing factor but is not the only cause of the shift in the earth's axis. Edgar Cayce described our earth as not one solid ball. Edgar Cayce stated our earth had a hard crust which covered a more fluid layer of molten rock. We now know Edgar Cayce's psychic prediction is true. The tectonic plates and earth's crust rest on a fluid layer of molten rock called the Asthenosphere (Figure 39) and this is a contributing factor in the shift of the earth's axis. The earth is not a perfect sphere and is relatively bulging around the earth's equator. This allows the moon, our sun and planets to exert a gravitational pull on the earth effecting the earth rotating on its axis. NASA scientists made an amazing discovery after the earthquake that hit Japan. The earthquake shifted the earth's axis 4 inches. Other contributing factors to the shift in the earth's axis will be the comet hitting northern Europe, earthquakes increasing in size and frequency and the most important of all is the power of God. This shift of the earth's axis has happened in the past and is not a one-time phenomenon. It is a natural phenomenon and once it occurs, scientists will study it and put this event in our history and science books.

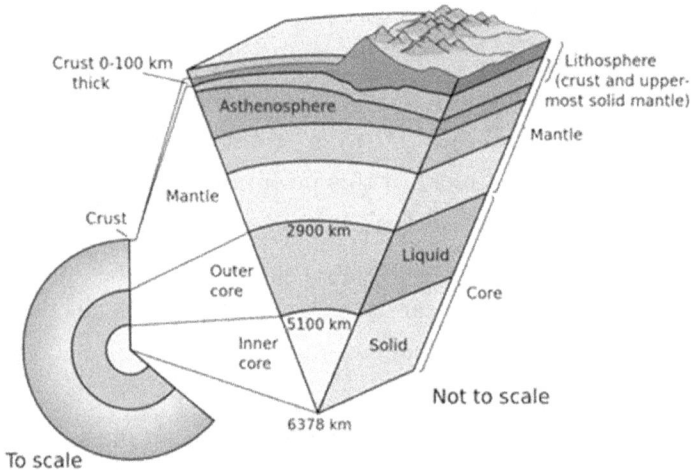

Figure 39- Layers of the Earth- Asthenosphere is Flowing Molten Rock and Not Rigid (from Wikipedia.com)

There is also a belief that the shift in the earth's axis will be a sudden violent cataclysmic event. If this were to occur, then probably no humans would survive. The shift of the earth's axis will occur over years (possibly ten to twenty years) and not days.

Look at a spinning top that is slowing down and you will see what will happen to our earth as she goes through a shift in her axis. First, the initial wobble becomes larger and more pronounced and then wobble will maximize. Next there will be less wobbling and more spinning of the top on a different axis. Finally, the top will be spinning on its side, spinning on a different axis. All the wobbling movement energy has been transferred and the top is now spinning on its side. So, it will be for the earth. The earth's axis will start to wobble, the wobble will maximize and then finally the earth will spin on her side. The North and South Poles shall be relocated to the earth's new equator and Japan shall be our new North Pole. Thus, fulfilling prophesy and the earth one step closer to its rebirth into a paradisiacal glory.

This wobbling of the earths on its own axis may only last ten to twenty years. The earth does not like to wobble for it is not a stable condition for the rotation of the earth. The wobble of the earth on its axis will cause great concern for our welfare and safety. Governments of the world will have a common enemy, and scientists and politicians of the world will come together to see what can be done. As far as the shift in the earth's axis there is nothing scientifically that can be done, except to weather the storm, let nature take its course, turn our hearts towards God and our fellow man and pray. Do not underestimate the power of God or the power of prayer. Prayer and faith can literally move mountains and soften the impact of cataclysmic events. The wobble in the earth's axis will right itself with time. As the top that was spinning vertically, eventually is lying on its side and spinning on the floor with a different axis, so it will be with planet earth.

The earth's stumbling to and fro like a drunken man, or in other words wobbling like a top before it is about to fall is not a safe time for the earth. The earth is not a perfect sphere. The earth's equator is longer

173

in horizontal circumference than the vertical circumference of the earth around its North and South Poles. In other words, the earth's equator is bulging outwards, while the North and South Poles are being compressed inwards. This is due to centrifugal force as the earth spins on its axis. As the earth shifts its axis, there will be new North and South Poles, and as it was prophesied Japan becoming the new North Pole. The Arctic and Antarctic will be relocated to the earth's new equator. As the earth shifts its axis and Japan becomes the earth's new North Pole, the earth's crust around Japan will be compressed inwards. The land masses of the Arctic and Antarctic will be relocated on the earth's new equator. The Arctic and Antarctic land masses are now compressed inwards but as the earth's axis shifts and these land masses become the new equator, these land masses will expand outward by the centrifugal force of the earth's rotation. This inward compression of the land around Japan, outward expansion of the land masses of the Arctic and Antarctic and the earth's crust floating on a layer of molten rock will place an enormous strain and tension on the earth's rigid crust. The result is earthquakes, volcanoes, tsunamis and floods. Eventually, there will be a ripping of the earth's crust created by centrifugal force of the earth's mass on the surface of our earth, culminating in an earthquake with the magnitude never known before on this planet. The result will be catastrophic.

CHAPTER 35

FLOODS

Mother Mary- *Foretells of coming floods which are biblical in size.*

Koran 55:20-21- *He has made the two bodies of water flow. They will one day meet. Between them there is a barrier; they cannot encroach one upon the other.*

Koran 25:54- *And He it is who shall merge the two seas together. This palatable and sweet, that saltish and bitter. And between them He has (presently) placed a barrier and a massive partition.*

Hopi- *there shall be rising waters*

Hopi- *the oceans could join hands*

Mayan- *world destruction by floods*

Hindu Gurus- *speak prophecy of the coming floods*

Hindu- *In the summer of 1983, Guru Bhagwan Rajneesh Chandra - "there will be floods which have never been known since the time of Noah,"*

Edgar Cayce- *the greater part of Japan must go into the sea... the coastline now of many a land will be the bed of ocean... Los Angeles, San*

Francisco will be destroyed before New York, or New York City itself, will in the main disappear. Southern portions of Carolina, Georgia, these will disappear. The Great Lakes will empty into the Gulf of Mexico.

Edgar Cayce-*As to conditions in the geography of the world, of the country -- changes here are gradually coming about ... For, many portions of the east coast will be disturbed, as well as many portions of the west coast, as well as the central portion of the U.S. In the next few years land will appear in the Atlantic as well as in the Pacific. And what is the coast line now of many a land will be the bed of the ocean. Even many battle fields of the present will be ocean, will be the seas, the bays, the lands over which The New World Order will carry on their trade as one with another.*

Edgar Cayce- *In 2100 AD The Pacific Ocean covers much of the western part of the country (United States).*

WITH THE COMING global warming, there will be melting of the polar ice caps and Greenland ice fields. This may not sound like much but the melting of these snow and ice fields will raise the level of the oceans and seas by 60 feet. This is a height that can submerge coastal cities and much of the low-lying land around the world. Many who believe in biblical prophecy point to the melting of these icecaps as the fulfilling of prophecy. The melting of the icecaps is only a part of the overall story. The melting of the polar and Greenland icecaps will continue and dwarf all current scientific predictions in how quickly they can melt. I don't know the extent of the melting of the icecaps, but this is only part of the story.

A major contributing factor to the coming floods is the coming earth changes. Mountains will be made low and valleys high. It is the coming earth changes that will produce most the floods predicted by prophecy. There shall be ocean floor that shall rise and become land and there shall be land that shall be submerged and become ocean floor.

I remember being told a prophecy of St. Patrick which stated Ireland would sink into the ocean before The Second Coming of Christ. I have not found a source for this and maybe one of the readers of this book shall send me a reference to St. Patrick's reported prophecy. Ireland sinking into the ocean does not imply total submersion of the entire country of Ireland. As countries around the world sink into the oceans and seas, so will Ireland.

Edgar Cayce is America's most widely known and most widely published psychic. Edgar Cayce had a spiritual gift and used it correctly. Edgar Cayce foretold most of Japan being flooded, flooding of Los Angeles, San Francisco, New York City, southern portions of Carolinas and Georgia, and the Gulf of Mexico to flood the Mississippi River states. Some with the gift of prophecy have spoken of California breaking off from the continental United States and becoming a series of islands in the Pacific Ocean, most of Florida submerged under water and the Grand Canyon to become Grand Canyon Lake. The Koran and Hopi prophecies state that the Pacific and Atlantic oceans will no longer be separated by Panama and Central America. These two great oceans shall merge with the rising waters and earth changes.

Messages from Mother Mary are of coming floods and are of the same order as were seen and foretold by Edgar Cayce. The coming floods are not an environmental natural cycle but are part of the earth changes and will be biblical in size. The prophecy of floods has started but the major floods will be another unmistakable sign when it occurs.

CHAPTER 36

---— § ---—

WATERWAYS OF THE WORLD TO BECOME UNSAFE

Doctrine and Covenants 61:14-16- Behold I, the Lord, in the beginning blessed the waters; but in the last days, by the mouth of my servant John, I cursed the waters. Wherefore, the days will come that no flesh shall be safe upon the waters. And it shall be said in days to come that none is able to go up to the land of Zion upon the waters, but he that is upright in heart.

Doctrine and Covenants 88:87- For not many days hence and the earth shall tremble and reel to and fro as a drunken man;

Hopi- The earth shall rock to and fro.

Hopi- the oceans rise to the sky

As CHRIST HAS stated in Doctrine and Covenants, in the beginning the waters were blessed. All those who lived by the sea and the ocean could prosper. The oceans, seas and lakes were blessed with life and calm waters so that all those who lived by the waters, fished and made their living upon the waters could do so.

In the last days, as Christ has stated, the waters will be cursed. The waters will no longer be safe to travel and make a living from. The marine highway shall become dangerous except for those with exceedingly great faith. The waterways of the world becoming unsafe will come from numerous causes. There will be earthquakes all over the world, in the oceans causing tsunamis. The world has only begun to see the extent of tempests, or fierce storms that are coming. These fierce storms will make the seaways and marine highways of the world unsafe.

The shift of the earth's axis is a major contributing factor to making the water ways of the earth unsafe. The earth shall reel to and fro as a drunken man and this turbulence in the earth will be translated into turbulence in the waters. The waters that in the past provided safe harbor, transportation of people and goods, will no longer be safe. The waters will be cursed and "no flesh shall be safe upon the waters." Giant waves and rogue waves shall rule the waters as Hopi prophecy states "the oceans shall rise to the sky."

CHAPTER 37

———— § ————

WAR AGAINST ISRAEL- PROPHECY TO BE FULFILLED

Zechariah 14:4 - *And his feet shall stand in that day upon the Mount of Olives, which is before Jerusalem on the east,*

Doctrine and Covenants 133:20- *For behold, he shall stand upon the mount of Olivet, and upon the mighty ocean, even the great deep, and upon the islands of the sea, and upon the land of Zion.*

THE LORD STANDS ON MOUNT OLIVET, ZION, ISLANDS OF THE SEA AND THE OCEAN

DURING THE WAR against Israel a wondrous event will occur. Jesus Christ shall **literally** stand on Mount Olivet leading his people to victory. A wondrous sight for all those who have waited, anticipated the return of the king.

This will not be the only appearance of Jesus Christ for he shall appear in other places, including islands of the sea and the land of Zion (New Jerusalem and United States). He will appear as he did when he walked the land with his apostles, but he may also appear ordinary under extraordinary circumstances. He may appear when all hope in your community has faded, as he appears as a volunteer worker. He may appear when your strength has left you, and you don't believe you can go any further. He may appear in a disaster, extending a helping hand when there are no other hands to reach for. He will not be wearing a robe and sandals, but there is a way you shall know him. The eyes of Christ cannot be mistaken for any other. The eyes of Jesus Christ are pure compassion and reveals the soul of the great Jehovah. A feeling will come over you and an awareness that the hand that reached out for you when all hope had faded was the hand of Jesus Christ. He has helped us so many times spiritually, but what a blessing to have been in the presence of the Christ. The stories of these appearances will uplift our hearts and spirits. He is here to give us strength and hope when times are darkest, and remind us that we will soon be with him in paradise.

It is widely believed that Christ appearing at Mount Olivet is the Second Coming of the Jesus Christ, but it is not. These appearances by Jesus Christ will be symbolic that we are not alone in our trials. The Second Coming of Christ which is culmination of all that we have worked for and the end of the grand plan of free will is near, but not yet.

THE TWO PROPHETS

Zechariah 14:2- *Jerusalem is taken captive, the houses riled, the women ravished.*

I will summarize Revelation 11. In a world of false prophets, there will come forth two true prophets and they shall prophesy for three and a half years. They shall travel on foot, be clothed only in sackcloth and they shall have all the power of the heavens, the power of God. They have come to teach and bring understanding into a world that needs love, hope and wisdom. It is likely that one of the prophets is Jewish and the other Muslim. They will bring healing and understanding to those of Jewish, Christian and Islamic faith. Anyone who tries to harm them shall be killed for they shall be protected by the one God, until they have completed their mission.

Once the prophets have finished God's work, they shall be overcome and killed. Israel shall also be overcome. People killed and women ravaged. The bodies of the dead prophets shall lie in the streets of Jerusalem for three and a half days and not be buried.

There will be rejoicing in the much of the Muslim world and other parts of the world that Israel was overthrown and defeated. After three and a half days, the spirit of God shall enter the bodies of the two prophets and bring life into their bodies. They will stand on their feet and great fear shall come to all those who witness this. A great voice from heaven shall say "Come up hither." The two prophets shall ascend into heaven in a cloud, witnessed by their enemies. In the same hour that the two prophets are called up into heaven, there will be a great earthquake, one tenth of the city of Jerusalem destroyed and 7,000 killed because of the earthquake. Those who were not killed will be afraid and give "glory to the God of heaven."

REBUILDING OF THE TEMPLE ON THE MOUNT

Daniel 9:26- Then after the sixty-two weeks the Messiah will be cut off and have nothing, and the people of the prince who is to come will destroy the city and the sanctuary.

Matthew 24:2- And Jesus said unto them, See ye not all these things? Verily I say unto you, there shall not be left here one stone upon another, that shall not be thrown down.

The Jewish people have had two temples on the Temple Mount. The first temple was built about 2,000 BC and destroyed in 586 by Nebuchadnezzar' armies, fulfilling Daniel's prophecy. A second temple was built, around 518 BC, destroyed by Roman armies in 70 AD, fulfilling the prophecy of Jesus.

Figure 40- Top- A drawing of Ezekiel's Temple by Henry Sulley
Figure 41- Bottom- Temple Mount and Dome of the Rock
(Muslim Temple) (Image from Wikipedia.org)

There has been a strong desire among those of Jewish faith and some in the Christian faith to rebuild the Temple Mount. The problem is the land of the Temple Mount belongs those of Muslim faith. There has been a strong resentment by some in the Jewish faith who want to reclaim this land and build a temple so they may worship at this sacred site.

The Temple Mount (Figures 40 and 41) is a site that is sacred to Christianity, Judaism and Islam. The Dome of the Rock (Figures 41) contains the exact spot where Abraham offered to God the ultimate sacrifice of his beloved son. It is at this holy site that Abraham bound his son, took up his knife to slay his beloved son and obey the will of God. According to the Old Testament, Judaism and Christianity the son that Abraham was about to slay was Isaac. What most Christians and those of the Jewish faith do not know is that this story of Abraham is the exact same story in the Koran (Islam). In the Koran, Abraham also takes his beloved son, binds him and is about to slay his son when the Archangel Gabriel sent by God stays Abraham's hand. Only in the Koran, the son who was to be offered by Abraham was Ishmael.

Is there any wonder that this sacred piece of land would be of great worth to Christians, Muslims and those of the Jewish faith? The site and the land upon which the Temple Mount is built are of enormous historical significance, but also one of the holiest places on earth. It is in the city of Jerusalem but the temple is owned by those of Muslim faith. During the war against Israel, the Temple Mount shall be destroyed. In the fulfilling of prophecy, the Temple Mount shall be rebuilt before the Second Coming of Christ. It will be a surprise and of great rejoicing to the whole world, that one religion shall not covet and claim this sacred site as their own. There will be great love and healing among all three religions when they symbolically rebuild the temple together.

CHAPTER 38

———— § ————

SIGNS ABOVE AND BELOW

Doctrine and Covenants 29-14- *stars shall fall from heaven, and there shall be greater signs in the heavens above and the earth beneath.*

Buddhism- *"the peoples of Agharti will leave their subterranean caverns and will appear on the surface of the earth."*

UFOs

Ezekiel 1:16- *This was the appearance and structure of the wheels: They sparkled like chrysolite, and all four looked alike. Each appeared to be made like a wheel intersecting a wheel.*

Ezekiel 1:4-5- *As I looked, behold, a stormy wind came out of the north, and a great cloud, with brightness around it, and fire flashing forth continually, and in the midst of the fire, as it were gleaming metal. And from the midst of it came the likeness of four living creatures. And this was their appearance: they had a human likeness,*

Ezekiel 10:9-11- *And I looked, and behold, there were four wheels beside the cherubim, one beside each cherub, and the appearance of the wheels was like sparkling beryl. And as for their appearance, the four had the same likeness, as if a wheel were within a wheel. When they went, they went in any of their four directions without turning as they went,* *but in whatever direction the front wheel faced, the others followed without turning as they went.*

Zechariah 5:1-2- *Again I lifted my eyes and saw, and behold, a flying roll! And he said to me, "What do you see?" I answered, "I see a flying roll. Its length is twenty cubits, and its width ten cubits."*

Doctrine and Covenants 76-24- *That by him, and through him, and of him, the worlds are and were created, and the inhabitants thereof are begotten sons and daughters unto God.*

Mother Mary- *Message to Gianna Sullivan- Children, God did not create only the Earth. God is the Creator of the cosmos, with its many galaxies, many orbits, different stars and different planets. God is the Creator! There are other planets like earth, far beyond your understanding.*

Koran 42:30- *among His signs is the creation of the heavens and the earth, and of whatever living creatures He has spread forth in both. And He has the power to gather them together whenever He pleases.*

Hopi- *The following is an excerpt from "The Book of the Hopi" by Frank Waters: After a time we will again walk with our brothers from the Stars, and rebuild this Earth. Our relatives from the Stars are coming home to see how well we have fared in our journey.*

Dogon People in Western Africa- *"And Dogon: "The Return of the Original Visitors" - The Dogon people in Western Africa attribute their acquisition of knowledge to the Nommos, divine supernatural visitors to the Earth who come from the Stars. The Nommos, also known as 'Masters of Water', the 'Monitors' and the 'Teachers', passed on Star* *knowledge to the Ancestors of the Dogon. According the prophecies of the Dogon, these Original Visitors will return to Earth from their place in the heavens in the form of a blue star.*

THE SOME OF the signs from below are the earth changes. The falling stars, moon turning red, and then sun turning as black as sack cloth are some of the signs from the heavens. One of the signs from the heavens will be the solving of the one of the greatest mysteries. Is there intelligent life somewhere else in the universe? Whether there is other life in the universe has been one of the great mysteries for mankind and for science. This mystery has had a huge impact on our media, movies, television and books. The media has numerous programs and books on the UFO (unidentified flying objects) phenomenon. There have been many reports of sightings of UFOs and even reports of contact with aliens from other planets. Is this phenomenon real or our imagination and fantasy?

Scientists, astronomers and engineers have developed telescopes that have brought the heavens into view. Our own Milky Way galaxy has 100 billion stars. Astronomers have discovered a vast universe full of 100 billion of galaxies, and this is just what they can currently see. Scientists and statisticians have estimated the probability of life forming on other planets, and then the probability of that life evolving into intelligent life. They have concluded statistically there must be other intelligent life in the universe.

Does intelligent extraterrestrial life have the technology to travel from other planets to our earth? There is a split decision among our scientists. There are those scientists thinking within a box and can't see out of the box, who say no. Their reasoning is that planets that could support life may be thousands of light years away and since man can't even approach light speed in travel, that life from other planets could not reach our planet. There are other scientists who can see and think outside of a box, who say it is possible. Look how much our technology has grown in just the past fifty years. Think how much it could grow in thousands of years. These scientists do believe it is possible for alien life to reach our planet.

From Bible scriptures Ezekiel and Zechariah both saw UFOs and Ezekiel saw aliens. Doctrine and Covenants, the Koran and Mother Mary stated there are other earths (worlds), and as Doctrine and Covenants states, "inhabitants thereof are begotten sons and daughters of God." The tribe of Dogon and Hopi prophecy state that extra-terrestrial life will come in the lasts days.

This is not the only world upon which God's children have come to have this third dimensional experience and schooling. There are other planets in this universe, with life as our own who are our brothers and sisters and children of the almighty God. We are not alone in the universe and that will soon become abundantly clear.

There have been thousands if not tens of thousands of reports of sightings of UFOs and some who claim contact with aliens from other worlds. UFO researchers claim that this phenomenon is real while the authorities from the government and skeptics state this is not real. Who is right?

Does our government know about UFOs and is giving the public misinformation? Who is the government? Our government includes millions of employees, and the vast majority of them are as much in the dark about UFOs as those not in the government. Is there a part of the government that knows the truth about the UFOs? YES. There may be one thousand in our military and government who know the truth about UFOs and have incontrovertible proof that this UFO phenomenon is real and aliens are here now visiting our planet. It will not be long, before **there will be incontrovertible proof for the entire world to see that UFOs are real and aliens are here now visiting our planet**. Those extraterrestrial beings are here now at this critical point in the history of mankind, and it is no accident that they are here. Planet earth is not just a brief layover as these beings travel across our galaxy or a popular alien tourist destination.

The claim of those in the government and military, who have covered up what they know, will be national security. The government and military have gained information from downed alien spacecraft which they do not want to leak out to the military of other governments. They are also concerned about panic that might occur if the public knew we are being visited by extraterrestrial beings. These are both legitimate concerns. There is a bigger issue, however, is our government telling those they serve, things that are not true. When it is uncovered that those who knew, did not tell the truth to those they serve, then the public will lose further trust in their government. This is the greater issue which will arise.

There is a collective fear in the back of our minds of invasion of our planet by alien beings. This is a fear that we will face, confront and move through. Independence Day and War of the Worlds were popular movies that illustrate our fear of alien invasion. The extraterrestrial beings that are here now are not here to conquer the human race, take over our planet and turn us into slaves. They are here as part of the divine plan. There will be those that look upon these alien beings as Gods, for their superior technology. This is a mistake and breaking of God's greatest commandment, to not have any other God's before Him. These extraterrestrial beings are our brothers and sisters and children of the One God. Some look like us while others do not. They are still children of the almighty God, here in service. You can call many of them older brother and sisters, not because they are any better than you and I, or because of their superior technology but because many are more conscious than we currently are. There are exceptions to every rule but they are here in love and service. They are here to lend a helping hand to mankind who is crossing the threshold into becoming conscious beings as earth becomes a conscious planet.

CHAPTER 39

———— ✧ ————

WORLD IN CHAOS

Daniel 12:1- *There shall be a time of trouble such as never was*

Matthew 24:15- *When ye see the abomination of desolation...then shall be great tribulation*

Matthew 24:21- *For then there will be great tribulation, such as has not been from the beginning of the world until now, no, and never will be.*

2 Timothy 3:1- *But understand this, that in the last days there will come times of difficulty.*

Luke 21:26- *Men's hearts shall fail them.*

Doctrine and Covenants 45-26- *The whole earth shall be in commotion.*

Doctrine and Covenants 29:15- *There shall be weeping and wailing among the hosts of men.*

Apache- *"Returning to Spirit and Sacred Law. The Fifth World of Peace is birthing"-The Apache say that we are now in the midst of transition. As always happens before there is a birth, there is labor. The birth of the Fifth World of Peace means transition and effort. As the Fifth World* *comes there will be growing pains. But there has been planted in our world a seed that is growing, and the efforts to nurture the seed have been successful. The prophecies have foretold of this time. It is happening even as I write these words. The old Fourth World was a paradigm where, when one individual has something, instead of using it to help the others, trying to keep it for themselves, with the result that in time a system was made that is now collapsing because its foundations were irresponsible in relation to the whole.*

Q'eros Inca- "Pachakuti - Earth's turnover. The Eagle and the Condor shall fly together again" This is a Time of tremendous crisis in the world, but as with any crisis it brings opportunity... opportunities to reinvent who we are, to reinvent what world we want to create for our children and our children's children. The upheaval of our way of life will be so turbulent that the Elders speak of "a tear in the fabric of time itself" as modern civilization collapses. No place on Earth will be safe, however the Elders say that there will be 'Safe People'. The paradigm of European civilization will continue to collapse, and the way of the Earth people will return.

Higher Power- Civil war.

THERE WILL COME a time when the whole world will be in chaos. It will not be difficult to see that when prophecy comes true one by one there will be more and more chaos. There will be earthquakes, volcanoes, tsunamis, fierce storms, floods, plagues, pestilence, the final great war, falling stars, the world trembling to and fro as a drunken man, water ways have become unsafe, one third the life of the oceans and seas dying, drought, crops failing, famine, UFOs landing, the earth to become hot and economic chaos. It is not difficult to see why the world will be in chaos.

In the midst of chaos, as we are all facing our fears, the hearts of many men shall fail them. It is one thing to have the love of God surrounding you protecting you and supporting you when you are facing fears or challenges, it is another to face your fears without the love, support and strength of God's love. The iniquity of men will cause the love of God that would normally fall upon them, to be withdrawn. We will all face our deepest fears, but some men and women will have God's love withdrawn from them. These brothers and sisters will have their hearts fail them and there shall be great fear among men and women. The whole world will be in commotion and there will be weeping and wailing among the hosts of men. Mankind will be losing the world that they had set their hearts upon. They will know in their souls that the prophecy of God is being fulfilled and we are all approaching that time when there shall be restoration of all things. There will be despair, heartache, loss, and the realization that the words of the prophets are coming to pass.

Mother Mary- Some will not like where they go.

God and the Christ are very concerned about every one of us. There is a caution given by Mother Mary that no matter how difficult things may become, never take your own life. Suicide is looked upon as murder of ourselves, and not an act of mercy. The repercussions are the same. Message from Mother Mary is "Some will not like where they go." Suicide will not take you back home but to a temporary, dark and foreboding spiritual realm. God and Christ are very concerned about suicide and mass suicide as people see death, dying and suffering all around them. In the midst of chaos, fear, despair, hardship, grief will come something quite unexpected. As the fear and despair is great so will be the love and compassion. The hearts of many shall be full of the love of God and there shall be great love and compassion. Men and women will see their fellow man who have lost much, their grief, sorrow and fear. They will turn their love into action and serve their fellow man. Amid commotion and fear, mankind will discover who they truly are; children of the Most High God, beings of love, compassion and courage. They will be the rock on a sandy beach when hurricane winds and crashing waves wash away the sand. They will provide strength, hope, love and courage to those whose hearts have failed them. In the time of greatest need those in fear will turn to their fellow men for help, and their brothers and sisters shall answer the call. Those who lose themselves in the service of their fellow man shall find themselves.

FINANCIAL CHAOS

I don't pretend to be an economist. The economy is not my education, training nor profession but I will talk about what I know. I personally believe in free enterprise. I believe that those with brains, and willing to work hard should be able to reap the rewards of good hard work, risk and insight. I also believe in sharing.

CONFIDENCE

The world revolves on confidence and faith. Confidence and faith are tied to each other and it is difficult to separate them, because they are so intertwined. Our financial, political and other institutions of the world are run largely on confidence. With confidence in the financial systems of the world, the finances of the world will flow smoothly. If there is confidence in our institutions, they will run fluidly. If there is confidence in the government of the money that we own, then the finances are stable and the government is stable. If the confidence in our financial and political systems declines and the world becomes unstable then our financial institutions can become chaotic.

GREED VS. ABUNDANCE

Before I proceed with calling things as I see them, I don't believe in blaming or judging anyone. I disagree with the character played by Michael Douglas in the movie Wall Street that stated, "Greed is good." I hear statements like "I made a killing on Wall Street." Who are they killing? They are killing the financial lives of their brothers and sisters. The motivation during the 1990's was to get rich quick.

It has been stated that money is the root of all evil, which is untrue. It is the love of money that is the root of all evil and another name for the love of money is greed. There are two forces in the world and they are ruled over by God and Christ on the one hand, and the antichrist on the other. These two forces are in opposition to each other and both at work in our financial system. Darkness works through greed and fear while light works through abundance.

People are seeing others make millions or billions of dollars and use the system and pay little to no taxes at all. Warren Buffet has talked to his financial colleagues and told the truth, that even though they make millions, they pay a less tax rate than their secretaries. It is the love of money and manipulating of the financial system that is causing many to lose faith in our financial system. I know of people who get elected or have others elected to government offices not for serving the public, but for serving themselves and making financial plans to benefit themselves and the groups from which they came. Again, this is legal but unethical.

Darkness says "There is only a certain amount in the world. If you want more then somebody else is going to have to have less. There is insufficient amount for everyone. Therefore, go and get what you want and don't be concerned about anyone else." No matter how much those motivated by greed have, they only want more and they are never satisfied with what they have.

A business associate is a stock broker and is very honest with me. He is upfront in telling me that Wall Street is mostly run on greed and fear.

Our forefathers created a constitution that would make the United States of America the shining light on the hill. Do we want our financial system, which is the back bone of our country, to be run on greed and fear? Greed is not only in Wall Street, but it is everywhere. Choose a profession and there you will find greed. Choose a profession and there you will also find charity.

ABUNDANCE

To God there is no such thing as lack, there is only abundance. God is a God of abundance. Once the world has been transformed into a paradisiacal glory then all will see that God is a God of abundance. There is no end to how much He can and will give. Our financial system works best when it runs on abundance and charity and not on greed and fear.

Those who receive abundantly believe in sharing. They have been blessed with abundance, they know the source of their abundance, and they know it was meant to be shared. The more you share and give back, the more you will receive abundantly.

I used to think that any one that made multi millions earned it out of greed. Not anymore. The higher power will often speak positively about those who have made a great deal of money. They have earned the money honestly and know since they have received abundantly, to share it. The higher power speaks positively about Warren Buffet. Here is a man who through honesty, hard work, intelligence and insight became the second wealthiest man on earth. He is a true humanitarian, giving away most his fortune to charity. There are a growing number individuals like Warren Buffet that are sharing their wealth. On the other side of the veil, Oprah Winfrey is referred to lovingly as Saint Oprah. Here is the wealthiest woman on the face of the earth and she is not bound by greed. The wealthiest woman on the face of the earth receives abundantly and shares abundantly.

Paul Newman is a shining example of abundance, giving and sharing. Here is a man who was not only a great actor but started Paul Newman's Salad Dressing that earns $250,000,000 per year. Paul Newman lived the principal of abundance. Paul Newman donated the proceeds of his salad dressing to charity to form the Hole in the Wall Charity Organization.

Love can do anything, produce abundance and defy common laws of known physics. There can be a limited amount of fish and bread in the baskets to feed the multitude, yet the number of fishes and the amount of bread can be multiplied by the act of love. This is a principal that is less understood and less well known, but exists none the less.

BALANCE

God and the universe are always seeking balance and it is a basic principal upon which the universe is built. If you work, you must rest and play. If there is a high, then there needs to be a low. Where there is excess the universe will intervene to bring things back into balance. The greater the excess, eventually you can plan on a deficit. There is a balance which is essential to life, health and well-being.

Look at nature which is the prime example of God's work in balance. The more biologists study nature and ecosystems the more they discover that there is a delicate balance in the web of life. If a part of the ecosystem is disturbed it will affect another part of the ecosystem and nature will act to restore balance. Whenever you see a boom, prepare for a bust. The bigger the boom, the bigger will be the bust. How can real estate keep going up 25% per year? It can't and eventually it must fall. The unrealistic stock market and real estate prices have been described as bubbles, but whatever you call them, what goes up must eventually come down. It is nature's way of restoring balance.

I remember the roaring 1990's and the economy was on a tear. People can get wealthy and never have to work again. Some economists said there was a bubble while others (probably ones making the money) said there is no end in sight. The roaring 1990s are what many will come to know as the equivalent as the roaring 20s (1920s). People believed the real estate boom would last forever, making 10 to 20% each year. It was a period of excess and the real estate bust soon followed.

Why was credit started? In the past if you wanted to buy something then you would have to work for the money before you could buy it. There are certain items that we all need credit for, like buying a home. It was greed and not philanthropy that created the bubble in the credit system. People were simply finding a way to make more money. Their motto was "Pay tomorrow for what you can buy today." There finally came a point when what people owed in America was greater than what they owned. This is a critical mass turning point.

Our financial institutions were not meant to run on greed or fear. We have collectively prayed for a change. The future is right around the bend and it is a paradise, a world of abundance. There will be a world where God will provide for all our needs. A fear of lack will not exist. To get to this paradise, we will need to go through change and that change will provoke fear. Use this opportunity to grow, to meet your fear head on.

I am not saying I know what will happen with the financial system and I am not saying there will be another depression. I am saying that there will be financial chaos as part of the biblical prophecy of the whole world in chaos.

We have prayed collectively for the end of darkness and the world to be renewed into a paradisiacal glory. We have prayed for this and we signed on for this, so we should accept responsibility for going through the change while God clears out the greed and fear.

The greatest cause of the economic downturn which is to come is God Himself and that we are at the top of the pride cycle (see chapter How God Will Save the World). It is God that has given to us all that we have. It is human nature to thank God initially as He blesses us, then forget about

Him and all that He has given us, once we have most of what we want. The downturn of the pride cycle is God's way of turning our hearts away from the things of the world and turning our hearts towards Him and each other. If ways if the world continued unchanged then the end of mankind, all life and the world would be closer than you would imagine.

CHANGE OF OUR FINANCIAL, POLITICAL, SOCIAL AND MEDICAL INSTITUTIONS

> **Mother Mary-** *message to Gianna Sullivan - Children, for the last 20 years I have oftentimes spoken of "change." I have told you that there is no time for fear; there is only time for change... After you see the two suns, there is only a short time before you will see a tremendous change in weather. After this, as you know, there are more changes to come.*

It is prophecy from Mother Mary that we are all going to go through a period of change. There has been a word reverberating everywhere, people want change. On the surface, we are saying things are broken and no longer working the way they should be working. From the depths of our souls we are praying for things to work the way they were meant to work. Change is coming, and it will be a little more change than people will say they wanted. There will be those who say, "I want the world the way it was." In the end, it will be well worth what we are about to go through. It is the financial chaos that will be a catalyst for the changing of our financial, political, social and medical institutions.

CHAPTER 40

———— § ————

TECHNOLOGY FAILS

Koran- 4:120 -*They will alter Allah's creation.*

Hopi- *This is the Fifth Sign: The land shall be crisscrossed by a giant spider's web.*

PROPHECY FROM THE Koran states that man *"will alter Allah's (God's) creation,"* which implies man will discover DNA and how to bioengineer (change DNA) with the science available. This prophecy has been fulfilled. Hopi prophecy states "The land shall be crisscrossed by a giant spider's web." This means initially telegraph and telephone wires will crisscross the land but eventually man will have the World Wide Web. This Hopi prophecy has been fulfilled.

RISE OF TECHNOLOGY

I have been amazed and at times mesmerized with the marvels, achievements, breakthroughs and even modern day miracles of dawning of the age of technology and the flourishing of technology. I was born at a time when technology was a fetus in the womb in the mother of creation. Little did I know the wonders that would await the world and all mankind when this fetus grew and up and became mature.

I was totally amused and amazed as a child when I picked up a phone and could talk with a friend or family member in another city of the United

States and have crystal clear sound almost instantaneously although they may be a thousand miles away.

I was entertained for hours at a time by television. I could watch a classic sports rivalry between the Boston Celtics and New York Knicks or Los Angeles Lakers as it was happening in the sports arena. I clearly remember sitting in the family TV room, as man landed on the moon. How excited I was to see man's first step onto the moon.

I remember being a teenager and going to the home of a friend of mine. He had at his home the first hand held calculator that I had ever seen. It fit in the palm of my hand and had keyboard of numbers and functions. The calculator had numbers light up behind a red screen so the numbers appeared red. The calculator could perform simple or very complex mathematical calculations in the twinkling of an eye with 15-20th decimal point accuracy. I remember being mesmerized by something so wondrous and amazing. I was completely captivated at such an amazing machine that fits in the palm of my hand.

I am still amazed when I look at the images of the CAT scan or MRI that shows clear images of the inside of the body, without the need for surgery. I have seen with my own eyes the modern-day miracles that modern technology can bring. I have administered the drugs during surgery that keeps the patient safely anesthetized during surgery. I have also given the drugs and utilized the technology that has saved the life of some of my patients. Without these drugs and this technology these patients would not have survived and returned safely to their families.

I remember the first computer I owned and loved the word processor which allowed me to write and edit without a typewriter. Again, I was amazed at the internet and how much useful information can be received so quickly. I am moved when I see the images of galaxies, stars and supernovas from deep space. These are beautiful images that show God's work and creations in process. Right out of Star Trek with Captain Kirk asking the computer information in the data bank, a cell phone translates our voice and gives us the answer we asked for.

There have been so many blessings, gifts and modern day miracles that have come from technology, and yet all things have their light side and their dark side. I have heard many say that technology is evil. Technology is not inherently evil; it is simply a tool. A powerful tool which can be used for good or for evil, and it is currently being used for both.

I remember in the 1990's people talking about technology and putting it on a pedestal. I saw people worshipping technology and the NASDAQ as if they were God. This is the dark side of technology; of which most are unaware that they are worshipping technology. The number one commandment is to have no other God's before God. Yet this is exactly what is happening, and so many are completely unaware of what they are doing.

It may help to understand the meaning of what it means to worship technology. If you say there was a need for God and superstition before the advent of science and technology, then you have put science and technology before God. If you put technology and those who control technology up on a pedestal, then you are worshipping technology. If you place technology in any higher role except what it was used for, a tool, then you worship technology. Technology like all the great scientific modern day marvels is not inherently evil, for they are from God, however, technology was and is meant to be a simple tool to use to make our lives better. God was aware that technology would be used for dark ends, but that is only the minor part of the story. Those who worship technology as if it were God, do more harm to themselves and humanity than they can imagine.

Revelation13:18- The number of the beast...is 666

So, comes the meaning of the number 666. 666 is a computer-generated number, and is symbolic of technology. It represents the evil that will come from technology and the breaking of God's greatest commandment which is to have no other God's before Him. Man's worshipping technology as if it were God, is the dark side of technology.

TECHNOLOGY FAILS

There will be several factors contributing to the failure of technology. Solar radiation is radiation from our sun, while cosmic radiation comes from outside our solar system. Every 12 years there is a shift in the sun's magnetic field. When this happens, there is a flare up in sun spot activity and the earth is bombarded by solar radiation from the sun. This solar radiation can knock out technology and has done so in the past. In 1853, solar flares and solar radiation from the sun was so intense that it knocked out the only technology of the day, the telegraph.

The earth's magnetic field is a protective shield that protects our earth from cosmic and solar radiation. It deflects solar and cosmic radiation towards our North and South Poles. Very soon, there will be a shift of the earth's magnetic poles and the earth will no longer have its protection from solar and cosmic radiation, and radiation will get through. This radiation can disrupt our current technology. Another potential source of failure of technology is an electromagnetic pulse or EMP. Governments of the world are developing electromagnetic pulse weapons designed to disrupt and cause the failure of technology.

Nations are hacking other nations computers. North Korea has hacked Sony Pictures computers and made corporations aware they are vulnerable. The United States hacked the computer system overseeing Iran's nuclear program. It is not farfetched to see someone or some nation creating a super malicious malware or super virus that can cause technology to fail. These are scientific reasons how technology might fail, but these do not give insight to the most important reason of all. Much of mankind worships technology as if it were God. It is the number one commandment of God to have no other Gods before Him. The failure of technology is symbolic to all of mankind that they have broken God's greatest commandment which is to have no other Gods before Him. Technology will fail and slowly the message will be received, that technology is meant to be a tool to serve all of mankind and not just a few. If mankind worships technology as if it were God again, then it will be taken away again.

CHAPTER 41

—— § ——

MARK OF THE BEAST

Revelation13:15- Image of the beast...speak and cause that as many as would not worship (it)...be killed

Revelation 13:17- No man might buy or sell, save he that had the mark or the number of his name

Revelation 13:16-17- And he causes all, the small and the great, and the rich and the poor, and the free men and the slaves to be given a mark on their right hand or on their forehead, and he provides that no one will be able to buy or to sell, except the one who has the mark, either the name of the beast or the number of his name.

MUCH HAS BEEN said and written about what the mark of the beast really means. There has been a significant amount of fear around this passage of revelation and fear of the unknowing. The mark of the beast refers to a plan by the United States government and technology companies to solve the problem of illegal immigration. The government has a tentative plan to insert a microchip under the skin of all the legal immigrants of the United States. This technology is used successfully for finding and returning the lost pets to their owners. This type of branding of the legal residents of the United States would make it much easier for the United States to deal with illegal immigration.

This branding of the citizens of the United States has the potential to do a great deal of harm. It is a power over the legal and illegal citizens of the United States, and like any power it can and will be abused. It starts simply and innocently. The government proposes a plan to deal with illegal immigration, and guarantees the public that microchips will not be used for any other purpose. The plan is implemented and then comes the exceptions to the rule. Initially there is just one exception to the rule. The government will state all the reasons why there should be an additional use for the microchip that has been inserted under the skin. The door has been opened and will never be shut, until the end of the world as we know it. The exceptions list keeps growing and the government will use the fear that is everywhere, to use this technology as they will. There will be those in positions of power who will use this technology for their own agenda. The potential for abuse of this technology is enormous, and the loss of our constitutional rights to privacy is gone.

CHAPTER 42

SYNTHETIC MATERIALS TO FALL APART

As OUR WORLD changes and the spirit of God floods forth, there will come a time when the synthetic materials produced by man will no longer be supported by spirit. Synthetic materials will fall apart. Clothes made of synthetic materials will fall off the body and there will be embarrassment for those who find themselves without clothes (Figure 42). Those who have clothes made of natural fibers and materials will have clothes covering their bodies.

Figure 42- Clothes Fall Off as Synthetic Materials Fall Apart

CHAPTER 43

§

ONE SOURCE OF ALL TRUE PROPHECY

HOPI PROPHECY

A MINISTER, DAVID Young, was driving in the desert in 1958 and offered a ride to an elderly Native American. The Native American said his name was White Feather and told the minister his story and related many Hopi prophecies. This story and the Hopi prophecies became a manuscript in 1959, which was distributed in many Presbyterian and Methodist churches. This story was reproduced and published in The Book of the Hopi, by Frank Waters in 1963. These prophecies have been published in other books and places.

> *My people await Pahana, the lost White Brother, [from the stars] as do all our brothers in the land. He will not be like the white men we know now, who are cruel and greedy. We were told of their coming long ago. But still we await Pahana.*
>
> *These are the Signs that great destruction is coming. The world shall rock to and fro. The white man will battle against other people in other lands -- with those who possessed the first light of wisdom. There will be many columns of smoke and fire such as White Feather has seen the white man make in the deserts not far from here. Only those which come will cause disease and a great dying. Many of my people, understanding the prophecies, shall be safe. Those who stay and live in the places of my people also shall be safe. Then there will be much to rebuild. And soon -- very*

soon afterward -- Pahana will return. He shall bring with him the dawn of the Fifth World.

This is the First Sign: We are told of the coming of the white-skinned men, like Pahana, but not living like Pahana men who took the land that was not theirs. And men who struck their enemies with thunder.

This is the Second Sign: Our lands will see the coming of spinning wheels filled with voices. In his youth, my father saw this prophecy come true with his eyes -- the white men bringing their families in wagons across the prairies.

This is the Third Sign: A strange beast like a buffalo but with great long horns, will overrun the land in large numbers. These White Feather saw with his eyes -- the coming of the white men's cattle.

This is the Fourth Sign: The land will be crossed by snakes of iron.

This is the Fifth Sign: The land shall be crisscrossed by a giant spider's web.

This is the Sixth sign: The land shall be crisscrossed with rivers of stone that make pictures in the sun.

This is the Seventh Sign: You will hear of the sea turning black, and many living things dying because of it.

This is the Eight Sign: You will see many youth, who wear their hair long like my people, come and join the tribal nations, to learn their ways and wisdom.

And this is the Ninth and Last Sign: You will hear of a dwelling-place in the heavens, above the earth, that shall fall with a great crash. It will appear as a blue star. Very soon after this, the ceremonies of my people will cease.

The gift of prophecy is of God and it can be given to anyone of any land, any culture, any religion of God or people who are worthy. All true prophecy comes from one source and that is God. Prophecy was given to some of the spiritual leaders of the Hopi Indians, whose tribe and reservation is in the southwestern United States. They are a very spiritual people who have honored their ancestors and teachings of the elders. The Hopi tribe was given prophecy as to the end of the fourth world and beginning of the fifth world. Many of these prophecies have come true but not all the Hopi prophecies have been fulfilled. These Hopi prophecies are a foretelling of future events as a prelude to the end of the fourth world and a period of destruction, then the beginning of the fifth world.

Let us take these prophecies one by one as the prelude to a time of destruction for the earth, the end of the fourth world and the beginning of the fifth world.

HOPI PROPHECIES THAT HAVE BEEN FULFILLED

"This is the First Sign: We are told of the coming of the white-skinned men, like Pahana, but not living like Pahana men who took the land that was not theirs. And men who struck their enemies with thunder."

The white man came. The first was Coronado and the Spanish Armada. Then came the landing of the white man on Plymouth Rock, colonization of the eastern seaboard and states, then eventual westward migration. The

Native Americans were struck down by thunder (guns and cannons) and forced out of their land. My teacher's own grandmother had to walk the Trail of Tears as the Creek tribe was kicked out of their land of Georgia and put on Indian reservation in Oklahoma. Many died walking the Trail of Tears. The Native Americans were struck with white man's guns, who lived by the law that "Might is right."

"This is the Second Sign: Our lands will see the coming of spinning wheels filled with voices. In his youth, my father saw this prophecy come true with his eyes -- the white men bringing their families in wagons across the prairies."

This prophecy told by white feather has already been interpreted by white feather. The white man came across the prairies and land in their covered wagons. The spinning wheels are the wooden wheels of the covered wagons.

"This is the Third Sign: A strange beast like a buffalo but with great long horns, will overrun the land in large numbers. These White Feather saw with his eyes -- the coming of the white men's cattle."

The white killed off much of the native buffalo, and brought with him cattle that looked like the buffalo, but had great long horns.

"This is the Fourth Sign: The land will be crossed by snakes of iron."

This is the building of the railroads that stretched across our nation. These railroad tracks connected the east and west coast and the north and the south. Eventually these snakes of iron connected all the major cities of the land that used to belong to the Native Americans.

"This is the Fifth Sign: The land shall be crisscrossed by a giant spider's web."

The fulfillment of the fifth sign was the invention of telegraph and telephones. With these marvelous inventions telegraph and telephone wires stretched across the nation, in crisscrossing patterns. They formed a web of black lines crisscrossing across our nation.

"This is the Sixth sign: The land shall be crisscrossed with rivers of stone that make pictures in the sun."

The fulfillment of the sixth sign came with the invention by Henry Ford of the first automobile. With the invention of the automobile came the need for roads which is the rivers of stone that crisscross our nation. Drive across these rivers of stone in the desert on a hot summer's day and you will see the pictures in the sun. These are mirages created by the heat waves coming off hot asphalt.

"This is the Eighth Sign: You will see many youth, who wear their hair long like my people, come and join the tribal nations, to learn their ways and wisdom."

The true spirit of the hippy movement was love, peace, happiness, freedom and getting back to the land. In a world becoming all about materialism, there was a movement away from materialism. This hippy movement became lost and could not handle the freedom of drugs and sexuality. The true spirit of the hippy movement was not totally lost. There were those searching for love, peace, happiness, freedom, brotherhood and getting back to the land, who were led to the Native Americans to learn the Native American ways. This sign has been fulfilled.

HOPI PROPHECIES CURRENTLY BEING FULFILLED

"This is the Seventh Sign: You will hear of the sea turning black, and many living things dying because of it."

There have been oil spills killing sea life but black is symbolic of pollution and death. Bible prophecy states that the sea will turn red and one third the creatures in the sea shall die. In biblical prophecy red is symbolic of death, but can also symbolize pollution. This prophecy is explained in chapters of Great Pollution on the Face of the Earth and One Third the Creatures of the Sea Shall Die. There has been pollution of our rivers, streams and oceans and fish dying because of the pollution, however, this prophecy is still being fulfilled.

"The white man will battle against other people in other lands -- with those who possessed the first light of wisdom."

This prophecy is being fulfilled with *"brother against brother and nation against nation. Wars and rumors of wars."* This prophecy also gives insight about the start of World War III, which will include those of Jewish and Muslim descent. It is those of Jewish, and Muslim descent whose ancestors brought forth the first light of wisdom.

"There will be many columns of smoke and fire such as White Feather has seen the white man make in the deserts not far from here."

This is the same as biblical prophecy of fire and smoke in distant lands. With climate change comes dying of our forests and vegetation, becoming great fuel for fires. This will create fire and smoke and this sign is currently being fulfilled.

"Only those which come will cause disease and a great dying."

This is the same as the biblical prophecy of plagues and pestilence. Although the plagues have started, there will be more plagues that will cause a great number of deaths.

HOPI PROPHECIES TO BE FULFILLED

"And this is the Ninth and Last Sign: You will hear of a dwelling-place in the heavens, above the earth, that shall fall with a great crash. It will appear as a blue star. Very soon after this, the ceremonies of my people will cease."

This is an important sign which has not yet occurred and is the same prophecy foretold in the Bible of the falling star. This comet will appear in the sky and shall land with a great crash in northern Europe.

"The world shall rock to and fro."

This prophecy is the same prophecy as Doctrine and Covenants prophecy and the world "reeling to and fro and stumbling as a drunken man." This prophecy refers to the wobbling of the earth with the shift of the earth's axis. This prophecy will soon be fulfilled.

"These are the Signs that great destruction is coming."

All these prophecies are *"signs that great destruction is coming."* The same destruction prophesied in the Bible. Those Hopis who listen to the prophecy and wisdom of the elders know the *"signs of the times."* They are preparing for the great destruction that is coming.

The Hopi prophecies are very accurate, and yet most of the Hopi prophecies are not let out to the white man. For the white man (I am Caucasian, so I am not pointing fingers) will take prophecy of the Native Americans, use it for their own purpose and not keep sacred knowledge, sacred. For this reason, most of the Hopi prophecies are kept secret and not let out to the white man.

Both the Mayans, Hopis, other Native American tribes have prophecy that talks about a time of great destruction that will come at the end of the fourth world and the beginning of the fifth world. This shows the same source of their prophecies. The Bible prophecies that speaks of the end of the world as we know it and then the earth being reborn into a paradisiacal glory again shows the common source of the prophecies. The ancestors of the Mayans, Hopis and Cherokees had the same great teacher, Jesus Christ. The Mayans called Jesus Christ the bearded Great White God, Quetzalcoatl, the Hopis called him their True White Brother, Pahana, while the Cherokees called him the Pale One.

JUDAISM, ISLAM, HINDUISM, BUDDHISM AND NATIVE AMERICAN PROPHECY

JUDAISM

The Christians and the people of Jewish faith share a close heritage. There is one basic difference between the people of Jewish faith and Christians, in that those of Jewish faith do not believe the return of the Jewish Messiah will be Jesus Christ.

Here are the beliefs why Jewish people do not believe Jesus is the Messiah. They believe the Messiah or the anointed one will come at a time of war and suffering. He will be charismatic and a great political leader and of the tribe of David. He will be a great military leader who will win battles for Israel and a great judge with great wise decisions and judgment. He will rebuild the temple, and reestablish worship and government in Israel. Most importantly they believe that the Messiah will be human and not divine.

Herein lies another great truth. Most of us have forgotten that our true nature is divine. We are children of the Most High God, created in His likeness and image having a human experience, not humans trying have a spiritual experience. Jesus Christ being born into the human experience was one of his greatest gifts to mankind, and showed how much God and Jesus loves us. All these prophecies are about to be fulfilled and the Jewish people will see that Jesus Christ is the promised Messiah of Judaism.

ISLAM

It is true that the followers of Islam, worship the same one God as did Abraham. Those who are of the Islamic faith and understand Islam and the Koran, accept the Old Testament as the word of God. The followers of Islam follow the Abraham covenant, they are the seed of Abraham and worship the Abraham one God. The Jews, the Christians and the Muslims worship the same God, whether the God is called Elohim, Allah or Jehovah. There is only one God and they worship the one God.

The Muslims recognize Christ as a true prophet and that He will return to earth and judge the Christians. This means they know the teachings of Christ are true and from God. They have love and respect for Mother Mary. They believe in the final battle of good and evil, the days of trials and tribulations, Judgment Day and the earth being renewed.

It is Satan's plan to put brother against brother and nation against nation. Make everyone appear to be your enemy when the ultimate truth is they are our brother and sisters. Those of Muslim faith share a close bond and heritage with those of Jewish faith and the Christians.

PROPHECIES OF THE KORAN THAT HAVE BEEN FULFILLED

Koran 81:4- And when the mountains are made to move.

This has already happened. Man's open pit mining, moving mountains to make highways and make way for construction.

Koran 82:3- When rivers are cut up,

Koran 81:7- And when the rivers are made to flow into each other.

Man is altering the course of rivers, which are now inland highways for boats and commercial vessels. Dams hold back the water and form man-made lakes.

Koran 81:6- And when the wild beasts are gathered together.

These are the zoos that we have all over the world.

Koran 81:7- When souls are joined with one another,

With world-wide travel and immigration there is intermingling and mixture of the races.

Koran 41:21- Their skins will bear witness against them as to what they have been doing.

We now can take fingerprints and track down those who committed criminal acts.

Koran 4:120- They will alter Allah's creation.

The great discovery of DNA has led many scientists to alter the DNA and God's creations. Genetic engineering is here and growing rapidly. Many scientists fascinated with what it can do with DNA and the benefits to mankind, while others without a higher consciousness and awareness are altering God's creations without respect for the One who created it.

Koran 81:5- And when the she-camels, ten months pregnant are abandoned.

Koran 16:9- And He has created horses and mules and asses that you may ride them, and as a source of beauty. And He will create what you do not yet know.

Koran- Highways in the sky,

We now have new forms of transportation, airplanes and jets with highways in the sky.

Koran 81:10- When the books are spread widely and propagated,

Koran 81:8- And when various people are brought together.

Books are now published and distributed all over the world and translated into the different languages for all to read. People from all over the world can now communicate through telegraph, phones, radio, TV and the internet. We now have international travel.

Koran 17:105- And after him We said to the Children of Israel, 'Dwell Ye in the promised land; and when the time of the promise of the Latter Days come, We shall bring you together out of various people.

This is the literal recreation of the state of Israel.

Koran- Tirmidhi- Allah's Messenger (saas) said, "In the End Times men will come forth who will fraudulently use religion for worldly ends and wear sheepskins in public to display meekness. Their tongues will be sweeter than sugar, but their hearts will be the hearts of wolves."

This is wolves in sheep's clothing.

HINDUISM

There are many who call Hinduism a false religion because it has many Gods. This is a misconception. The Hindus believe in one supreme God, who is the God of all things. The Hindus give more description to the different aspects of the one God. There is God the creator and God the destroyer which are different aspects of the one God. Hinduism does not have many supreme Gods, but one supreme God with many helpers. This is no different than other religions who have angels, archangels, great spiritual beings like the Christ, Abraham, Moses and Saint Peter assisting God in his work.

BHUDDISM

There is a great deal of misconception about the religion and practice of Buddhism. I have heard that Buddhists do not believe in God, even though

I know many Buddhists that do believe in God. After researching this question, I reached a different conclusion. There are some Buddhists that believe in God, there some that do not and there are some that don't know.

There is something more important, however. One of the great teachings that came from Jesus Christ, was a concept of the kingdom of heaven. Until the birth and teachings of Jesus, it was taught that depending on how one lived their life, when people died they would either go to heaven or hell. Jesus taught us that the kingdom of heaven is within. It is important to escape the hell that we enter into by our choices and enter into the kingdom of heaven right now; heaven on earth. The goal of Buddhism, Hinduism, Zen, Sikhism, yoga and meditation is enlightenment.

Mother Mary- *Your goal is enlightenment.*

Luke- 17:20-21- And when he was demanded of the Pharisees, when the kingdom of God should come, he answered them and said, The kingdom of God cometh not with observation: Neither shall they say, Lo here! or, lo there! for, behold, the kingdom of God is within you.

The message from Mother Mary is *"Your goal is enlightenment."* Messages from Mother Mary speak of enlightenment and consciousness in the same truthfulness as the importance of her son, Jesus, the atonement and the sacrament. As if they are not separate but different sides of the same coin. My goal, being a follower of Christ, is the same as those who practice Hinduism, Buddhism, Sikhism, Zen, yoga, martial arts, meditation and Native American ways and teachings. The end goal of these disciplines is enlightenment, which in Christianity, Judaism and Islam is entering the kingdom of heaven, here on earth.

The teaching by Jesus Christ, that the kingdom of God is within us a great pearl of great value. One may come to the wrong conclusion that God and the kingdom of God do not exist on the other side of the veil.

God and the kingdom of heaven do exist on the other side of the veil, however, God gave us a great gift as we passed through the veil. He gave us a microcosm of God's kingdom(s) in the human heart. Dorothy did not have to go to Oz to find what she was looking for, she had what she was looking for all the time. We can enter the kingdom of heaven at any time. When we die, we will pass through the veil and enter the room (kingdom) in God's spacious mansion that we have created in our own heart and mind.

NATIVE AMERICANS

I have been very blessed to have had a Native American medicine man, Bearheart, as a teacher and friend. I was adopted by Bearheart and taken into the tribe. Bearheart was also a Christian minister. I was taught Native American ways, the honoring of mother earth and all living things. It was very clear to both Bearheart and I, both being Christians, that as we prayed to the Great Spirit in prayer we were praying to the one God, God the Father. Bearheart had the gift of prophecy and from time to time would speak prophecy. As I read the prophecy of the Hopis, Mayans and other Native Americans it is very clear to me the source of their prophecy, which is the one God.

THE SOURCE OF ALL TRUTH AND ALL TRUE PROPHECY

The prophets and enlightened masters of the Bible, sacred Christian and Jewish texts, Koran, Hinduism, Buddhism and Native American tradition can receive the gift of prophecy and other gifts of God. All truth and all true prophecy comes from one source, the one God.

CHAPTER 44

—— § ——

THE RAPTURE

Revelation 7-4- And I heard the number of them which were sealed: and there were sealed a hundred and forty and four thousand of all the tribes of the children of Israel.

Luke 9:28-29- And it came to pass about an eight days after these sayings, he took Peter and John and James, and went up into a mountain to pray. And as he prayed, the fashion of his countenance was altered, and his raiment was white and glistering.

THE RAPTURE IS a common belief among many Christian churches. In this belief, Christ will come before the Second Coming of Christ and Judgment Day. A select number (some believe 144,000) of those who have lived God's laws will be called up into heaven before the start of the trials and tribulations of the last days. The rest of the world, who have not lived God's laws, will suffer God's judgments before the Second Coming of Christ.

This common belief among many Christians was started by Preacher John Nelson Darby of the Plymouth Brethren in 1827. This unique interpretation of the biblical scripture is believed to be inspired by a Margaret MacDonald, a 15-year-old girl in northern Scotland in 1830. Margaret had a vision while reading the Bible. In this vision, she saw Christ coming in the clouds, the faithful were called up, and then tribulations come upon the earth. Preacher John Darby taught that before the Second Coming of Christ the faithful would be called up to heaven and would not have to experience and endure God's judgments in the last days. This doctrine taught by John Darby was published in 1909 in the Scofield Reference Bible and became popularly known as The Rapture. This interpretation of Revelation scriptures became popularized and established doctrine in many Christian churches.

It is a wonderful thought for those who believe in The Rapture that some brothers and sisters will ascend into clouds with Jesus Christ and watch as their brother and sisters go through trials and tribulations. This is a nice thought and belief but only partially true. Enoch and the prophet Elijah ascended into heaven never having died. This will happen to those of sufficient faith and the earth angels who were brought to earth to assist mankind in end times. They will ascend into heaven before Judgment Day (not all at the same time), receive teaching and knowledge and have spiritual freedom. Most importantly they can do as Jesus can, descend from heaven on to the earth plane to assist those brothers and sisters in their trials and tribulations.

God has sent forth faithful, valiant spirits to assist mankind at a time of great need. Would a loving Father then call these valiant spirits back when they are needed the most? Are these valiant spirits solely on a pulpit or in a distant cave where none can reach in the hour of need? These valiant spirits have been placed in every country and every city, every religion and every people. They have gone where they are needed. They are fathers, mothers, children and a newborn baby. They are the butcher, baker and candlestick maker; they are everywhere. They will be the eye of a great hurricane, the center of a great storm. They will be a solid rock where there is not much to grab hold of, lest people are swept away. They shall provide calm in total chaos and a world in fear. You shall know them not by their position or title but the quality of their love.

SEALING OF 144,000

The sealing of 144,000 relates to a unique calling of God, after the Second Coming of Christ. There will be 144,000 brothers and sisters of the tribe of Israel chosen and honored with a special task or mission. It would be a great honor, if chosen.

CHAPTER 45

— ◊ —

PERSECUTION OF THE SAINTS

Mark 13:20- *And if the Lord had not cut short the days, no human being would be saved. But for the sake of the elect, whom he chose, he shortened the days.*

Matthew 24:8-9- *But all these things are merely the beginning of birth pangs. Then they will deliver you to tribulation, and will kill you, and you will be hated by all nations on account of my name.*

Matthew 24:22- *Except those days be shortened, there should no flesh be saved*

Luke 21:16-17- *Ye shall be betrayed...and some of you...put to death*

Revelation13:7- *To make war with the saints, and to overcome them, and power given him over...all nations*

Mormon 8:27- *And it shall come in a day when the blood of saints shall cry unto the Lord, because of secret combinations and the works of darkness.*

Buddhism- *For many centuries, the mystical tradition of Agharti (or, Aghartha) and its ruler, the King of the World, has existed in Tibet and Mongolia. "There will be terrible war between all the earth's peoples; entire nations will die --- hunger, crimes unknown to law, formerly* *unthinkable to the world. The persecuted will demand the attention of the whole world."*

I HAVE WONDERED about the timing of fulfilling of certain prophecies. I was sure certain signs should have taken place already, and did not understand why they had not been fulfilled, yet. Finally, I understood. The days of trial and tribulation had been shortened, for the benefit of the saints and all mankind. **If the last days were not shortened then no man, woman or child would survive.**

Some believe that Auschwitz could never happen again. That was long ago and we have much more important issues to focus our attention on. This crime against humanity, is not an isolated incident and unfortunately prophecy states it will happen again. Hitler committed war crimes and he tried to exterminate the Jews and many others. If Hitler had not lost to the allies, he may have succeeded in genocide.

It is the history of man to blame; it is part of our animal nature. Whenever things don't go the way we want it to, there must be someone responsible. We cannot be responsible for our pain, who can we blame? The saints, Christians and God's elect shall be persecuted in the last days. The world shall say "Things are not going well, horrible events are happening, who can we blame for the mess that we are in?" It is darkness that wants to persecute and destroy the saints and God's elect. For the benefit of the saints and all mankind, those days shall be shortened.

CHAPTER 46

——— § ———

FAILURE TO BELIEVE AND DISCERN THE SIGNS

2 Peter 3:3-4- Knowing this first, that there shall come in the last days scoffers, walking after their own lusts, and saying, Where is the promise of his coming? For since the fathers fell asleep, all things continue as they were from the beginning of the creation?

THERE WILL BE those who read my book and cannot or will not understand what is written in plain simple English. Those who understand the Bible, Koran, sacred Jewish and Christian texts and prophecies of Buddhists, Hindu, Native Americans and Aborigines understand the "signs of the times." As prophecies are fulfilled and it becomes very clear to most of us, about the fulfilling of prophecies and God's word there will still be unbelievers and scoffers.

The unbelievers and scoffers will say, "Show me a sign and then I will believe." This book is full of signs. The unbelievers will say, "No, show me now that I have you here and I have a few minutes. Show me a sign and then I will believe." If God did show them a sign, they might believe for a week or so, and then fall back into their unbelief. This book is full of signs and for those who have faith will be able to discern the signs.

The signs will be clearer as each prophesy is fulfilled. The faithful will know in their hearts the signs as they come true. Those of less faith will in the end know that what others have told them concerning the end times. There will be others, that Jesus called the scoffers who even in the end will fail to discern the signs of the times. There will be unbelievers scoffing at those who would believe in such superstitious nonsense as the end of the world as we know it. In the end the signs shall become crystal clear and even those who have scoffed at those who believe, shall fear in their hearts. They shall sense in their hearts something biblical is happening.

CHAPTER 47

ASSISTING NOT RESCUING MANKIND

THERE IS so much anxiety, fear, heartache, pain, suffering and lack of direction in this world that it is easy to see why so many of us want to be rescued. Many of us are calling upon anyone with power to rescue us from this condition in which we all find ourselves. Neither God nor Christ, who is also known as the Savior, would rescue us from the world of affairs in which we find ourselves. To do so would undermine our reason for being here, and everything we have worked for. To rescue us, would be to say that Christ's plan of free will has failed, we cannot make it, so please send us a lifeboat. To rescue us would be telling us that God no longer believes in His children and their ability to make it home again. God has not lost faith in us or our ability to make it back home. He believes more in us than we believe in ourselves. He is quietly, patiently waiting for us to return home to him, where a celebration will be awaiting all of us who choose to return home.

Rescuing is much different than assisting. Who can come to this world and make it on his own? "I am a rock or an island and I don't need yours or anyone else's help." Soon there will be so much trouble, disasters, chaos in the world that we will all need assistance just to survive. We will call upon each other for assistance and help. It is the calling for assistance from our fellow man that will open our hearts towards our fellow man. Assisting our fellow man and divine assistance from God and his angelic host is not only good, but part of the plan of the salvation of the world and mankind.

CHAPTER 48

————— ∮ —————

HOW GOD WILL SAVE THE WORLD

THERE HAS BEEN so much in the movies, television and books about how the world is in distress and there is need for a hero or heroine to save the world. It has been a love affair of the world to search for their hero or heroine. There are the mythical super heroes like Superman, Spiderman and the Fantastic Four, Batman and Robin, and other heroes and heroines like Lara Croft, Indiana Jones and James Bond. Many look to our spiritual, political, scientific, medical, environmental and financial leaders to save our world. Others look to the everyday unnamed heroes and heroines who are saving our world. Everyone can lend a helping hand in the saving of our world but the true savior of our world and mankind will be God and Jesus Christ.

ULTIMATE CHOICE

Let me also say that the future is not fixed. Mankind's future and the future of the world hang in a delicate balance of survival or destruction. This fate is not in the hands of the few but in the hands of mankind as a whole. It is the whole of mankind that will decide the fate of mankind and the world and all life. The reason is our greatest gift of all. Truly there are other planets in the universe with life as our own, but it was earth and us that were chosen for this grand experiment in free will. It is because of this greatest gift of the plan of free will that it is forbidden even by God to interfere with our free will. If not for man being given free will and the ability to choose between good and evil, God would be able to save us and the world with a word. We were chosen out of all of God's children in this plan of free will. This places responsibility on us and no one else. The saving of the world is up to us, although more assistance is available than you might imagine. The choice between good and evil will be made clear to everyone and then we will all have to make a choice. Choose God and your fellow man or choose the things of the world. For those who are agnostic or atheist, do not feel you must believe in God. If you love your fellow man, then you love God. It is that simple.

RESPONSIBILITY

Spiderman's father said it eloquently when he told Peter Parker "With great power comes great responsibility." This great gift of free will is more powerful than you might think. Returning to God with free will, will give all of us great power in the hereafter. "With great power comes great responsibility." Now it is time for the whole of mankind to except the responsibility for free will, the state of affairs of the world, and the ability to save ourselves and our planet. The first step in responsibility is don't point the finger of blame. There will be groups of people who will be blamed for the affairs of world. Some will say "It is this group's fault and all the woes of the world can be blamed on this group. If it wasn't for this group all would be well." In the history of the world, certain groups have been blamed and genocide taken place and it has never resolved the problems of men. The problems in the world are not caused by any one group or groups but is caused by the hearts of men. This has been the history of man, and history has the tendency to repeat itself. We are all in this together. Even though there are some who are hurting more and some that are helping more, blame is the opposite of taking responsibility. Blame takes away the power that we need. If we succeed, it will be the whole of mankind and the plan of free will that will succeed. If we fail, then it will be the whole of mankind and the plan of free will that has failed.

GOD'S LOVE IS THE ULTIMATE FORCE IN THE UNIVERSE

Everything is unfolding according to divine plan. The unleashing of the forces of darkness is part of the divine plan. The resulting chaos, with brother against brother and nation against nation was foreseen and had to happen. You are witnessing the eternal battle between good and evil. The darkness is very clear to see; it is everywhere. Don't be fooled into believing there is not much light, love and goodness in the world; there is. As darkness is unleashed, there will be an increase in the light and love in the world. As our fellow man calls for aide, the compassion in the hearts of men shall answer. It is wise not to point fingers at the other side, no matter which side of the battle of good and evil you choose. Darkness must be unleashed in the last days, as well as the flooding forth of God's light. How else would we be able to make a clear choice between good and evil, light and darkness? For this plan of free will, we must all make the ultimate choice.

GOD IS IN CHARGE

God is flooding forth His love and light at this very moment. There is nothing more powerful than God's love in the universe. Darkness is a real force, and as Darth Vader stated correctly, "Do not underestimate the power of the dark side." It is a strong, powerful universal force that shall deceive many, and cause many to fall. Some say, "With darkness so powerful, how can God manage and overcome?" The opposite is true, with God's light and love being the strongest force in the universe, how can darkness persevere? It is all unfolding according to

232

divine plan. It is God that is unleashing darkness, not Lucifer. There is only one who is in charge at this very moment and in this whole process and that is God.

Since God is in charge does that mean we have nothing to worry about? NO. Our fate is up to us. Whether we make it or not, is our choice, not God's. We will make the ultimate choice and determine our fate and the fate of the world. God is giving us his love and assistance. Any more than this would be to destroy our free will and our whole reason for being here. Then again, don't underestimate the power of God's love and assistance.

It is true that God has other children on other planets and in the spiritual realm. God has many things that He is attending to in his kingdom and in the universe. It is also true that His eyes, heart and attention are turned here at this critical moment, for this is the culmination of this plan to give some of His children free will. He very much wants us to succeed.

DIVINE PLAN

There is a plan for the salvation of the world and mankind. For without this plan, God's love and God's assistance all would be lost, and the result would be man's destruction of himself. Never before has man held the nuclear weapons, technology and biological weapons that can destroy all life on our planet. The following is the divine plan to save mankind, all life and the world.

GOD'S ASSISTANCE

God has called forth angelic beings to assist mankind. These angelic beings are more numerous than we can imagine, and exist on different spiritual levels in God's Kingdom. They are turning their hearts and their attention here to mankind and the world. They carry God's power and are here in love and assistance.

God has sent forth what I refer to as earth angels. They are spiritual beings born into human bodies, but were called forth now to assist mankind at this critical point in the history of mankind. They are everywhere. They have been sent to every religion, every sect, every country and city. They are everywhere and are more numerous than you would think. Their role is to assist mankind through the difficult times ahead.

THE PRIDE CYCLE

The Bible was written by those who were the communicators with God. We were all meant to have a one on one communication with God, but we believe we don't have this ability so God sent prophets that we may have His word. The Bible is the word of God, but also a history book in man's relationship to God. Those who study history and world leaders know that history repeats itself. A famous statement was "Those who do not learn from the past are condemned to repeat the past." The great leaders and historians know this. That is why it is so important to have a record of history, so that we may all learn from the past. Throughout the Bible and other holy books is God's word but also a history of man in relationship to God. Needless to say, mankind does not learn the lessons of the past and history repeats itself.

The pride cycle is important to understand. It starts out with those who have little land, food and possessions. Life is difficult and there is need for abundance. These people call upon the One who created us all for help in providing food and taking care of their basic needs of life. God, who is a loving, caring, compassionate God gives to His children. They turn their hearts, love and prayers towards each other and the One who loves us without end. Goodness is everywhere. The people continue their hard work and prayers, and the loving God pours forth abundance. The land blossoms, the people flourish for God has given abundance to them. They forget the hardship they came from and who was mostly responsible for their abundance and fortune. They set their hearts upon the things of the world and the praise of the world, and not upon the One who gave them the abundance. The goodness and love for their fellow man and God turns into what they want, and goodness and the spirit of God leaves. There begins the downward cycle and loss of abundance. They forget and get caught up in the world and worldly possessions. There is no time line on this, but they eventually lose what they had. It is only after losing what they had that their hearts are turned back towards God. They turn their hearts away from the worldly things, probably because they no longer have them, and their hearts are turned towards God. They ask the One who created us all to give them their basic needs. Once their basic needs are met, then they ask for more. God who loves His children gives abundantly. The people receive abundantly and so the cycle continues. This cycle has repeated itself repeatedly, from the beginning of time and it is important to understand; the pride cycle that will be a key in God saving the world.

Look all around you and you see a world full of pride and people who have set their hearts upon worldly things, possessions and accolades of the world. As a whole, mankind has set its heart upon the worldly possessions rather than upon God and their fellow man. It is God's love for us, in answer to our collective prayers that He is orchestrating the breaking of our collective pride. He is allowing us to fall on our knees then turn our hearts towards Him and each other. There will be those who believe this is punishment and done by the hand of an angry God. The challenging times ahead are done because God loves us and not out of punishment. Once we have passed through the trials and are safely on the other side, we will see how much love it took to save us from our own destruction.

Before the last day, God's name will be taken in vain more often than I care to speculate. He will be cursed and blamed for the hardships that come to all of us. These hardships are necessary and part of God's plan to save the world and save mankind. It is the coming hardships that will prevent us from destroying ourselves. The coming hardships will not discriminate, for the challenges will fall on all of us, for we are all part of the human race.

I will now tell a short synopsis of my life in the hope that you will understand that hardships can be a blessing and not a curse. My life has been full of hardship and challenges, yet I am thankful for everything that has transpired in my life. I lost my only daughter to brain cancer, lost our money due to her illness, nearly lost my only son who was in an automobile-pedestrian accident, gone through a bitter divorce, lost the relationship with my son as a result of the divorce, lost my dog and cats, and I was diagnosed with cancer. These hardships are not all but a tip of the iceberg. How can I, who have endured so much and be thankful for these challenges in my life. These hardships were not without pain, for I have endured more pain and shed more tears than any one I am aware of. There was pain and the wounds may never heal. I don't wish upon my worst enemy to lose their child for I can think of no greater pain for anyone to endure. Through all that I have been through I felt the hand of God. He is not someone who hates me or enjoys seeing me suffer, but one who loves me without end. At the part of road that I am currently on in this adventure of life, I can look back and see where all this hardship has brought me. Now I value God and the welfare of my fellow man and not the riches of the world. All this hardship has brought me to God. My heart has been broken so many times that there is nothing left and only God's love can fill the void. I was at times prideful and could have gone in the wrong direction in life. It was God's love for me that sent me hardships, broke my pride, humbled me, brought me to a better place and got me headed in the right direction. So, I am eternally grateful to God for having the compassion on me, to love me so, to give me trials that I may have a change of heart and turn my eyes, soul, spirit and heart towards God. I don't wish any harm on any one. I am pained to know what must happen, and the hardships we will all go through together.

THE LOVE OF MANY SHALL WAX COLD

I have written a whole chapter on this topic because it is one of the signs of the end of the world as we know it. This is one of the ways that God chooses to save the world. God's love falls upon all for He loves all His children. This is a unique time in the history of mankind where those who choose darkness will have God's love withheld. This is not because these children of God are not loved, but because they are being forewarned about the ultimate choice they are about to make. Living without God's love is hell on earth. These children of God will be given a type of preliminary feedback to help them understand more clearly the consequences of their choice.

NUCLEAR WAR

Mother Mary- *I will not allow nuclear weapons.*

This is the time prophesized in the Bible where man could destroy himself. Darkness is being unleashed and there are many leaders with nuclear weapons that could start a nuclear attack that could escalate to nuclear holocaust and nuclear winter. This could destroy all life on this planet except possibly those insects and animals living underground. We are already in "piece-meal World War III" and nuclear war a very real possibility. In our subconscious there is a fear that we all dread. It is not only nuclear bombs that can level cities but the nuclear fallout that would follow. I have read the accounts of Japanese who suffered radiation poisoning after the nuclear bombs were dropped on Japan and it is a sickness and death that we fear. There is a decree from God, prophesied by Mother Mary, that nuclear weapons will not be allowed. This does not mean that a terrorist cannot explode a nuclear device or dirty bomb or some nations using small nuclear bombs, but it does mean the world will not end with nuclear holocaust and nuclear winter. God is saving us from destroying ourselves.

THE PLAN OF DARKNESS

GET WOMEN TO FALL, AND THE MEN SHALL FOLLOW

It is important to understand the plan of darkness. Part of the plan of darkness is to get women to fall. This was the plan in the Garden of Eden, for Satan knew if Eve fell, that Adam would follow. If the women of the world choose those enticements of darkness, then the Dark Lord has won a crucial battle. The men will follow the women.

DIVIDE AND CONQUER

What is the cause of wars, brother against brother and nation against nation? This is due to the unleashing of darkness that you are seeing the fruition of the plan of darkness. There is war and discord among the brotherhood of man. One of the greatest weapons available to darkness is deception and the wolf in sheep's clothing. It is the plan of darkness to divide and conquer. It is darkness in the hearts of men that causes them to see their fellow men as the enemy. It is the unleashed darkness that brings anger and hatred into the hearts of men, and that anger and hatred is turned towards their fellow men. Have mankind fight among themselves and they will destroy themselves. The great military minds will tell you the strength of this plan and it has been used successfully throughout the history of mankind. If you want to conquer a nation, first divide then conquer.

GOD'S PLAN

FAITH IN WOMEN

God believes in us although at times we may not believe in ourselves. The Father has a special relationship with his daughters. God knows the plan of darkness but is confident in his daughters. The daughters of God have the strength, courage and faith that most are unaware of. The daughters of God will make the ultimate decision in the fate of mankind and the world and chose love and their fellow man.

GOD'S PLAN IS UNIFICATION

There is a plan that strikes fear in the heart of darkness. God is aware of the plan of darkness. There are also great military minds within the force of light. God's plan is unity of the brotherhood of man. If this plan succeeds, then darkness shall fail. How does God plan to unite the brotherhood of man? Leaders of countries have used the principle of unity to unify their countries for battle and war. Unify your country and you become a strong nation and will survive the attacks of your enemies. If your country fights among itself, then it will destroy itself. A leader of Israel stated, "If our enemies would leave us alone we would destroy ourselves, but since they continue to attack us, we are unified and strong." The salvation of mankind will come from God finding a common enemy of man that will cause mankind to unite; unity of the brotherhood of man. God will not find a nation, or a religion, or a belief for all mankind to fight against. He will not send aliens to attack us. The enemy that He will send is hardship. He will send natural disasters, plaques and pestilence in the form never seen before in the history of the earth. It is these hardships sent to all men that will be the common enemy. Men and women shall unite and turn their hearts one to another. The unity of the brotherhood of man will be key in the failure of the plan of darkness.

BATTLE OF ARMEGEDDON- THE FINAL GREAT BATTLE OF GOOD AND EVIL

Luke **17: 21-** *Kingdom of God is within you.*

Revelation **16:16-** *And he gathered them together into a place called in the Hebrew tongue Armageddon.*

Joel **3:14-** *Multitudes, multitudes in the valley of decision: for the day of the LORD is near in the valley of decision.*

Edgar Cayce- that the so-called "Battle of Armageddon" described symbolically in the Bible would begin in 1999. Cayce foresaw that this "battle" will not be a war fought on Earth. Rather, it will be a spiritual struggle between the "higher forces of light" and "lower forces of darkness"

The Battle of Armageddon has symbolic reference to a plain 50 miles north of Jerusalem. This plain is where several important battles were fought in the Old Testament. Many theologians believe this is where the final battle between good and evil, Christ and the antichrist will be fought. They believe all nations shall be gathered on the battlefield of Megiddo for the greatest battle the world has ever known. Christ will come at the height of the conflict, Israel will be saved, darkness defeated and bound for a thousand years and the great millennial era will be ushered in.

Just as modern day Babylon and spiritual Babylon gets its name and has symbolic reference to the Babylon of old, the final battle referred to the Battle of Armageddon is symbolic of the final battle of good against evil. The Valley of Armageddon is most appropriately named the Valley of Decision.

The spiritual human heart is one of God's most magnificent creations for it contains a microcosm of God and the universe. In the spiritual human heart exists the kingdoms of heaven and hell and the Light of Christ. Every one of us has both kingdoms in our hearts. They both exist and the choices we make determines in which of these kingdoms we will live and go. To say there is only heaven and hell is an oversimplification for there are many kingdoms of God and many kingdoms in the human heart. There is another profound gift that God gave every one of us and this is the Light of Christ. Whether you are Christian, Jewish, Muslim, Buddhist, Hindu, Native American, agnostic or atheist; the Light of Christ resides in every one of our hearts. The Valley of Decision, which is also called the Valley of Armageddon, is a place in the human heart and this is where the final great battle between good and evil will be fought. **The Battle of Armageddon is the final battle for the hearts of men.**

Soon we will all be asked to make the ultimate choice and choose good or evil, God or the world, our fellow man or only what serves our pride and egos. This will be clearly displayed on the world stage as there will be two camps, those who choose the world and those who choose God and their fellow man. As these two camps are polarized on the world stage, so will it become clear in our hearts. The choice will be clear and then we will all have to make the ultimate decision. It does not matter what you have done in your lifetime when it comes to God's infinite love. You are more precious and worth more than you may ever know. All that matters is our decision. You can be living your life in hell, and truly your heart has been consumed with hell, but with your free will if you choose God and your fellow man, will come God's promise. God gave us the Light of Christ and

241

it is now when the Light of Christ will do battle against darkness. There is nothing more powerful than God's love and the Light of Christ, and no amount of darkness or evil can overcome them. If your choice is God and your fellow man, then darkness and the chains of darkness shall be broken and darkness shall have no more power over you. The Light of Christ is going to battle for the hearts of men.

OPENING OF OUR HEARTS
There will be hardship and challenges come to all of us. Here is another opportunity to open our hearts and turn our hearts away from the riches and accolades of the world and towards our fellow man. As the opportunities arise to share and give to our fellow man it will not be as important how much we give but how much love we put in the giving. As our governments give to other countries that are facing challenges, there is a golden opportunity to send love with the economic aid that is sent. As our loved ones face challenges and we share with them, it will not be as important how much we share as how much love we put in the sharing. It is not money but the opening of our hearts and love of our fellow man that will save the world.

WE ARE ALL IMPORTANT AND AFFECT THE WHOLE OF MANKIND
Every one of us effects the whole of mankind. Let me illustrate this with the help of a building block of the universe, the electron. The electron has mass, just like the proton and the neutron, although its mass is about $1/1,000$ of the mass of a proton or neutron. The electron has a very small amount of mass. According to Sir Isaac Newton's law of gravity, anything with mass will affect on another particle with mass. The closer the two particles are the greater will be the gravitational attraction, and the

further apart the two particles are the less will be the gravitational attraction. Even the small electron exerts a gravitational pull and affects an electron on the other side of the Universe, however small that might be. All particles in the universe are affected by every other particle in the universe and in a certain sense every particle in the universe is connected to every other particle in the universe whether by a gravitational field or divine cosmic force.

The same is true of humans and the human heart. We are all connected to each other and one of us affects all of humanity. Change one heart towards God or his fellow man and all of mankind is uplifted. Turn one heart towards darkness and it lowers all of mankind. We are all connected; we are one.

The next is called the concept of critical mass. In making nuclear weapons there is a term called critical mass. If the amount of plutonium ignited in a nuclear bomb exceeds a certain critical mass, then the entire mass of the plutonium in the bomb turns into energy. So, it will be with the hearts of men. Every one of us is part of the human race. Our fate and the fate of the world will not be determined by one or two individuals but by all of us. Each one of us influences the whole. Change one heart towards God or their fellow man and all of mankind is uplifted. Once a critical mass, or percentage of human hearts, is turned towards God and their fellow man, then war for the hearts of men and the plan of free will, will be victorious.

GOD'S OPTIMISM

I have often thought about the world and my fellow man and where we are in the history of mankind. I was concerned about the future of man and the world, because of the amount of darkness that I know is in the world. I would often ask myself, "Will mankind make it?" Let me tell you a story about my beloved daughter Michelle. My only daughter Michelle was diagnosed with a malignant glioblastoma brain tumor which was inoperable. I don't wish upon my worst enemy what I, my daughter and my family went through. We eventually lost my daughter to the brain tumor, but something miraculous happened along the way. There was such an outpouring of love and compassion for my daughter Michelle and our family and I was no longer doubtful about where man was going. There was so much goodness among people from all walks of life that my resounding conclusion was "YES, mankind and the world will make it!" It is this same optimism that swells in my heart that swells in the hearts of the angelic beings, Mother Mary, Christ and the Eternal God. Their love, compassion and optimism for us are off the chart. With the love and assistance from the higher power, there is a confidence in mankind that says, **"WE WILL MAKE IT!"**

NEVER DROP YOUR GUARD
It is human nature to relax and drop our guard knowing that a greater power is at the driver's seat. This is also one of the greatest weapons of darkness. For the second you drop your guard, the enemy will attack. The second you think you have made it, is when you have lost it. It is prudent and wise never to drop your guard until Judgment Day and the war for the hearts of men and the plan of free will is victorious. There will be a great celebration and an outpouring of love and gratitude, then we can drop our guards and join in the celebration.

CHAPTER 49

---- § ----

DESTRUCTION OF BABYLON

Revelation 14:8- And there followed another angel, saying, Babylon is fallen, is fallen, that great city, because she made all nations drink of the wine of the wrath of her fornication.

Revelation16:19- And the great city was divided into three parts, and the cities of the nations fell: and great Babylon came in remembrance before God, to give unto her the cup of the wine of the fierceness of his wrath.

Revelation 17:5- And upon her forehead was a name written, MYSTERY, BABYLON THE GREAT, THE MOTHER OF HARLOTS AND ABOMINATIONS OF THE EARTH.

Revelation 18:1-19- And after these things I saw another angel come down from heaven, having great power; and the earth was lightened with his glory. And he cried mightily with a strong voice, saying, Babylon the great is fallen, is fallen, and is become the habitation of devils, and the hold of every foul spirit, and a cage of every unclean and hateful bird. For all nations have drunk of the wine of the wrath of her fornication, and the kings of the earth have committed fornication with her, and the merchants of the earth are waxed rich through the abundance of her delicacies.

Therefore, shall her plagues come in one day, death, and mourning, and famine; and she shall be utterly burned with fire: for strong is the Lord God who judgeth her. And the kings of the earth, who have committed fornication and lived deliciously with her, shall bewail her, and lament for her, when they shall see the smoke of her burning, Standing afar off for the fear of her torment, saying, Alas, alas that great city Babylon, that mighty city! for in one hour is thy judgment come. And the merchants of the earth shall weep and mourn over her; for no man buyeth their merchandise any more:

The merchants of these things, which were made rich by her, shall stand afar off for the fear of her torment, weeping and wailing, and saying, Alas, alas that great city that was clothed in fine linen, and purple, and scarlet, and decked with gold, and precious stones, and pearls! For in one hour so great riches is come to naught. And every shipmaster, and all the company in ships, and sailors, and as many as trade by sea, stood afar off, And cried when they saw the smoke of her burning, saying, What city is like unto this great city! And they cast dust on their heads, and cried, weeping and wailing, saying, Alas, alas that great city, wherein were made rich all that had ships in the sea by reason of her costliness! for in one hour is she made desolate.

ANCIENT BABYLON

THE BABYLONIAN EMPIRE existed from 18th to 6th century BC and was located principally between the Euphrates and Tigris Rivers in modern day Iraq. Babylon was the capital city and was located on the east side of the Euphrates River.

Babylon, the largest city on earth during 600 BC, had a sophisticated legal system and King Hammurabi established a famous code of laws. Literature, history and science were well developed and medicine, surgery, pharmacology, chemistry, math, geometry, alchemy, botany, zoology, astronomy and astrology were practiced. Babylonians were skilled in making metals, made dyes, pigments, paints, perfumes and cosmetics. They built dikes, reservoirs, canals, irrigation ditches for water and farming. It was a center of trade for this region of the world. They divided the day into 24 hours, hour into 60 minutes and minutes into 60 seconds. This system of keeping track of time has lasted 4,000 years.

One of the seven wonders of the ancient world was built by King Nebuchadnezzar II about 600 BC. The hanging garden of Babylon was built in the palace for his wife or concubine (mistress) who loved the mountains. It was like a mountain of terraces filled with various plants. It was an architectural wonder with arch ways, a delivery system for the water to be delivered to the top of the terraces. The wealth, luxury, color and sophisticated society in Babylon became legendary during the reign of Nebuchadnezzar.

Slavery was alive and well and someone could sell his family and children into slavery as payment of debt to their creditors. Marduk became the supreme God, over heaven and earth.

The Babylonian Empire was enemies and persecutors of the Jewish people in the Middle East and became symbolic of worldliness and iniquity. The prophets Isaiah and Jeremiah prophesied that Babylon would become a desolate heap. Prophecy fulfilled, the modern-day ruins are located 90 kilometers (56 miles) south of present day Baghdad, Iraq.

Modern Day Babylon

Babylon has become symbolic of worldliness, materialism, wealth and iniquity. There is absolutely nothing wrong with advancements in science, medicine, architecture, chemistry, mathematics, astronomy, botany, metallurgy, agriculture, law, financial system, trade and luxury items. There is absolutely nothing wrong with abundance. This is where you can have your cake and eat it too; you can have God and abundance. It is the history of mankind, to turn their eyes to the wealth of the world and away from God. Once wealth is attained, all the things which are not good for the soul and money can buy becomes the pursuit in life. It is not advancements in society that is mankind's nemesis but the falling away from God that follows prosperity, wealth and luxury.

Babylon has become symbolic of the world, worldly possessions, ego, pride, boastfulness, "whoredoms," deceit, murders and evil doing. The prophets could easily have changed Babylon's name to Rome to symbolize all worldliness, for Rome was another Babylon.

There are three modern-day Babylons. There is the modern-day remnant of ancient Babylon which is in modern-day Iraq. With Desert Storm and Desert Shield, there was destruction of modern-day remnant of ancient Babylon. There is also modern-day Babylon and these are the modern-day port cities of the world. In the modern-day port cities, there is worship of money, "whoredoms," lying, cheating, robbing, murder, mayhem, raping and breaking of everyone of God's commandments. Modern-day Babylon is where the breaking of God's commandments is concentrated. There is also a spiritual Babylon, which is the most important of the three Babylons.

Doctrine and Covenants 133:14- *Go ye out from among the nations, even from Babylon, from the midst of wickedness, which is spiritual Babylon.*

Spiritual Babylon exists all over the world and is in every country and every city. We are building kingdoms at this very moment where we will end up going at Judgment Day. They are kingdoms of heaven and hell, and one of the kingdoms of hell is spiritual Babylon. You do not have to live in a major port city to live in spiritual Babylon; you can live in small town USA. If you live your life doing every manner of evil against your fellow man, then you live in spiritual Babylon.

THE SIGNS YET TO COME

I do not believe in judging my fellow man and this is another reason why. Spiritual Babylon exists in the heart of every man, just as the kingdom of heaven exists in the heart of every man. This is not a curse but part of the divine plan and our third-dimensional schooling. It is our task to leave the spiritual Babylon in our hearts and walk into the kingdom of heaven which is also in our hearts.

DESTRUCTION OF MODERN DAY BABLYLON

> ***Revelation 16:18-19****- And there were voices, and thunders, and lightnings; and there was a great earthquake, such as was not since men were upon the earth, so mighty an earthquake, and so great. And the great city was divided into three parts, and the cities of the nations fell: and great Babylon came in remembrance before God, to give unto her the cup of the wine of the fierceness of his wrath.*

> ***Koran****- "Az-Zalzalah"- In the Name of God, the Compassionate, the Merciful. When the earth is shaken with its (final) earthquake. And when the earth throws out its burdens. And when man will say: what is the matter with it?*

The earthquakes associated with the earth changes have already started but will continue and will increase in magnitude and frequency. Things will get better for a short season and then the fear of many men will lessen. There will be great rejoicing among many in the world, as it appears the worst is over and prophecy and the words of the prophets shall not come to pass. As stated in the chapter Shifting of the Earth's Axis, the earth wobbling on its axis will put great tension and stress on the outer layer of the earth's crust which is rigid. This will cause earthquakes, volcanoes, and tsunamis, but there will be a final tear or break in the earth's outer crust. Without warning, there will be a great earthquake, the kind never seen before in the history of the earth. A great earthquake shall shake the earth and the great cities and the major port cities (modern day Babylon). Following the great earthquake will be a mega-tsunami occurring all over the world. The result of the greatest earthquake the world has ever known and the mega-tsunami will be the destruction of modern day Babylon. In one hour, the port cities of the world are gone. There will be weeping and wailing for the loss of modern-day Babylon and all those who loved modern-day Babylon and all the wickedness within her.

CHAPTER 50

NIGHT OF SCREAMS

Mother Mary- There will be three hours of darkness, there shall be no light and it will be the night of screams.

NEAR THE END of our ordeal, when men have dealt with more than they believed they ever could, comes the climax of our trials and tribulations. There will be three hours of darkness and nothing shall give forth light. There will be no light from candles, fires, light bulbs nor any earthly device or technology. The earth shall not receive light from the sun or any heavenly body. The light by divine command shall be withdrawn from the earth for a period of three hours.

So, begins the night of screams. With all that mankind has gone through, you would believe enough is enough. How much more do we need to go through? This will not be a walk in the park. It may be the hardest three hours that anyone, except the Christ has gone through. Each one of us must face the fears that we avoided until this point. For many this will be their worst nightmare come true. The pain, the suffering, and the screams will be plain for all to hear.

This is the point where there will be nothing to grab on to for security except God and God's love. For those who know what is happening, it will help to know that there will be an end to the night of screams. It is darkest before the dawn. Just on the other side of the greatest darkness is the dawn and a beautiful morning, and soon the earth reborn into a paradisiacal glory.

This appears to be a great curse or punishment but it is really the opposite. Before we can be reborn of the spirit we must face our fears, every one of them. The fears that we have avoided facing until this time will show up for us to confront in the night of screams. The blessing comes at the end, when our fears can be let go and our light can shine brightly. The children of God will make a quantum leap forward in waking up from a dark dream and the planet will have made a quantum leap in becoming a conscious planet.

We will look back at what we have come through and thank God, not curse him for having given us such a great gift. We will look back at every one of our fears that we faced and walked through and see how much we have grown in such a short period of time. We will see the love, compassion and support that God and His angelic beings had for us. We will see how we reached out to each other in our hour of greatest need and what a gift God has given us when we reach the other side and we are in paradise.

The night of screams will not be terrifying for everyone. For those who have done the work, faced their fears and taken these monumental challenges as an opportunity to purify themselves, the night of screams will be a spiritual triumph. They will have no fear or terror. As in Egypt, with the plague of death passing over the city, for it will be an angel carrying all the remaining fears. This angel shall pass by those who have done the work, and they shall have three hours of enlightenment.

An important question in the minds of many "Is there a God?" This question will be answered. It is important to know that God is a God of miracles. If there was no God than there would be no miracles. There will be no light during the night of screams and this will be a miracle for every one of us to witness. With all of us witnessing this miracle, there will be absolute proof that miracles exist, and if miracles exist then God exists. QED

CHAPTER 51

—— § ——

WORLD CHANGED

CHANGING OF OUR MEDICAL, FINANCIAL, SOCIAL AND POLITICAL INSTITUTIONS

I HEARD STORIES while I was growing up that scientists may have a cure for dental cavities, but that much of the dental profession did not want a cure for dental cavities because it would put dentists out of work. I was amazed at the audacity of this statement, but I could see this point of view. Although I did not agree with it, I could see a part of the profession of dentistry that would not want a cure for dental cavities.

I have heard other stories for other professions. One is oncology, the profession, practitioners and researchers in the field of cancer. I heard stories that part of the profession of oncology does not want a cure to cancer, for if there was a cure then those in the profession would be out of a job. Again, I was amazed at the audacity of this statement and that some of those in the field of oncology who would not want a cure for cancer, for fear of losing their jobs. If I were a researcher or oncologist treating cancer, I would shout a cheer of joy if a cure for all cancer was found. There are many fields in the medical profession and diseases that need good well trained researchers and physicians. I would not hesitate for a moment to find another profession if I could only find cancer in the history books.

I have heard similar stories in the field of anesthesiology. There are stories of the perfect anesthetic and an anesthetic so safe that anesthesia could be achieved without the need for general anesthesia. I heard first hand by another anesthesiologist, "Does the profession of anesthesiology want the perfect drug that will produce anesthesia without potential for harm? If that drug was discovered, we (anesthesiologists and anesthetists) would be out of a job or the profession drastically changed." Again, I see this point of view but I disagree with it. Any advancement in medicine and science should be taken, and being an anesthesiologist I would welcome the perfect anesthetic. The benefits greatly outweigh the redirecting my line of work. I will further state that the perfect anesthetic does exist and will become known, at the proper time and proper place.

Is it too much of a stretch of the imagination to see how the medical profession could be changed if the world was born into a paradisiacal glory and everything, everyone and all institutions had been changed as well. Although there will be the world changed, there will be evolution of all things. Everything will not appear in perfect form, for the world will still be according to our beliefs. There will be an evolution of the earth, all things, all life and all institutions renewed into its paradisiacal glory. The future will bring an end of diseases that have plagues mankind for far too long. With the end of diseases as we know them, would there be a need of physicians and the health profession? There will be, but the health profession will not look the same as it does now. The future of the medical and health professions will be preventative medicine and recognizing and treating diseased spirit, as well as knowledge and technology. There will be a changing of financial, social, political and medical systems as mankind and the planet becomes more conscious.

ELEVATION OF CONSCIOUS- GIVING OF UP OF JUDGEMENT

CONSCIOUSNESS AND ENLIGHTENMENT

1 Thessalonians 4:13- But I would not have you to be ignorant, brethren, concerning them which are asleep, that ye sorrow not, even as others which have no hope

1 Thessalonians 4:15- For this we say unto you by the word of the Lord, that we which are alive and remain unto the coming of the Lord shall not prevent them which are asleep

We all came from God and Heaven, a place where there is love, light and consciousness. When we lived in the presence of God we were conscious beings. We made a decision to come to earth for third dimensional schooling and the grand plan of free will. As we came through the veil which separates us from God and our true home, we went through a *"forgetting."* We forgot what we knew, to experience good and evil in this third dimensional school. This was part of the divine plan and eventually we would return home to God and our true home. As we passed though the veil, we went from conscious beings (knowing and seeing God's kingdom) and became unconscious beings (forgetting the truth, love and knowledge we once knew).

Enlightenment and becoming conscious is passing back through this veil that separates this third dimensional world from God, the kingdom of heaven and our true home. We can go back to God and the kingdom of heaven right now, heaven on earth. In the eastern religions, this is called enlightenment. It is a path of waking up out of our sleep, unconsciousness, and becoming conscious. The western religions call it becoming righteous, holy or in Christ's teaching, entering the kingdom of God (kingdom of heaven).

What are the synonyms of enlightenment? To become enlightened means to wake up (spiritually) out of our sleep, become conscious, fully aware, holy, righteous, overcome our animal nature and be divine children of God, be with God's love and light and enter the kingdom of heaven, here on earth. They all mean the same thing.

The opposite synonyms exist. Unconscious means to stay asleep (spiritually), remain unaware, unrighteous, sinful (bad karma), unholy, wicked, succumb to our animal nature and to live without God's love and light, which is hell on earth. All these mean the same thing.

Examples of conscious or enlightened beings are helpful. **God is the ultimate awakened, conscious being.** My goal is to keep my eyes focused on Him and become like him; a conscious being. It helps to have a role model. Buddha is an awakened, enlightened being. Jesus Christ is a fully awakened conscious being. Who is more enlightened than the Christ? The true prophets Moses, Abraham, Noah and Mohammed did God's work and were enlightened conscious beings.

Who are examples of an unconscious beings? Hitler and Colonel Kaddafi are examples of great Antichrists. Not only were they unconscious beings, but they used their political and financial power to deceive and do great harm to their fellow man.

It is helpful to see the way God sees us and the world. God knows we have passed through the veil and became unconscious, but He sees His children in our divine state. He is aware of our fallen, unconscious state, but that is not how He sees us. To awaken or become enlightened means to be aware of our true nature, and be the children of God that we are. To live in the kingdom of heaven that exists right here on earth, right now at this very moment. It means we see our fellow man as our brothers and sisters. It means we see this earth and all living things as divine in creation and becoming good stewards in watching over their welfare. To become conscious means to live with God's love and light. A world where miracles, healing, prophecy, wisdom, communications with God, angels, spiritual beings is an everyday reality.

The opposite is to remain unconscious. To be unconscious means we see our brothers and sisters as our enemies or competition. This unconscious world is about reverting to our animal nature and taking as much as you can, because soon it will be gone. The only one that matters is me. To deny our divine nature, miracles, healing, love, truth and all of God's gifts is to remain unconscious.

There is also inner awareness, for the kingdom of heaven is within us. Most psychologists and psychiatrists will tell us we are not aware of most of what is going on inside ourselves. Much of our behavior is unconscious

(Sigmund Freud's unconscious). As we discover why we live and act the way we do and bring this unconscious part of our mind to conscious awareness, we become more conscious and aware.

Doctrine and Covenants 132:8- *Behold, mine house is a house of order, saith the Lord God, and not a house of confusion.*

Wherever you go in God's kingdom there are laws to maintain order. God's house is not a house of chaos or confusion, but of divine order. To attain enlightenment or enter the kingdom of heaven here on earth, we must live the laws of that heavenly kingdom. Living the teachings of the Christ or the Buddha will take us to the kingdom of heaven. Breaking all of Christ's teachings (commandments) will take us to spiritual realms where there is no love or light of God, which is hell on earth. Living the laws of the kingdom of heaven is the key to getting into heaven, here on earth.

Mother Mary– *Unconscious beings in an unconscious world.*

It has been described by many that we are asleep and this is a very clear way to understand consciousness. The world as a whole is asleep, but as the new day is dawning, the world and mankind is waking up. We have all been in a long deep sleep, and it is time to wake up and see the world, mankind and all God's creations as they truly are. Slowly but surely, we are waking up. It is true that some of us enjoy our sleep, maybe having a nice dream, and some of us will have to be shaken (literally as well as figuratively) out of our deep sleep.

Message from Mother Mary is we are "Unconscious beings in an unconscious world." Yes, there are planets with life as our own. Yes, on the overall view of the planets and life on those planets, by comparison we are unconscious beings in an unconscious world. Do not look at this statement and hang your head down. This planet was chosen for the grand plan of

257

free will because it had a significant amount of darkness. Also, know that it was valiant spirits (I am talking about us) who volunteered to undergo this grand experiment in free will. We should lift up our heads; open our eyes and hearts and mind to a greater reality. All this darkness is potentially light. Hold on to your hats, for Dorothy's Kansas and the rest of the world of unconsciousness is going bye-bye.

Mother Mary- *Your goal is enlightenment.*

Mother Mary- *Just being here and being who you are, that is enough. God cannot ask more of anyone than to be who you are.*

I am Christian and a physician. One might think that if I wanted to serve God and my fellow man that my goal would be to build a free medical clinic in India, or inner city New York City or Los Angeles. Message from Mother Mary is *"Your goal is enlightenment."* The next message from Mother Mary put my heart at rest. "Just being here and being who you are, that is enough. God cannot ask more of anyone than to be who you are."

Who are we? Ask people this question and you will get different answers. "I am an executive, the head of this whole company." No, an executive is who you are not. "I am a talk show host, everyone knows that." A talk show host is who you are not. "I am a mother. Look at my children and what a great job I have done with them." A mother is who you are not. "I am a financial tycoon, look how many G's I pull down each year." A financial tycoon is who you are not. "I am a failure and my whole life has been a series of failures." A failure is who you are not. If we are not all these labels, that society and friends label us with, then who are we? We are children of the Most High God and created in His likeness and image. I do not say this lightly or minimize what I am saying. To be a child of God is humbling to know of the immense worth that we are. That is who we are and no one, no matter how much they try to pull us down, can ever take that away from us.

God is flooding forth His spirit and will be shaking up our world in every sense, to slowly wake us up. We live in a parched desert where God's love can be difficult to find. Christ and Buddha were trying to show us a way to an oasis of God's love that exists in this parched desert. When we return home and there is love everywhere and we realize again that love is who we are, then we will understand and be enriched for the experience.

GIVING UP OF JUDGMENT

With the elevation of consciousness will bring closure to the judgment of our fellow man. It is one of the final steps to enlightenment for mankind. Mankind will no longer condemn, or judge their fellow man, but extend a helping hand and say "You are my brother and my sister. Your welfare is my welfare, your pain is my pain, your happiness is my happiness and I am here for you."

CHAPTER 52

———— § ————

REBUILDING OUR PLANET

Hopi- Then there will be much to rebuild.

THE NIGHT OF screams was our darkest hour and it is darkest before the dawn. The dawn has come and it will be a glorious day. It would be premature to say the earth has become a paradise; it has not. Before God creates a masterpiece, He must start with a blank canvas. The canvas is cleared and purified, and brilliant colors of rich oils are ready to create a magnificent work of art.

Mankind is part of this work of art, and with all priceless works of art, they take time and effort. The cities and towns will have sustained much destruction and now it is time for the rebuilding. It will not be easy to rebuild our planet and the time will still be challenging for many. As the planet and mankind has become more conscious the cities and towns will be built with love and renewed motivation. We have done a great thing for our children and children's children, but the time of paradise is not yet.

The Christ has not returned, and there will be many who say, "My Lord delays his coming." This is not wise or truthful. The timing of the Second Coming of Christ is only by the holy command of the one God. Christ has not delayed his coming, but is waiting for divine command.

CHAPTER 53

———— § ————

MOTHER MARY

MOTHER MARY IS the mother of the Christ, the blessed virgin with a special place in the heart of God, heart of Christ, in Christianity and the collective Christian church. She is honored in Christianity and Islam but she is not bound to only a certain group. She is the mother of the Christ, loves her son and those that follow him.

Mother Mary has appeared in visions to people all over the world. Some you may have heard about. One of the most famous is Our Lady of Guadalupe. In 1531, in Guadalupe, Mexico a poor 57-year-old Aztec Indian, named Juan Diego was converted to Christianity. One day while walking to the chapel, he saw a beautiful woman surrounded by brilliant light standing on a hill. She spoke to Juan and said "I desire you to know who I am. I am the ever-virgin Mary, Mother of the true God who gives life and maintains its existence." Mother Mary instructed Juan to tell the bishop what had happened. The bishop did not believe the story of Juan Diego and wanted a sign. Juan went back to the hill and told Mother Mary. She instructed Juan to cut Castilian roses and bring them to her. He gave Mother Mary his cloak, which was made of cactus fibers, and she arranged the roses. Juan returned to the bishop, with the roses arranged by Mother Mary. Juan opened his cloak and the flowers fell out, and on the cloak was the image of Mother Mary. The bishop fell to his knees and knew the story of Juan Diego was true. Mother Mary told Juan, "Call me and the call my image Santa Maria de Guadalupe" (Saint Mary of Guadalupe).

The cloak of Juan Diego (Figure 43) exists today in the Basilica of Our Lady Guadalupe in Mexico City. The cloak has been scientifically examined and shows no deterioration (with no preservation done) in 480 years and no brush strokes. The surface of the cloak containing the image of Mother Mary feels like silk while the rest of the cloak feels like coarse cactus fiber. One of the scientists who studied the cloak concluded the image of Mother Mary must have been created by a supernatural force.

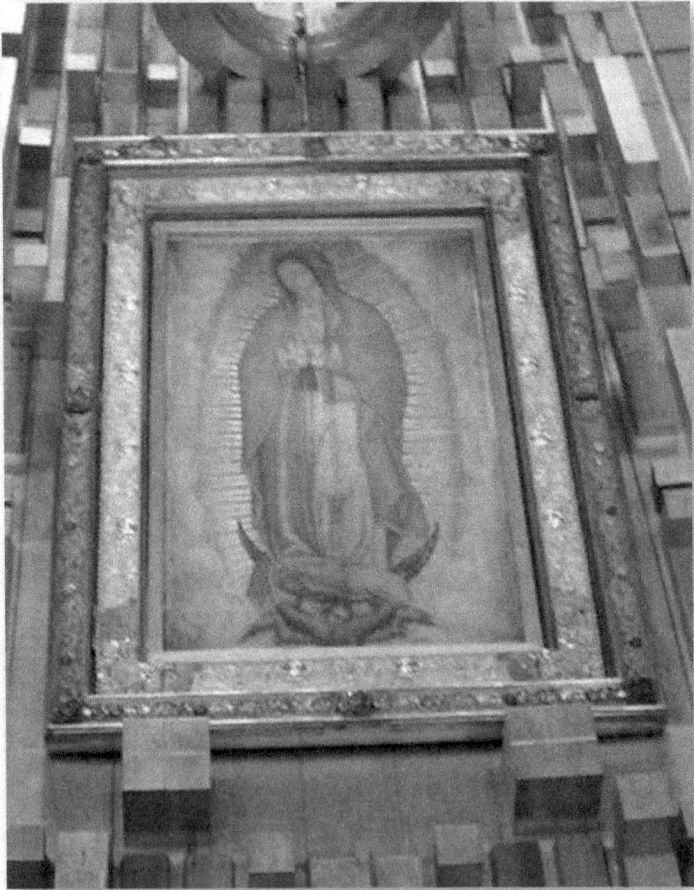

Figure 43- The Cloak of Juan Diego with the image of Our Lady of Guadalupe

Figure 44- Close Up View of Our Lady of Guadalupe (Photo by Lyricmac)

OUR LADY OF LOURDES

In 1858, Bernadette Soubirous was 14 years old in Lourdes, France and was collecting firewood. In a grotto, she saw a lady dressed in white who spoke to her. The people of the town and the parish priest gave a great deal of skepticism and criticism of Bernadette's story of the lady dressed in white.

On the ninth vision of Mother Mary by Bernadette, Mother Mary asked Bernadette to drink from the spring. Bernadette did not see a spring and began digging in the mud. She was ridiculed and mocked by onlookers, as she drank a few drops of muddy water. Water flowed up from this spring, and people from the town began having miraculous healings. Many come from around the world to Lourdes seeking healing miracles. Cases that are believed to be miracles are examined closely by the Lourdes Medical Bureau and then reexamined by the International Medical Commission. As of 1954, the Lourdes Medical Bureau had "upheld" 1,200 miraculous cures in Lourdes.

OUR LADY OF FATIMA

In October, 1917 Mother Mary appeared near the town of Fatima, Portugal. She appeared six times to three children. The Blessed Virgin Mary gave messages to the children to be given to those in the church and the faithful. In one of these messages the children were given a secret with three parts. The first part they were shown a place where none of us want to go after this life, hell. The next part was a prophecy of the start of World War II and the last part was reportedly given to the Pope, and no one else. The Catholic Pope did visit this sacred site kissing the ground where the Blessed Virgin appeared, as an unofficial acknowledgement of this appearance by Mother Mary.

OUR LADY OF MEDJUGORGE

June, 1981 in a village in western Herzegovina two girls saw a brilliant silhouette of a woman. "It is Our Lady," one exclaimed. They went down the hill and returned with four other children. The beautiful woman was dressed in white and called herself the Queen of Peace. Mother Mary appeared almost daily for years with messages and then once a month. She has given thousands of messages. During the visitations, the children do not react to light, do not hear sounds around them and do not react to being touched. The Blessed Mother has given a prophecy to the children; at the site of the apparitions she would eventually give a sign. This would be a sign as to the truth of what happened at Medjugorge and the messages given.

MRS GOD

Mother Mary- *I am the humble representative of Mrs. God.*

Mother Mary calls herself the humble representative of Mrs. God. It is very appropriate for someone to say, "I had a message from God, and She said..." Just as we have a Mr. God, we also have a Mrs. God. They both exist and both are real. If you are Christian, they may be called our Heavenly Mother and our Heavenly Father. It is interesting that the mother of the Christ would prefer to call her Mrs. God and not Heavenly Mother. Both names are appropriate but calling our Heavenly Mother, Mrs. God, shows that even the mother of Christ knows God is a God of all children, no matter their religious beliefs. The ultimate truth is we are all children of the one God, and our hearts and souls want to return home. Mother Mary and Christ are here in service of God and all God's children.

MOTHER MARY TO VISIT EVERY SOUL BEFORE THE SECOND COMING

Mother Mary- *My goal is to visit every soul before the Second Coming of Christ.*

Mother Mary has said her goal is to *"visit every soul before the Second Coming of Christ."* This has several purposes. The first is to give witness to her son, the Christ, and his part in bringing souls back to God and out of darkness. Second, is to make them aware that they have a choice. This is not a choice of heaven or eternal damnation in hell, although there are spirit prisons in hell. It is a choice to graduate out of the third dimensional experience or to stay behind in the third dimensional experience.

The visitation will be to all souls, those in a third dimensional bodies and those in the spirit world. With the visitation of Mother Mary to all souls, we will have the truth right in front of us and we will all know there is a God, and what has been communicated by the prophets and God's chosen is true. All mankind will know the truth and none will be able to say, "I cannot be held accountable, for I did not know." At the Second Coming of Christ and the heavenly host, all mankind will know the truth about God, heaven, good and evil and then make a choice.

CHAPTER 54

SIR ISAAC NEWTON

SIR ISAAC NEWTON was a mathematician and physicist and is referred to as the father of modern physics. Some biographers and scientists have referred to him as one of the most brilliant minds ever. Author's statements about Sir Isaac Newton include: "A mind like Newton's comes along once every 500 years." "One of the foremost scientific intellects of all time." "The single most important contributor to the development of modern science." Brian Green, author of the Elegant Universe refers to Isaac Newton as the most brilliant mind ever. The accomplishments of Sir Isaac Newton are well known. He developed the Law of Gravity and the Three Laws of Motion. It is these fundamental laws of physics that are the same laws used today to put a man on the moon. He realized that it was gravity that kept the planets in motion around the sun and moon around the earth. This would apply to all celestial bodies.

Newton made many contributions in optics and to the field of mathematics. He was famous for his contributions to geometry. He developed "fluxions" and "inverse fluxions" in mathematics "which are the equivalent of modern day differential and integral calculus." He was considered by many as the developer of the scientific method.

Figure 45- Sir Isaac Newton (Portrait of Newton in 1689 by Godfrey Kneller)

Scientists embrace Sir Isaac Newton as a pioneer, brilliant mind, father of modern day physics and one the most important scientists leading to some of the most important scientific discoveries. They respect this genius and his accomplishments. They do not embrace the other side of his life of which he was just as passionate and devoted. Sir Isaac Newton was a chemist, alchemist, astrologer, metaphysician and one who passionately studied the Bible.

Unpublished Newton's papers were discovered by a Jewish collector and original manuscripts now reside in the Hebrew National Library in Jerusalem. "Newton spent over 50 years studying the Bible trying to unlock the secret laws of the universe." Thousands of pages of Newton's works were dedicated to decode the Bible. According to Dr. Stephan Snobelen, from the University of King's College in Nova Scotia who examined Newton's papers, "Newton predicted that the Second Coming of Christ would follow plagues and war and would precede a 1,000-year reign by the saints on earth—of which he would be one." Producer Malcolm Neaum, of the BBC documentary Newton: The Dark Heretic says: "Newton prayed daily for the end of the world which he believed would herald the Second Coming of Christ. This would usher in the 1000-year rule of the Saints and Newton believed he would then take his place as Chief Saint."

""Although his methodology was strictly logical, Newton still believed deeply in the necessity of a God. His theological views are characterized by his belief that the beauty and regularity of the natural world could only "proceed from the counsel and dominion of an intelligent and powerful Being." He felt that "the Supreme God exists necessarily, and by the same necessity he exists always and everywhere." Newton believed that God periodically intervened to keep the universe going on track."" Sir Isaac Newton is a legendary scientist who discovered universal laws that govern the entire universe. He was concerned that his discoveries would lead mankind away from his belief that God had a divine hand in all things.

The scientists who are mainstream will continue to embrace and give accolades to one of the most brilliant minds mankind has produced, and most will continue to downplay his beliefs in alchemy, metaphysics, astrology and theology. Is it possible that in addition to being a scientific genius, that Sir Isaac Newton was also an enlightened being, composing the rare combination of genius and enlightenment? Was Sir Isaac Newton a scientist as well as a saint?

Possibly the most brilliant mind ever and devoted to study the Bible, Sir Isaac Newton, calculated the Second Coming of Jesus Christ to be in the year 2060. It is not terribly important what the exact time and day of Christ's arrival will be. All that we know is the signs are being fulfilled and now we are patiently waiting the return of the Anointed One.

CHAPTER 55

——— § ———

A THIEF IN THE NIGHT

2 Peter 3:10- But the day of the Lord will come as a thief in the night; in which the heavens shall pass away with a great noise, and the elements shall melt with fervent heat, the earth also and the works that are therein shall be burned up.

Mother Mary- Every two thousand years God sends a great teacher to the earth. Jesus was the last of the great teachers.

MOTHER MARY HAS stated that "Every 2000 years God sends a great teacher to the earth. Jesus was the last of the great teachers." It has been 2,000 years since Jesus Christ came to the earth and taught great truths about God and his kingdom. Since God sends and great teacher to earth every two thousand years and Jesus was the last of the great teachers then it follows that we are due for the Second Coming of Christ.

What is meant by a thief in the night? If you are prepared for a burglary, with burglar alarms, watch dogs, surveillance cameras and a watchful eye, then a burglary is much less likely to be successful. If, however, you have taken no precautions and have not prepared your house against burglary, then your house is easier prey for the burglar and more likely to be burglarized. So, it is with our souls, and hence the meaning of Jesus coming as a thief in the night.

It is human nature to want our cake and eat it too. It is human nature to want everything even though at some point we must choose between things we want. There are many who want to go play and do whatever they want, with idea in mind that when it is the eleventh hour and the Day of the Lord is midnight, then and only then will they start preparing. They want to clean house in the eleventh hour, put it their house in order and say, "Look Lord my house is clean at Judgment Day and therefore I will make it back to heaven." God and Christ both know this, and therefore the dreadful Day of the Lord shall come as a thief in the night. The day will come when "no man knoweth."

We don't know when God will call us back home. There might be a sudden motor vehicle accident or heart attack and then God takes you. God will take you when you don't expect it to come. Those who have prepared their homes for that day will go where they want to go. Those who play and do what they will, without preparation, will be caught off guard. They will not be able to prepare in the eleventh hour.

CHAPTER 56

—— § ——

SECOND COMING OF CHRIST AND JUDGEMENT DAY

SECOND COMING OF CHRIST

NO ONE KNOWS OF THAT DAY AND HOUR OF CHRIST'S COMING, ONLY THE FATHER

> *Matthew 24:36- No one knows about that day or hour, not even the angels in heaven, nor the Son, but only the Father.*

> *Islam- Ahmad-The Last Hour will not be established until there will remain those people who will neither be aware of the virtues and never prevent the vices.*

> *Islam- Tirmidhi- The day of Judgment will not come until the very lowest people are the happiest*

GOD HAS NOT given me one single absolute date, nor will I ask God to give me and any dates. It is unnecessary and counterproductive to the writing of this book. I feel everything, see certain things, have some knowledge and understanding of what is about to happen. As Matthew 24:36 states, *"No one knows about that day or hour, not even the angels in heaven, nor the Son, but only the Father."*

Acts 1:9-11- And when he had spoken these things, while they beheld, he was taken up; and a cloud received him out of their sight. And while they looked steadfastly toward heaven as he went up, behold two men stood by them in white apparel; which also said, Ye men of Galilee, why stand ye gazing up into heaven? This name Jesus, which is taken up from you into heaven, shall so come in like manner as ye have seen him go into heaven.

Matthew 24:27- For as the lightning cometh out of the east, and shineth even unto the west; so shall also the coming of the Son of man be.

Matthew 24:30- And then shall appear the sign of the Son of man in heaven: and then shall all the tribes of the earth mourn, and they shall see the Son of man coming in the clouds of heaven with power and great glory.

Revelation 1:7- He cometh with clouds, & every eye shall see Him

1 Thessalonians 4:16- For the Lord himself shall descend from heaven with a shout, with the voice of the archangel, and with the trump of God:

Doctrine and Covenants 29:11- For I will reveal myself from heaven with power and great glory, with all the hosts thereof, and dwell in righteousness with men on earth a thousand years, and the wicked shall not stand.

Doctrine and Covenants 133:48-49- And the Lord shall be red in his apparel, and his garments like him that treadeth in the wine-vat. And so great shall be the glory of his presence that the sun shall hide in shame, and the moon shall withhold its light, and the stars shall be hurled from their places.

Judaism - *The Coming Messiah- The Mashiach is the one who will be anointed as king in the End of Days.*

Islam- *Islamic tradition holds that Jesus, the son of Mary, was the promised Prophet and Masīḥ (Messiah) sent to the Israelites, and that he will return to Earth at the end of times,*

Islam- *Muslims believe that Jesus will return to earth near the Day of Judgment to restore justice and to defeat al-Masih ad-Dajjal ("the false messiah", also known as the Antichrist).*

Koran- *13:15-50-60 And the Trumpet shall be blown; that will be the Day whereof Warning.*
Then, when one blast is sounded on the Trumpet,– On that Day shall the (Great) Event come to pass.

Koran 89:22- Your Lord comes with the angels row after row.

Koran 25:25- The day when the sky will be filled with clouds, and the angels will be sent down in succession.

Koran- *2-210- Will they wait until Allah comes to them in canopies of clouds, with angels*

Buddhist- *Az-Zalzalah: "The Coming of Maitreya Buddha" In those days, brethren, there will arise in the World and Exalted One named Metteya. He will be an Arahant, Fully Awakened, abounding in wisdom and goodness, happy, with knowledge of the worlds, unsurpassed as a guide to mortals willing to be led, a teacher of gods and men, an Exalted*

One, a Buddha, even as I am now. He, by himself, will thoroughly know and see, as it were face to face, this Universe, with its worlds of the spirits, its Brahmas and its Maras, and its world of recluses and brahmins, of princes and peoples, even as I now, by myself thoroughly know and see them. The Law, lovely in its origin, lovely in its progress, lovely in its consummation, will he proclaim, both in the spirit and in the letter; the higher life will he make known, in all its fullness and in all its purity, even as I do now.

Hindu-*The spiritual master Sri Aurobindo was given a vision of the "Great Man", the coming Messiah, which he transmitted in poetic form: "To bring God down to the world on earth we came, To change the earthly life to life divine... A mutual debt binds man to the Supreme: His nature we must put on as He puts ours; We are children of God and must be even as He:*

For man shall not know the coming till its hour And belief shall not be until the work is done. God must be born on Earth and be as man That man being human may grow even as God."

Hopi–*The transformed elder brother, the True White Brother, will wear a red cloak or a red cap, like the pattern on the back of a horned toad. He will bring no religion but his own, and will bring with him the Tiponi tablets. He will be all-powerful; none will be able to stand against him. He will come swiftly, and in one day gain control of this entire continent. The True White Brother and his helpers will show the people of earth a great new life plan that will lead to everlasting life.*

Hopi- My people await Pahana, the lost White Brother, [from the stars] as do all our brothers in the land. He will not be like the white men we know now, who are cruel and greedy. We were told of their coming long ago. But still we await Pahana...He will bring with him the symbols, and the missing piece of that sacred tablet now kept by the elders, given to him when he left, that shall identify him as our True White Brother...These are the Signs that great destruction is coming. ...Then there will be much to rebuild. And soon -- very soon afterward -- Pahana will return.

Mayan- Quetzalcoatl (the great white God) will return.

Cherokee- "The Rattlesnake Prophecy and the Time of the Beloved Woman". And in the Year 2012 the Cherokee Calendar Ends. But upon the times just prior shall be the Feathered Serpent and its prophecy. And all is reborn. For the Feathered Rattlesnake comes and shall be seen in the heavens in the year 2004 to 2012. In the south of the Americas ... it is related as the coming of Quetzalcoatl. The Ancient Cherokee relate it as the coming of the Pale One once again.

It is widely taught and widely believed that Christ will come to a great plain and battle field in Palestine, called the hill of Megiddo. Here Christ will defeat the armies against Israel, battle and defeat Satan. There will be Judgment day, darkness will be bound for a thousand years, and then the earth be changed into a paradisiacal glory. This is only partially true. **The Battle of Armageddon is the battle for the hearts of men.** Once we have made the ultimate choice of choosing God or darkness then it is Christ that will go to battle for the hearts of men. The Second Coming of Christ will not be on the battle field, the hill of Megiddo, in Palestine. The Second Coming of Christ will be experienced all over the world at the same time, and at a time that no one knows, only God the Father.

In all the history of mankind and the universe, what events would I want to be there, see and experience for myself. They would be the creation of the universe (yes, the great Jehovah oversaw every aspect of the big bang and organization of the galaxies, stars and planets), the parting of the red sea with Moses, meeting Jesus in Jerusalem, and seeing the Second Coming of Jesus Christ in all his glory. I must say, this would top the list to see and experience the Second Coming. I cannot imagine any event being more magnificent and glorious than the coming of this day and this event.

Christ will come in the clouds of heaven, dressed in wine red cloak with great power and great glory. So great will be the brightness of his coming that it will LITERALLY block out the brightness of the stars, moon and even the sun. All mankind will know in their heart what is happening, and there will be those with joy and eager anticipation of this very moment and those in fear, knowing that prophecy has been fulfilled. Christ will return accompanied by Buddha, Krishna, Adam, Noah, Abraham, Elijah, Moses, Mohammed, the archangels, enlightened masters and rows and rows of angels; the heavenly host. Every eye all over the world will be able to see the coming of the Christ with the heavenly host. With prophecy fulfilled, the Second Coming of Christ is also Judgment Day. It shall be announced with a trump (loud noise) of God and the voice of the Archangel Gabriel that the great day of the return of the king is here. What a glorious sight to behold.

The faithful in all religions have eagerly awaited this day. The coming of the promised Messiah has come. They have known him by different names and yet they have always known him in their hearts. All mankind will see the coming of the promised Messiah, the anointed one. **The Second Coming of Jesus Christ (Christian and Islam), the promised Messiah (Judaism), the Great Man and Messiah (Hindu vision), the Maitreya Buddha (Buddhism), the true white brother Pahana (Hopi),**

the great white God Quetzalcoatl (Mayan), the pale one (Cherokee), is all the same being, Jesus Christ.

It was Jesus Christ that descended into the American continent after he ascended into heaven in Jerusalem. He taught, and ministered in America to those living on the American continent. This is why the Mayans, Hopis, Cherokees and other Native Americans talk about the return of the great white God and true white brother. As Jesus taught and ministered on the American continent, two thousand years ago, he taught that he would return at some point in the future and this is the Second Coming of Christ.

Once Christ has returned and there is Judgment Day, there will not be one soul that will not know the truth about God and heaven. Sir Isaac Newton, considered by many to be the most brilliant mind ever, prayed for the end of the world as we know it, as this would be a necessary step before the Second Coming of Christ.

JUDGEMENT

Romans 14-:10- But why dost thou judge thy brother?

Matthew 7:2 -For with what judgment ye judge, ye shall be judged: and with what measure ye mete, it shall be measured to you again.

Matthew 7:1- Judge not, that ye be not judged.

Luke 6:37- Judge not, and ye shall not be judged: condemn not, and ye shall not be condemned: forgive, and ye shall be forgiven:

John 12:47- And if any man hear my words, and believe not, I judge him not: for I came not to judge the world, but to save the world.

Judaism-Teachings- Don't judge, don't judge, don't judge.

I don't believe in judging my fellow man and I have heard the sacred Judaism teachings, "Don't judge, don't judge, don't judge." There is another reason not to judge. There are some of us that are more conscious now, and there are some of us that are more unconscious. In other words, some of us are more aware while some of us are less aware. It is best not to judge, for the sinner can become the saint and the saint can become the sinner. There are those who hold a lot of light today, but if they turn and focus on darkness, can become very dark. Some of the darkest stars, become some of the brightest stars.

Christ warned us about judging our fellow man and asked us not to judge our fellow man. Christ knew the universal laws and that we reap what we sow. The Christ taught us not to judge our fellow man for as we judge our fellow man we will be judged and to the same degree we judged our fellow man. The Jews were stoning a prostitute, and Jesus protected her and said, "He that is without sin among you, let him cast the first stone." The holiest being ever to walk the earth, did not judge the prostitute, yet the Jews were about to stone her.

If we could only see ourselves the way that God sees us. We are absolutely special and precious. There is no one and nothing worth more to God. We are children of the Most High God. We are created in the likeness and image of greatest of all and what can be more precious than a child of God. It is also true that none of us is more special, valued or loved more, than the rest of God's children. Would a good Father say "This is my favorite son or favorite daughter who I love above all my other children," so his other children would feel less than?

I have seen many who are on the fast track and they want to go higher faster. I honor their path, their work and their effort. Does this make them any better than anyone else? If some of us want to smell some of the roses, and enjoy a beautiful sunrise, a vibrant rainbow along the way, does this mean we will not get to our final destination? We will make our destination and it is anticipated that we will smell some flowers along the way. We are not less than those who are on a fast track. Sometimes it pays to be the tortoise rather than the hare. **We were not put here to judge and condemn each other, but to love and help each other.**

WE JUDGE OURSELVES

Matthew 5:45- While one portion of the human race is judging and condemning the other without mercy, the Great Parent of the universe looks upon the whole of the human family with a fatherly care and paternal regard; he views them as his offspring, and without any of those contracted feelings that influence the children of men, causes his sun to rise on the evil and on the good, and sendeth rain on the just and on the unjust.

John 12:47- And if any man hear my words, and believe not, I judge him not: for I came not to judge the world, but to save the world.

Alma 41:7- These are they that are redeemed of the Lord; yea, these are they that are taken out, that are delivered from that endless night of darkness; and thus they stand or fall; for behold, they are their own judges, whether or not to do good or evil.

Here is Eternal Supreme Being God and the holiest of them all. If anyone could judge or had the right to judge it would be God. Yet God, the holiest of them all, would not and will not judge us, but loves us unconditionally as any loving Father would. Yet we continue to judge and condemn each other without mercy.

Here is the Christ, the holiest being ever to walk the earth who tells us he did not come to judge the world, but to save it. If there were two beings worthy to judge us, it would be God and the Christ, yet even they do not judge us.

I have a good friend who had a unique experience, she died and was brought back to life. This is commonly called a near death experience. My friend became very ill and entered the hospital for treatment and succumbed to her illness. She died and her spirit left her body. She saw the world from the spirit world perspective and how differently it looked from the viewpoint of the spirit realm. She could see flowers breathe, as if they were lungs breathing in air. She eventually went down a long dark tunnel to the other side of the veil and she stood before Jesus Christ. There was no judgment of my friend from this immaculate being, but unconditional love. My friend was eventually led to what looked like a television monitor where she viewed her entire life. She saw her entire life in a short period of time. She found herself, judging herself for what she had done in her lifetime and sometimes very harshly. My friend stood in front of the Christ and yet the Christ would not judge her, yet she judged herself and at times very harshly. The ability to see herself clearly, was only possible by standing in the presence of the Christ. My friend returned to her body and her body came back to life. I am grateful to have this good friend.

At Judgment Day, it will not be the Eternal Supreme Being that judges us, nor the Christ, for we will judge ourselves. It is not the personality or the ego that will judge ourselves, but our soul. It is the part of us that came from God that will place judgment upon ourselves. It is the ego that would say, "I am so great and wonderful, I can go wherever I want and there is no accountability for my choices." It is the soul that says, "We are all brothers and sisters of the one God and today I am accountable for all my choices. Today, I will make the best choice for my spiritual development and path. It is not my personality or ego that is great; it is God that is great."

HEAVEN AND HELL

> *Luke 17: 21- Kingdom of God is within you. The kingdom of God and heaven is within you. The man that has all love in his heart and mind has the kingdom of heaven in his heart and mind. So it is with hell. The man who is without love in his heart and mind is living in hell.*

> *2 Nephi 2:11- For it must needs be, that there is an opposition in all things.*

> *Pope John Paul- Hell is not a real place.*

Yes, there is a heaven, but what is hell? The Pope John Paul had revelation and it was revealed to him that hell is not a real place. If an enlightened spiritual being such as the former Pope John Paul has said hell is not real, then I give that credibility.

> *Mother Mary- You will not be tested to the extent my son was tested.*

Mother Mary has a message for me, "You will not be tested to the extent my son was tested." I will call my period of testing by another name, the *Dark Night of the Soul*. This does not represent badness or evil, or doing evil deeds, it is a descriptive term to describe a period of testing that is part of our spiritual journey. Job went through a period of testing as part of his spiritual path. It is during my period of testing that I was tested by the forces of darkness. As I have stated before, I don't wish upon my worst enemy to go through what I have gone through. I do know that this was part of my spiritual journey and for my benefit. I have been to hell and back, and it was not a curse but a blessing. It was all part of the spiritual journey and it makes me appreciate what I have. How do I truly know joy, if I have not gone through sadness and depression? How do I truly know heaven until I have descended into darkness? How do I know joy and ecstasy until

I have experienced pain and suffering? How do I know love and compassion until I have been without them?

I grew up in the Rocky Mountains and lived minutes away from the mountains and the outdoors. I lived 20 minutes away from some of the best skiing in the world. I spent seven years in New York City, for my medical training and one of the best educations in my life. As much as I love New York City, I never knew what I had growing up. The mountains and the outdoors were so much a part of who I was and I didn't know what I had until I no longer had them. The same is true about heaven and hell. To truly know heaven and love, I must know what it is like to be without them.

***Doctrine and Covenants 88**- Christ descended below them all. Art thou greater than he?*

Doctrine and Covenants 88 states that *"Christ has descended below them all. Art thou greater than he?"* Christ descended into darkness and farther into darkness than we will, to lead by example. It was also part of his spiritual path. This is not to say that Christ did something wrong to descend into hell, and neither did I. It is part of the spiritual path, a period of testing. When Christ descended into darkness and was surrounded by all the darkness (absence of God's light and love), it was his light that enabled Christ's ascension out of darkness. To be without God's love and light is hell; a living hell. Christ did this out of his love for us and he would not ask us to do anything that he has not been through himself. If Christ can descend into darkness far below the depth that we will and make it back to God, then we can to.

There is an antichrist, Lucifer, who is also called Satan. He is the Prince of Darkness, as Christ is the Prince of Light. The antichrist rules over darkness as Christ rules over the light. He stands in opposition to Christ and the teachings of Christ. 2 Nephi 2:11 *"For it must needs be, that there is an opposition in all things."* He has dark angels that assist and counsel him. He rules over his kingdom of darkness, which is in the spiritual world but also here on earth. Lucifer has power over his kingdom.

I occasionally see someone in their own self-created hell. The hell is in his heart, sometimes in his mind and sometimes both. I occasionally see someone in heaven, for heaven is in his heart, sometimes his mind and sometimes both. Heaven and hell exist in the spirit world and right here on earth. **Heaven is being with God's love and light, while hell is the absence of God's love and light.**

For two thousand years, Christian teachers have taught about heaven and hell. They have taught that if you are good you will go to heaven, if you are bad you will go to hell. It has become a major belief system in Christianity. The Catholic world was in shock when Pope John Paul announced that hell was not a real place. The cardinals, arch bishops and priests were even angered that what they had taught for years was informed by the Pope to be incorrect. This was an interpretation of the Bible that was taught and believed, so that all of us that believed in God's word were taught to believe in the popular interpretation of the eternal damnation of hell.

I have prayed for understanding and I write what I now understand. Although the writings of Bible are the word of God, it is the interpretation of the word of God that goes awry. John L Allen Jr. who is a journalist for the National Catholic Reporter has stated, The International Theological Commission (Chief advisory body to the Vatican) is working on a document that "Christians can hope that hell will be emptied." No matter what we have done, the hope is that we can all return to God and heaven. Hell is being without God's love and God's light.

WHAT IS REAL?

I have a friend whose daughter was in the hospital and had a break from her reality. Her mother would look into her eyes and she wasn't there; she was gone. Her mother spent days with her, telling her daughter that what she was experiencing was not real. After days of telling her daughter what she was experiencing was not real, medicines, professional help and most importantly love, her daughter woke up from her hell. The staff, mother and family knew the world she went to was not real, but it was only after she had woken out of the dream state that her daughter could see it was not real. Her daughter was very thankful for all the love, support and help to bring her out of her hell.

Try to tell someone, who is in a state of mind where there is a break from their normal reality, that their experience is not real and they will not believe you. Tell someone who is suffering because of their break with reality that what they are experiencing is not real and they will want to belt you. Although their pain and suffering are real, their monsters and demons are not.

There are syndromes where pain is created in the brain and has no peripheral stimulation of pain receptors. Some doctors say it's all in your head. It may be from their brain or mind that is producing the pain but the pain is very real to them. Hell may be very real to many but when we all wake up we will understand it was all a dream.

Most of mankind is asleep, in a dream and don't know they are in a dream. Their demons and monsters are very real to them, even though the monsters and demons do not really exist. When we get back home, we will see that it is only love and the kingdom of heaven that are real. Our bad dreams were not real. Jesus is trying to show us the way out of our hell. The experience, the knowledge and the love we create is real, and we will bring back home. The knowledge and experience will benefit God and all those in heaven.

SPIRIT PRISONS

Isaiah 42:7- to bring out the prisoners from the prison.

1 Peter 3:18-20 preached unto the spirits in prison. The Son visited the spirits in prison,

Mother Mary- *Some will not like the place they go to.*

Although there is probably no eternal hell, what does exist is temporary holding areas after we die, which are without God's love and light (hell). Mother Mary has stated *"Some will not like where they go."* There are spirit realms and prisons without God's love and light (hell), and where none of us want to go after this lifetime here on earth.

So much can be learned from our spiritual experiences and those who have died, crossed over the veil to the other side and then returned to their earthly bodies. These are referred to as near death experiences. George Ritchie MD died in an army hospital for nine minutes and then returned to life. He wrote a book "Return from Tomorrow" about his afterlife (near death) experience and I will include what he wrote and his experience of the afterlife.

In the after-life, George Ritchie MD traveled across the veil to the other side, stood before Christ and then was taken on a tour of the afterlife with Christ. Dr. Ritchie was taken to earth and viewed people from the viewpoint of the spirit realm. He writes,

"Gradually I began to notice something else. All of the living people we were watching were surrounded by a faint luminous glow, almost like an electrical field over the surface of their bodies. This luminosity moved as they moved, like a second skin made out of pale, scarcely visible light."

Dr. Ritchie was then shown the spirit prisons. He writes,

"Now, however, although we were apparently still somewhere on the surface of the earth, I could see no living man or woman. The plain was crowded, even jammed with hordes of ghostly discarnate beings; nowhere was there a solid, light-surrounded person to be seen. All they were the

most frustrated, the angriest, the most completely miserable beings I had ever laid eyes on.

"Lord Jesus!" I cried. "Where are we?

At first I thought we were looking at some great battlefield: everywhere people were locked in what looked like fights to the dearth, writhing, punching, gouging. It couldn't be a present day war because there were no tanks or guns. No weapons of any sort, I saw as I looked closer, only bare hands and feet and teeth. And then I noticed that no one was apparently being injured. There was no blood, no bodies strewed the ground; a blow that ought to have eliminated an opponent would leave him exactly as before.

Although they appeared to be literally on top of each other, it was as though each man was boxing the air; at last I realized that of course, having no substance, they could not actually touch one another. They could not kill, though they clearly wanted to, because their intended victims were already dead, and so they hurled themselves at each other in a frenzy of impotent rage.

If I suspected before that I was seeing hell, now I was sure of it. Up to this moment the misery I had watched consisted in being chained to a physical world of which we were no longer part. Now I saw that there were other kinds of chains. Here were no solid objects or people to enthrall the soul. These creatures seemed locked into habits of mind and emotion, into hatred, lust, destructive thought-patterns.

Even more hideous that the bites and kicks they exchanged, were the sexual abuses many were performing in feverish pantomime. Perversions I had never dreamed of were being vainly attempted all around us. It was impossible to tell if the howls of frustration which reached us were actual sounds or only the transference of despairing thoughts. Indeed, in this disembodied world it didn't seem to matter. Whatever anyone thought, however fleetingly or unwilling, was instantly apparent to all around him, more completely that words could have expressed it, faster that sound waves could have carried it."

Dr. Ritchie was shown the spirit world and spiritual prisons. There are spiritual prisons that exist, realms of pain and suffering, which we do not want to go to when this life is over.

THOSE IN SPIRITUAL PRISON BROUGHT FORTH

Nephi. 9: 12- hell must deliver up its captive spirits.

Those who are in those prisons of hell shall be released and brought forth to stand before the judgment seat of God.

RESURRECTION

Isaiah 26- 19- Thy dead men shall live, together with my dead body shall they arise. Awake and sing, ye that dwell in dust: for thy dew is as the dew of herbs, and the earth shall cast out the dead.

Acts 24:15- Having a hope in God, which these men themselves accept, that there will be a resurrection of both the just and the unjust.

Koran- 13-5- When we are (actually) dust, shall we indeed then be in a renewed creation?

Koran 75:3-4- Does man think that We cannot assemble his bones? Nay, We are able to put together in perfect order the very tips of his fingers.

Koran- 20-55- From the (earth) We created you, and into it We shall return you, and from it We shall bring you out once again

Koran- 82:4-5- And when the graves are turned upside down; (Then) shall each soul know what it has sent forward and (what it has) kept back.

The resurrection means that the soul will be reunited with the physical body. The rising of the dead from the graves is quite literal. The spirits of those who have died and those released from spirit prison will be reunited with their physical bodies. All mankind will be present for Judgment Day. Every one of us will stand before the Christ (who is one with God), and then every knee shall bend for the return of the king.

JUDGMENT DAY- DAY OF ACCOUNTABILITY

Romans 14- 10-12- for we shall all stand before the judgment seat of Christ. For it is written, As I live, saith the Lord, every knee shall bow to me, and every tongue shall confess to God. So then every one of us shall give account of himself to God.

Corinthians 2 :5-10- For we must all appear before the judgment seat of Christ; that every one may receive the things done in his body, according to that he hath done, whether it be good or bad.

Revelation 22:12- And, behold, I come quickly; and my reward is with me, to give every man according as his work shall be.

Daniel 12-2- And many of them that sleep in the dust of the earth shall awake, some to everlasting life, and some to shame and everlasting contempt.

Koran25:26 - *The true kingship on that day will be to the Gracious. It is a day which will be very hard on the ingrates.*

Koran 22:7- *day of reckoning approaches "the hour approaches without any doubt."*

Koran 99:6-8- *On that Day, people will come forward in separate groups to be shown their deeds: whoever has done an atom's weight of good will see it, but whoever has done an atom's weight of evil will see that.*

Koran 2:82- *And those who believe and do good deeds, they are dwellers of Paradise, they dwell therein forever.*

Koran- 4-141, 159- *...on the Day of Judgment He (Jesus) will be a witness against them. ...Allah will judge. Betwixt you on the Day of Judgment.*

Koran- 17- 29- *And all things have We preserved on record.*

Koran- 17:13-14- *Every man's fate We have fastened on his own neck: On the Day of Judgment his own neck: On the Day of Judgment We shall bring out for him a scroll, which he will see spread open. (It will be said to him:) "Read your (own) record: sufficient is your soul this day to make out an account against you."*

Koran- 18-49- *And the Book (of Deeds) will be placed (before you); and you will see the sinful in great terror because of what is (recorded) therein; they will say: "Ah! woe to us! What a book is this! It leaves out nothing small or great, but takes account thereof!" They will find all that they did, placed before them: and not one will your Lord treat with injustice.*

Hindu- *Shortly before he was assassinated, Mahatma Gandhi predicted the future of the human race to a group of friends and associates: "Mankind is approaching hard times, because as soon as the measure of its sins will be full, it will be called to account by the superior power above us. You may call this event as you wish: Judgment day,*

It was part of the divine plan that we would pass through the veil, be born into the world of good and evil and experience this world first hand. We were meant to come and play in the garden. This does not mean that we are not responsible and accountable for what we do here. We are. We were meant to make choices and learn from those choices. Experience right and wrong, good and evil first hand, for this was all part of the divine plan. At some point, we were meant to make the decision to come home. We would be receiving help and guidance to assist in our journey back home.

Judgment Day is a day of accountability. It is a day we stand before God (Christ is one with God the Father) and give an accounting of our time here on earth. All that we have done and choices we made, we will all be held accountable. On Judgment Day, we will see ourselves, everything we have done, see all our strengths and our weaknesses, all our love and kindness and meanness, our truth and our deception, our charity and our greed. We will see ourselves clearer than we have ever seen ourselves before, and stand before our God to give an accounting of what we have done. It takes the presence of God before we can see ourselves clearly.

It is not the personality or ego that will judge ourselves, it will be the soul or part of us that came from God. You can say it is God that is judging, for it is our soul that came from God and made of the substance of God. It will not be the Eternal Supreme Being, by whatever name you call Him or Christ that will judge. It will be our soul that judges, for it is self-judgment. It is not actually judging ourselves to be good or bad, for there is not one of us that is inherently evil. The soul will choose where it wants to go next to better receive the knowledge and experience it wants on its spiritual path. God is not in a hurry but misses us and patiently waits for us to return home.

Traditional Christian teaching is that at Judgment Day, according to our faith and our works, we will either go to heaven or hell.

THE KINGDOMS OF GOD

John 14-2- In My Father's house are many dwelling places; if it were not so, I would have told you; for I go to prepare a place for you.

Revelation 11:15- The kingdoms of this world are become the kingdoms of our Lord, and of his Christ; and he shall reign forever and ever.

Doctrine and Covenants 132:8- Behold, mine house is a house of order, saith the Lord God, and not a house of confusion.

Koran- 56:1,7-8- When the Inevitable Event comes to pass... you shall be sorted out into three classes. Then (there will be) the Companions of the Right Hand...

Koran-79:35-39- Then, for such as had transgressed all bounds, and had preferred the life of this world, their Abode will be Hell-Fire;

Koran- 80:38-41- Some faces that Day will be beaming, laughing, rejoicing. And other faces that Day will be dust-stained; Blackness will cover them.

Wherever we go in God's kingdom there are laws to maintain order. God's house is not a house of chaos or confusion, but of divine order. To attain enlightenment or enter the kingdom of heaven here on earth, we must live the laws of that heavenly kingdom. Living the teachings of the Christ or the Buddha will take us to the kingdom of heaven. Breaking all of Christ's teachings (commandments) will take us to spiritual realms where there is no love or light of God, which is hell on earth. Living the laws of the kingdom of heaven is the key to getting into heaven, here on earth. These kingdoms of heaven and hell, which we are entering here on earth, are the kingdoms we will go at Judgment Day.

To say that we go to heaven or hell at Judgment Day is an oversimplification. There are many dwelling places in the Father's house, many kingdoms. These kingdoms of heaven are bound by laws and if someone wants to live in that kingdom then they must abide by those laws. As the Koran states, we will all be separated into three groups which correspond to three basic kingdoms. Those who love Babylon will stay behind on the third dimensional plane. This will become their kingdom. (See below There Will Be Those Who Chose to Stay Behind). There will be another group which has chosen God and live many of the laws and commandments of God. They will live in the fifth dimension, as our earth has been reborn into a paradisiacal glory. There joy and happiness will be great. There is another group that has accepted God and the Christ, and lived ALL the teachings and commandments. This group will receive the greatest reward for their faithfulness. They will live in the higher dimensions of God's kingdom and their joy and happiness will be exceedingly great.

FALL OF SPIRITUAL BABYLON

Revelation 14:9-10- And the third angel followed them, saying with a loud voice, If any man worship the beast and his image, and receive his mark in his forehead, or in his hand. The same shall drink of the wine of the wrath of God, which is poured out without mixture into the cup of his indignation; and he shall be tormented with fire and brimstone in the presence of the holy angels, and in the presence of the Lamb:

There are three Babylons. Babylon of old, which is in present day Iraq, has fallen. The current Babylon is the major port cities of the world. There is also a spiritual Babylon that exists throughout the world. It is a real kingdom that exists in the spiritual realm but has a physical world presence. It exists in every country, every city, and most towns throughout the world. It is our brothers and sisters who choose to live the laws of the kingdom of Babylon. The kingdom of Babylon and the consciousness it has, says "Eat, drink and be merry, for there is no God and life goes on as it always did." "Rape, steal, murder, lie, boast, take, hate, get even, destroy marriages and families, do whatever brings you pleasure, for are no consequences of your actions." These are the laws of the kingdom of spiritual Babylon, or you might say lack of spiritual laws.

Judgment Day is the final hour for spiritual Babylon. It is a kingdom that has deceived many of our brothers and sisters. Christ shall defeat and bind darkness and so will spiritual Babylon will fall this day.

FINAL PURIFICATION

Malachi 4:1- For, behold, the day cometh, that shall burn as an oven; and all the proud, yea, and all that do wickedly, shall be stubble: and the day that cometh shall burn them up, saith the Lord of hosts, that it shall leave them neither root nor branch.

Doctrine and Covenants 38:11- all flesh is corrupt in my eyes...

With the Second Coming of Christ there is an opportunity to go back home. A time when all our sins (spiritual pollution, negative karma, and unconsciousness) will be removed and we will be given the opportunity to graduate and go back home. Every one of us will need purification before we can progress on. None of us would make it back to where we came without divine assistance. All our sins shall be taken upon the Christ, and we shall once again be purified before our God. All our relatives and those that have died shall be purified. This is a great act of love by God and the Christ. How many of us would take all our brother's and sister's spiritual pollution, sickness, hate, evil doing onto ourselves that others may be clean enough to return to heaven?

This is a unique and special day for all of us to rid ourselves of our sin, as the Christians, Jews and Muslims call it, or our negative karma and unconsciousness, as the eastern religions call it. Christ knew very well of karma and the law of karma and stated this law in the simplest of terms, *"You reap what you sow."* It is divine law that keeps account of all that we do. *"Those who live by the sword shall die by the sword." "Blessed are the merciful, for they shall receive mercy."* All these sayings come from the divine law of karma.

THERE WILL BE THOSE WHO CHOOSE TO STAY BEHIND

Mother Mary- There will be those who will choose to stay behind.

Doctrine and Covenants 88- And these are the rest of the dead; and they live not again until the thousand years are ended,

Mormon 9:4- Behold, I say unto you that ye would be more miserable to dwell with a holy and just God, under consciousness of your filthiness before him, than ye would to dwell with the damned souls in hell.

I said in the night of screams that we would face all of fears that we have not yet faced; almost. For some of us there is one more fear to face. To most Judgment Day will be a day of excitement and anxious anticipation and a day that many have been longing and waiting for. The day is also going to make many afraid, for this is the day that was prophesied and the day that has come to be.

There are many of our brothers and sisters who have been deceived by darkness. Mother Mary states, *"There will be those who choose to stay behind."* It is the soul of these brothers and sisters that will make the decision to stay behind. There are reasons that these souls will choose to stay behind. First, is described by Mormon 9:4 *"Behold, I say unto you that ye would be more miserable to dwell with a holy and just God, under consciousness of your filthiness before him, than ye would to dwell with the damned souls in hell."*

Second, the soul has not received everything that they signed on for. It is like going to an outstanding university that is foremost in the country in the field that you are studying, and by the end of the normal four years when most of their colleagues are graduating, they say "I do not have all the knowledge and the training that I wanted, and I am going to complete another year of school to complete my training." I admire the courage and the integrity of the souls of these individuals for making the choice to stay behind and complete the training.

These souls will not remain on earth renewed into paradise but they will receive additional schooling and training for a thousand years. They will stay behind on the third dimensional plane. At the end of the thousand years, darkness shall be unleashed on the earth and shall entice and deceive our brothers and sisters again. It is during this time of earth when darkness has been unleashed in the world, that these souls will be born back into the world to complete their schooling and their training.

I honor the souls of my brothers and sisters who know they have not received all that they signed on for in this third dimensional schooling. These brothers and sisters are not lost and their adventure into this third dimensional school will not be in vain. They shall be given another opportunity to graduate from this amazing school and join the rest of their brothers and sisters who will be waiting for their return.

SATAN BOUND FOR A THOUSAND YEARS

Revelation 20:1-3 *- Satan...bound 1,000 years...cast into bottomless pit*

Lucifer, his angels and his kingdom will be bound for one thousand years and there shall be no more darkness in the hearts and minds of men on earth. There will be no more darkness in the world. The root of all lies, hatred, fear, greed, envy, lust, glutton, murder and pride will be bound and have no place or power in the world as it is renewed into a paradisiacal glory.

We will look at each other and treat each other as that special brother or sister that we loved without end. Their concerns and welfare will be ours, and our concerns and welfare theirs. The joy, happiness, love and abundance will be everywhere.

CHAPTER 57

TIME OF CELEBRATION

WE ARE COMPLETING our time here on earth and our third dimensional schooling. There are many, many planets in the universe and yet it was the planet earth that was chosen for the grand plan of free will. We are graduating from this most challenging of God's schools. To be graduating and to have made it with free will is a great honor; a job well done. Commencement is about to take place and the celebration well deserved. God, Christ, Mother Mary and the heavenly host have been planning this celebration for a long time, for they never doubted our love for each other would be victorious in the end. Celebration for victory in the grand plan of free will. The celebration at the end of Star Wars in Return of the Jedi, or the end of The Lord of the Rings will not be able to compare with this celebration.

Great love, joy and gratitude will be shown by those that we have helped bring back home. Our hearts and souls will be beaming. One of our brothers or sisters will come to us and say, "Thank you. I didn't think I was going to make it, but you reached out with your hand and helped me walk through my trials when all hope in my heart had faded." With joy in your heart, you will reply, "I know, for when my heart was failing, someone grabbed my hand and gave me strength."

Jesus who gave his life for us, who took upon himself all our sins, was there for us when we lost our way. He did so much, and gave us so much. He was there to catch us when we fell, and even carried us when we had no strength left. We could not have returned without his help and assistance.

God, Christ and Mother Mary will be there to congratulate us on a job well done.

Our family will be there, along with our relatives and friends that have passed on. All those that passed away at such a young age. The grandmother or father that you had such a close relationship with. Friends that you miss so much to this very day, will be there for the celebration. You will be amazed who will be there for the celebration. Adam, Eve, Noah, Abraham, Elijah, Isaiah, Moses, the disciples, Buddha, Krishna, Mohammed, Archangels Gabriel, Michael and Raphael, other amazing glorious angels and spiritual beings, and enlightened beings from other worlds. They will all be there for the celebration.

God with His infinite patience has waited for His children to return home. Who will be happier to have their children return home, than our Father and our Mother. Returning home from a difficult and courageous journey, and there are many patiently waiting for us to return. There is something about home that soothes the soul and brings comfort. We will have returned to our family, Father and Mother, and finally we are back home.

CHAPTER 58

―§―

THOUSAND YEARS OF PEACE- A PROMISED PARADISE

Revelation 20:1-3- Satan...bound 1,000 years...cast into bottomless pit

Revelation 20:7- When the thousand years are completed, Satan will be released from his prison, and will come out to deceive the nations which are in the four corners of the earth,

Hindu- The end of the age of Kali Yuga marks the beginning of Satya Yuga, the Golden Age of Truth, Wisdom and Virtue. Again golden age will come.

Edgar Cayce- predicted the result will be 1000 years of building a world of peace and enlightenment.

Pueblo Native Americans- indigenous prophecies- Under the symbol of the rainbow, all of the races and all of the religions of the world would band together to spread the great wisdom of living in harmony with each other and with all the creations of the Earth. Those who taught this way would come to be known as "the rainbow warriors". Although they would be warriors, they would carry with them the spirits of the Ancestors, they would carry the light of knowledge in their heads and love in their hearts, and they would do no harm to any other living thing. The legend said that after a great struggle, using only the force of peace, these rainbow warriors would finally bring an end to the destruction and desecration of Mother Earth and that peace and plenty would then reign through a long, joyous and peaceful golden age here on Mother Earth.

***Quechua- South America**-Indigenous Prophecies- He says that the native Quechua Incan prophecies predicted the white man's coming would bring 500 years of materialism and imbalance. However, this era is coming to an end and the Age of Aquarius will "signal the return of Light to the planet and the dawn of a golden era. The Aquarian Age is an era of light, an age of awakening, an age of returning to natural ways.*

WITH THE FINAL purification and the Christ taking upon the sins of the world upon himself, and the binding of darkness (Satan). The darkness that was unleashed in the last days is bound for a thousand years. The jealousy, hate, envy, greed, unbridled destructive lust, glutton and fear will be gone from the hearts of men. Men and women will see their brothers and sisters as we knew them on the other side of the veil with their hearts now open. Hearts turned toward their fellow man. The earth will become a world of love and compassion and the concerns of your brothers and sisters will be just as important as your own. Brotherly love will have new meaning and mankind will be their brother's keepers.

Heaven that we came from was full of God's love. The earth has become a desert, with so little of God's love to quench the parched tongues of those looking for God's love. During the millennium, it will be creating heaven on earth with God's love everywhere. There will be no emptiness or void within us; we shall be complete.

Isaiah 8- Yea, the fir trees rejoice at thee, and the cedars of Lebanon, saying, Since thou art laid down, no feller is come up against us

The world will have renewed. The soil will be rich and fertile, and everything grown in abundance. The nutrition received from the fruit of the vine will not only provide all the nutrients that are needed, but be full of God's light and love. Fruits and vegetables, grains will be everywhere and provide wholesome nutrition. There will not be processed foods, but whole foods, and there will be no starvation. The world will become the Garden of Eden once again.

Man will live in harmony with the environment, the way God created it. The forests will no longer be decimated and leveled, the environment no longer ravaged. The forests will remain lush, green, vibrant and healthy. Clear water for all of mankind and all living things. Man will become good stewards of the paradise they have inherited. Clear blue streams and mountain lakes, green lush forests, sandy white beaches, green fields and pristine mountains. There will clouds, cleansing rain, vibrant rainbows and stunning sunrises and sunsets.

No more natural disasters of hurricanes, tornados, floods, earthquakes, volcanoes and tsunamis. There will be no more nuclear reactors, coal burning plants, toxic chemicals nor pollution. We will discover a clean renewable source of energy. This energy shall power our lights, technology, cities and transportation.

Isaiah 2:4- ...and they shall beat their swords into plowshares, and their spears into pruning hooks: nation shall not lift up sword against nation, neither shall they learn war any more.

Isaiah 14:7- The whole earth is at rest, and is quiet: they break forth into singing.

No more war, violence and bloodshed of our fellow man. Man shall not learn warfare any longer and there shall be peace on earth. The Second Coming of Christ will start an era of peace and harmony on the earth for one thousand years. The Battle of Armageddon was fought and won in our own hearts. Darkness in our own hearts will be bound and cast away; peace, harmony, love and understanding will flourish in our own hearts and the world.

Isaiah 20- There shall be no more thence an infant of days, nor an old man that hath not filled his days: for the child shall die a hundred years old;

Doctrine and Covenants 101:31- And when he dies he shall not sleep, that is to say in the earth, but shall be changed in the twinkling of an eye, and shall be caught up, and his rest shall be glorious.

Inca- Q'eros Inca: "Pachakuti - In this life, we need to share and live in community with no jealousy, no competitions, united, sharing, not only between people, but sharing with the earth and mountains.

Apache- As people develop their gifts, which all come from Spirit, and use them for the benefit of All Our Relations, we are building a system founded on that which is eternal and based in love. The light of Spirit is penetrating the darkness that once was, and out of chaos and disorder there is being built the Fifth World of Peace, where there is no inequality, no injustice, no division of those who have too much from those who have too little, where all the gifts will be divided and all the bounty will be evenly shared. There will be abundance in everything and with abundance there will be no more greed and hoarding. The new theme of mankind will be sharing. The wealth, the harvest, the advancements, God's love shall be shared with all. Communities will look after and take care of each other.

No more death and dying; no more infant and child deaths. Mothers and fathers will no longer have to bury their children. We shall live a long healthy life, no longer suffering old age, Alzheimer's or decaying bodies. When it is time to go back to heaven and God, we will be changed in the twinkling of an eye, never experiencing death or dying.

There will be the end of disease as we know it. An end of the plagues that destroyed our health and happiness. No cancer centers or hospitals full of the sick and terminally ill. Yes, we will still have physicians, but the way that we look at health and the way to heal the body, mind and spirit will be entirely different. The physicians will be taught by the master physician, Jesus Christ.

Isaiah 21:4- And God shall wipe away all tears from their eyes; and there shall be no more death, neither sorrow, nor crying, neither shall there be any more pain: for the former things are passed away.

No crying, sorrow, despair, pain or suffering. The new theme will be happiness with lots of smiles and happy people. There is a yearning within all of us to be happy. There will be happiness everywhere and it will be contagious. Instead of catching a virus or some other annoying microorganism in the schools or work place, we will catch more happiness. It will go beyond happiness, to something called exquisite joy. It will be good to have gone through the trials, tribulation, pain and suffering, for now mankind will appreciate joy and happiness.

Isaiah11- The wolf also shall dwell with the lamb, and the leopard shall lie down with the kid; and the calf and the young lion and the fatling together; and a little child shall lead them. And the cow and the bear shall feed; their young ones shall lie down together: and the lion shall eat straw like the ox.

Animals will be changed in the twinkling of an eye. The wolf shall dwell with the lamb, the lion with the calf, and a little child shall lead them. There will be no need to kill the animals for food, for far more nutritious food will be found everywhere. Man will not need meat as a source of protein. There will be no more predators and the animals that were carnivores will become herbivores. Mankind will become herbivores and animals will no longer fear man. Animals and man shall live in peace.

Isaiah 65-17- For, behold, I create new heavens and a new earth:

Mankind and God will be creating heaven on earth. There will be building of cities, transportation and there will be much growing. There will advancements, universities, learning, the arts, writing and creative arts. Along with the universities and there shall be teachings by the greatest spiritual teachers. Bringing forth the knowledge and wisdom of God and the ages.

Mankind will have a greater understanding of what the brotherhood of man means. Man shall see all as brothers and sisters, and eventually, the brotherhood of man will be one color, one race and speak one language.

Living side by side with us will be intelligent beings from other planets in the Milky Way Galaxy and other galaxies. These beings are also our brothers and our sisters and have come to assist us in our evolution of consciousness and will share their teachings, knowledge and technology. The brotherhood of man is a universal brotherhood of man. Mr. Spock will teach us "The needs of the many outweigh the needs of few," and ways of the universe. We will travel at speeds currently unthinkable, travel to outer space and go for a Sunday afternoon flight. Star Trek fans are going to love it.

TECHNOLOGY

You might believe because mankind placed technology before God and worshipped technology, that technology and the age of enlightenment cannot coexist. They can and they will. Bill Gates and the other techies would stand in amazement if they knew what is coming. We are barely entering the first day of preschool when it comes to the advancements in technology and science. Technology can and will serve all mankind. There will be evolution of technology and sharing of the advanced technology of our extraterrestrial brothers and sisters. There will be technology advancements that astounds our imagination. If you like what technology can do now, then hold on to your hats for we have not seen anything to compare to what is to come.

Buddha, Mohammed, Krishna and other enlightened masters will be there from time to time. There will still be different religions, but all will all honor the Christ who stands at the head. All these enlightened beings, masters and prophets will continue to worship the one God.

Figure 46- Mahatma Gandhi

Hindu- *Shortly before he was assassinated, Mahatma Mohandas Gandhi predicted the future of the human race to a group of friends and associates: Whoever will survive this settlement will see an entirely new earthly existence manifested. For a long, very long time the world war will be crossed out from the dictionary of mankind, perhaps even for all time. Christmas, the festival of Christianity, will be accepted by all* *religions as the true festival of Peace. Blessed be, who will live to see this epoch!*

Mahatma Gandhi (Figure 46), brought home rule and liberation to India. He is an old soul, enlightened one, in addition to being a great leader of men. Mahatma means great soul and he is revered in India. In his revelation shortly before his death, it was revealed to him, that Christmas will be celebrated in all religions. All people and all religions shall recognize and honor the Christ, his importance and all that he has given us. God's and Christ's teachings will be taught but much more importantly lived in all parts of the society

Isaiah 2:2-4- And it shall come to pass in the last days, that the mountain of the Lord's house shall be established in the top of the mountains, and shall be exalted above the hills; and all nations shall flow unto it. And many people shall go and say, Come ye, and let us go up to the mountain of the Lord, to the house of the God of Jacob; and he will teach us of his ways, and we will walk in his paths: for out of Zion shall go forth the law, and the word of the Lord from Jerusalem. And he shall judge among the nations,

Isaiah 22:27-28- All the ends of the world shall remember and turn unto the Lord: and all the kindreds of the nations shall worship before thee. For the kingdom is the Lord's: and he is the governor among the nations.

The government will be from those who want to serve the whole of mankind, and not the few. It will start at the very top with Jesus Christ as the head of government. Jesus Christ and the enlightened ones shall bring forth truth and wisdom into government and will organize government and laws, more in divine teaching than laws that need policing. We will discipline and govern ourselves with divine teachings. Government and all of us shall look after the whole and not the few. The teachings of Christ shall be brought into all professions.

Passion, talk about passion! Nothing can match the fulfillment of having all your passion with all of God's love. Passion will be part of the paradise, but it will be far more complete, rich, fulfilling, and rewarding.

Luke 9:28-29- And it came to pass about an eight days after these sayings, he took Peter and John and James, and went up into a mountain to pray. And as he prayed, the fashion of his countenance was altered, and his raiment was white and glistering.

Koran 39:69- The earth will shine with the light of its Lord

Pacific Maori- The Elders' prophecy says that in 2012 an event called the 'Ka hinga te aria' will occur which translates to the 'fall (hinga) of the curtain/veil (aria). The falling of the curtain will allow the world of humans and other physical entities to merge with the world of spirits and Deities.

We will be creating heaven on earth, an enlightened planet. The world and those of us choosing paradise will be totally changed in the twinkling of an eye. "*John, Peter, John and James went up into the mountain to pray and Jesus was transfigured. His countenance altered, and his raiment was white and glistening.*" We will be transfigured. There will be falling of the veil that separates heaven and earth. Earth will have changed from the third dimensional planet to a fifth dimensional planet. Our bodies will become lighter and less dense. We will be able to see and communicate with those who have passed on. We will be able to see spirit that surrounds all of us. We will become conscious beings on a conscious planet; an age of enlightenment.

There will be working of miracles by all of faith, for the benefit of all mankind. This will not be a rare event commanded by Christ nor extraordinary to those living in paradise. Christ and the masters teaching the secrets of God and universe. Those of sufficient faith shall be able to levitate, fly, be in two locations at one time and communicate by mental telepathy.

Doctrine and Covenants 130:9- This earth, in its sanctified..., whereby all things pertaining to an inferior kingdom, or all kingdoms of a lower order, will be manifest to those who dwell on it; and this earth will be Christ's.

The earth will become a fifth dimensional planet. Living on a higher dimensional plane allows us to look down into the lower dimensions, although those on the lower dimensions cannot look up into the higher dimensions. We will be able to look down (be able to see) upon the third dimensional plane and those that have chosen to stay behind.

Doctrine and Covenants 133:23- He shall command the great deep, and it shall be driven back into the north countries, and the islands shall become one land;

The earth was once one land before the continental drift broke up the land into islands and separate continents. During the millennium, Christ will command the seas and oceans to move north and all the continents and islands will become one land, within 1,000 years and not over millions of years. There will be one land, recreation of Pangaea.

1 Corinthians 2:9- But, as it is written, What no eye has seen, nor ear heard, nor the heart of man imagined, what God has prepared for those who love him.

No one can imagine what God and Christ have prepared for us. We should eagerly look forward to paradise, at the end of the period of challenges. What a gift we shall leave for our children, our children's children and our posterity. We remember our fathers as they laid down their lives, that we may have a land of freedom. Our posterity will remember the sacrifice that we made for them and the cost of their paradise.

CHAPTER 59

─────────§─────────

THE ADVENTURE CONTINUES

THERE ARE THOSE that feel they understand all that there is to know about God, heaven, hell and the hereafter. To those who try to put God into a nice little box, I say you cannot put God into a box. The prophecies of God through the prophets will be fulfilled. After Judgment Day and the rebirth of the earth into paradisiacal glory our journey is not over. It is eternal progression and eternal is a long, long time. As we ascend the magnificent mountain of God's paradise we finish one leg of the journey, come to a plateau and enjoy a magnificent view. The view is spectacular and we look back and see how far we have come and there are few words that can describe our joy. There is a great celebration for having made it so far and with such a high degree of difficulty. We look at each other and know we couldn't have made it so far without each other. We understand a little more about God and His kingdom. We take a rest, get ready for the next climb and adventure, for next plateau is in sight and our journey continues. With us roped to each other and God as our guide, we will make it to the next plateau in God's kingdom, together.

CHAPTER 60

---- § ----

HOW TO SURVIVE THE COMING EARTH CHANGES

GOD IS IN CHARGE AND CONTROL

I LOVE SPORTS and high thrill sports. I love windsurfing and I am learning kayaking. Learning any sport, it is helpful to take lessons and to watch the professionals or best in the field. I will watch people in their element and see what I can learn. In learning windsurfing I had a learning curve of getting beat up by high winds. I noticed that the experts in windsurfing can sometimes be very small women and yet they could do quite well in high winds. These windsurfers had discovered not to fight the wind but use the wind. They knew how to deflect wind if they had to and use the weight of their body so they made windsurfing seem effortless.

In kayaking the same thing occurs. Those who understand how to use the force of the river and go with the flow and force of the river, make kayaking seem effortless. Those who try to muscle through and fight the river are eventually overcome by the force of nature.

There are two opposing forces on earth, the light and the darkness. There is only One in control and that is God. Everything is unfolding according to divine plan. Trying to hold on to what once was, is to fight nature and the universe. Those who understand what is happening and why, will be able to move with the force of nature, the universe and God's power and will fare the best. Those who try and fight nature and the universal force will be exhausted in futility. We will eventually succumb to fear or surrender to love.

Many believe it is the military who is in charge and controls our world. Many believe it is those who have the money in the world that is in charge and controls the world. Many believe it is the powerful political leaders that are in charge. Others believe it is the media that is in charge and controls our planet and mankind. We believe that we are in control but we are not. It will soon become very clear that there is only One in control. Universal forces, Mother Nature and ultimately God will shake the world to wake us up and finally we will understand it is not us in control but the One who created us all. The key is not to fight it. To fight the changes that are coming is to be overcome by them. God wants us to do what we can to help our loved ones and each other, but leave 95% of the work to God.

ONLY SECURITY THERE IS

What is your security? Is it money, living on an island, guns and weapons, expensive security systems or even a body guard? It will soon become clear, that these will provide limited security. Buying your own island, security guards, guns, weapons, fortresses, stockades will not provide the safety and security you are looking for. God will be the only security there is. Being able to communicate with the One who created us will be an invaluable tool to have. It can lead you to a safe place to live, a source of food and water when you have none, people who are there to help you and not take advantage of you, be a source of strength, courage, hope, optimism, encouragement where none can be found. God will be that source of strength and the beacon of light when other lights go out. Yes, it does help to prepare as you should, but very soon God will be the only safety and security there is. The world will come to know this very clearly as the world begins to shake and the forces of good and evil are at war in the world. The higher power and your inner voice will be your guide in times that are darkest.

The higher power is the rock that shall weather the storm. The storm has begun but you haven't seen anything yet. Those that build their houses on sand when the high winds, and high waves come will have their houses washed away. Those that build their houses on the rock will weather the storm. The higher power will be light when all other lights fade, will provide strength when strength fails, wisdom and insight when none can be found and hope when men's heart's fail them. God will be eye of the hurricane, the still quiet place at the center of a major storm.

For those who are turned off to the word God, because of a negative experience, then I will state it another way. If you love your fellow man and see them as your brothers and your sisters, then the choice has been made. You have chosen love. I know of people who are not timid in calling themselves atheists, and yet they love their fellow man and serve their fellow man. If you love your fellow man, then you love God. If you serve your fellow man, you serve God. If you believe in your fellow man, then you believe in God.

Some will try and find security in every way possible with money, guns, security systems, position in society, etc. There is only one security, and that is with God, and the only protection. There is wisdom in being prepared and even expecting the unexpected. In the end, however, people will only find security in God. No amount of money, number of guns or sophisticated emergency system will provide security you are looking for.

BE PREPARED

SPIRITUAL PREPARATION

No one is guaranteed physical safety in the last days, only spiritual safety. However, God and the spirit will be the closest you can come to physical safety. He knows where you should be and not be. If you want to survive the coming changes, live to see the earth renewed to a paradisiacal glory and personally see the Second Coming of Christ, then God is the way. No guarantees for any of us, but you have increased your odds 100-fold.

One of my goals is to be there at the Second Coming of Christ. I am looking forward to being there to meet Christ and the heavenly host. Although this is my goal, I am not guaranteed physical safety in the years to come. No one is. If I prepare, spiritually and physically, I am 100 times more likely to be there at his coming. It is wise to live every day as if it were your last day on earth.

TEMPORAL PREPARATION (MATERIAL WORLD PREPARATION)

EXPECT THE UNEXPECTED

What did you learn from Hurricane Katrina? I will tell you some of the things that I learned. **Be prepared and expect the unexpected.** Don't expect some government agency to guarantee your safety, to take care of you and rescue you in a timely manner. Take full responsibility for yourself and your loved ones.

COMMUNITY

Community will provide strength in challenging times. Social order will break down and there will be need to form communities that look after each other. No man is an island, and we will call upon each other and depend on each other very soon. Friends and family can be a great source of strength. People of like mind and spirit will come together, for we are all in this together.

THREE DAY EMERGENCY PREPAREDNESS KIT

There are many web sites and government organizations that have a great deal of information in how to prepare your three-day emergency preparedness pack. This is usually all contained in one back pack, but this will depend on the size of the family. This will contain food, water, utensils, medications, necessary clothing for weather and conditions, radio, flashlight, money, identification and sleeping materials. This list is not all inclusive but the back pack should contain everything that you need if there is a disaster and you must leave your home with only a few minutes notice.

TEST DRILLS

Practicing the fire drills at school, work or at home are a great idea. Practice makes perfect. Nothing helps more in an emergency than to have practiced what you will do if an emergency happens. The same is true of disaster drills. It is of enormous value for a family, group or individuals to have planned what they will do in an emergency or disaster. There is no need to alarm any one, but to have an intelligent, thoughtful understanding of what to do in an emergency is paramount for the coming challenges.

THREE MONTH SUPPLY OF FOOD AND WATER

There is debate on how much food and water is necessary when the disasters outlined this book happen. This is between you, your family and God, but three months' supply of food and water should be sufficient. There should be a three-month supply of food, water, medications and what you would need to survive if you were cut off from your normal source of food, water and necessary supplies. People often do not think water is that important, or that water will always be there. Water can be cut off very abruptly and without notice. Water is essential to life and a three-month supply of water is wise. It is important to keep in mind those who may call on you in an emergency or disaster. If Uncle Fred and Aunt Mary have no intention of preparing for the coming challenges and you would like to help them, then this should be planned for.

HOW TO SURVIVE THE COMING EARTH CHANGES

There are some creative ways of having enough water for a disaster. A swimming pool is a great source way for water storage. Having ways to purify the water will help if the water might not be as good as bottled water.

CASH NEST EGG

Did you learn anything from Y2K? Fears of a Y2K meltdown and panic never happened yet the practice drill, information given and dialogue, I found helpful. It will be necessary to have enough cash if normal ways of attaining money break down. A prudent amount of cash in your home safely tucked away so it cannot be stolen can be helpful in emergencies and disasters. If you cannot afford it, then do what you can and let God do the rest.

PREPARE FOR FAILURE OF TECHNOLOGY

I have worked in hospitals and surgery centers when the computer has crashed. There was a sense of panic in the places I worked because so much of the daily work is centered around information in computers and computer files. It was very easy for me to go back and work with paper and create a medical record on paper. For others, this situation became awkward and anxiety provoking. Emergency test drills and preparedness are very important for when emergencies occur. Preparing for a breakdown or failure of technology is wise. So much of our everyday life is surrounded by technology. Our cars, transportation, work, wall street, communication, military and emergency programs are largely dependent on modern technology. Very few could imagine widespread failure of technology, and the panic and chaos that would result. Ask yourself, "What would I do if technology failed?" Would your business and household have a backup in place so you could function and you and your family survive?

DEBT

The world does not fully understand how close the financial markets of the world came to a complete financial meltdown in 2007-2008. Swift action by those in power averted this economic disaster. A warning shot was fired over the bow of our boat, but will the world listen.

The days of the easy, fast money are coming to an end. Some with the greatest finances can suffer the most when the challenges come. There is acceptable debt and there is debt that is ill advised. I am not a professional financial advisor, but there is wisdom in not living beyond your means. It is not wise to buy a home and luxury items that you cannot afford. It is important to expect the unexpected. If you were to lose your job and had no income for six months would you lose your home or your car? Would you have enough to feed your family and pay your bills?

There are two good reasons to go into debt. The first is buying a home that is within your means and the other is education. Both are good sound investments. There will soon be financial chaos that will be part of the world in chaos. Those who have not lived beyond their means and have acceptable amount of debt or the best scenario which is no debt, will fear the least. There is wisdom to living within your means and getting out of debt.

There will be many people and many groups who will come and say give us this amount of money and we will guarantee your safety and that you will make it through the coming catastrophes. Don't believe them and don't waste your time or money. There is not one person on this earth that is guaranteed safe passage through these earth changes. The greatest safety there is, is with God. He is the only one that can see you safely through the coming changes.

COMMUNICATION WITH GOD

There are two opposing forces in the world and this is all according to divine plan. It is divine plan that there is opposition in all things. The dark side of the force will tell you "There is no God and it is foolish to believe in Him. Look at the riches and the fame, and things of the world. Go out and grab it now, before it is gone. It is foolish to believe in the prophets and what is written in the Bible. Do not believe in the end times or Judgment Day, for the world goes on as it did before. Even if there was a God, you are not worthy of His love and His time. He would be much too busy to talk to you."

There is another force that says "You are a child of the Most High God. You are more valuable and precious than you could ever imagine. He wants to give you more than you think possible, and He wants a one on one relationship with you. He is there any time to listen, be a friend, help and simply love His child. You do not need to go to someone else who will communicate to God for you, for He wants to talk with you Himself."

There is only going to be One source that will see you safely through the coming changes and challenges that are coming. There is only One that can watch over and take care of His child who is loved more than you know. It is God or the higher power that can provide safety when fear and chaos is everywhere. There are different ways that the higher power can watch over you and communicate with you, for you and your loved ones. I will describe each of these communications with the higher power.

COMMUNICATION CAN COME IN ORDINARY WAYS

I heard a poignant story. A man's boat had capsized in the middle of the lake and he believed God would save him. He prayed earnestly and there appeared a boat that could take him to safety. The man replied, no I have faith that God Himself will save me and he told the boat to go to shore. The man prayed earnestly again. Another boat appeared and the man again told those in the boat to go to shore, for the man believed God Himself would save him. This happened a third time and the man again sent the boat to shore believing that God Himself would save him. The man died went to heaven and stood before God. "God, I prayed earnestly to you and believed that you would save me, but you didn't." God replied, "I don't know what happened, for I sent three boats to save you." The point of the story is that sometimes the communication is as obvious as the nose on your own face, but you may not see it is your answer to your prayers coming in a form you least expected.

YOUR FRIENDS AND FAMILY AND FELLOW MAN

These can be a source of love, support and communication from the higher power. The answer to your prayers can come in a form you least expect it. A loved one can come to you and give the insight to a problem that you have been seeking for years. God does speak through all of us, even though we may not be aware of it.

God communicates through our loved ones, in ways we never see and are not fully aware of. I will tell you a story of one of my in-laws and a 9/11 story I doubt you have heard. I will call my in-law Jeff, and he worked at the Twins Towers in New York City. Jeff is a hard worker and very dedicated to his job. He was part of a firm located on the higher levels of the Twin Towers and would travel from New Jersey to work every day. He never missed work and I will repeat, never missed work. He was the first to work and didn't leave work until the work was done. His wife was rarely sick and when she was sick, she could always manage. Very early on the morning of September 11, 2001 Jeff's wife complained she didn't feel well. Jeff attended to her, felt she would be fine and he would come home early from work to be with her. She was more emotionally ill than physically sick. She begged Jeff to stay home today and be with her. This was quite a dilemma for Jeff who never missed work and believed his wife would be fine. The more he said he needed to get to work, the more she would ask him and plead with him to stay home. This continued, but she did not want Jeff to go to work and continued to plead with him to stay home. He relented and stayed home. Jeff stayed with his wife a few hours, and then she said, "I am feeling better, I will be alright now." Jeff couldn't understand why a few hours would make a difference to her, but he looked at her, felt she would be fine, gave her a kiss and he was off to the office. Jeff parked his car walked across the plaza of the Twin Towers and was about to enter the front doors of the South Tower when first jet hit the South Tower with a thunderous roar. Debris began falling on the plaza and then bodies began falling with the debris. Jeff made it across the plaza without being hit by falling debris or bodies and made it to a place of safety. The airliner hit the South Tower and all that worked in his office were killed. If Jeff had not listened and acquiesced to his wife's incessant pleas, Jeff would have been in his office and been killed. God works through our loved ones in ways we do not fully see and understand, but it is another way that God communicates to us.

PETS

I recall a story on television. A woman owned a dog which she loved very much. The feeling was mutual, I am sure. This woman's dog would repeatedly put his nose on the exact same spot on her breast. There was an intention and urgency that the woman picked up from her dog. This brought to the woman's awareness maybe she should have a breast checkup. She made an appointment with her doctor and exactly where the dog had put his nose on her breast, the doctor found cancer. The cancer was removed and the woman's life saved, thanks to her dog. Some dogs can smell cancer, but God can and does communicate through our pets.

FEAR

I have written a whole chapter on fear and that fear is tied into darkness. Fear is part of being human and has kept our ancestors away from dangers that allowed our ancestors to have offspring. If it were not so, we would not be here, for our ancestors would have been eaten by saber tooth tigers or fallen prey to some other danger. If we have this mode of survival, we might as well use it.

Our bodies and spirit are geared for survival. If we cared not if we lived or died or the well-being of our offspring then we would be much more likely to fall prey to the predators, not have offspring and we would not have our posterity. Our fear mechanism is geared for survival, and will be useful in the coming years. The problem for many in these modern times is that it is always turned on. When fear is always on there will be anxiety, depression, sadness, pain and insomnia. It is important to have the fear mechanism turned off until it is needed. If it is off most of the time and turned on only when we need to be alerted to impending danger, then our fear mechanism can be a useful way for our spirit and the higher power to communicate to us. It is important to use fear as a tool, and not to succumb to fear or make decisions out of fear.

INTUITION

"Never underestimate the power of a woman's intuition." I don't know who originally coined this phrase but it is true and full of wisdom. It is not only woman who have intuition, men have it also. Intuition comes from feelings and more of a gut feeling and can be a very powerful way for our soul and the higher power to communicate and bring something to our conscious awareness. You may even say sense of something.

Let me give some examples of intuition. I am amazed at how many stories I hear on a recurring theme. Who we marry can either provide much happiness or much unhappiness. Finding the right one to spend the rest of your life with is one of the most important decisions we will ever make. I have talked to many women who have told me the exact same story. These women were all dating men who had a position of authority. Here is the story that I heard repeatedly. A man would tell the woman she was to marry him. Every one of these women at some point had a gut feeling that something was wrong with the plans for marriage. Something was wrong and something was telling them not to marry. They were faced with a choice, do I trust my gut feeling (intuition) that is telling me something is wrong and not marry, or do I trust this man who has a position of power, influence and authority. These women ended up trusting the man and not themselves and their relationship with God. Every one of these women whose stories I heard, ended up in an unhappy marriage and divorce.

What can be learned from these stories? Trust yourself, your intuition and what God is trying to communicate to you. If a woman (or man) chooses to trust someone else more than herself and her relationship with the higher power, then she needs to accept and be responsible for her choices. It is imperative to trust yourself, trust in God and all the ways that God chooses to communicate with you.

FEELINGS

I am a pure empath and I feel everything. This is also a way to communicate with others and the higher power. This is similar to intuition. I can talk to someone and if they are in pain, I will feel what they are feeling and feel their pain. I can talk to someone else and if they have a headache I will feel their headache. Once I know that this is their headache that I am feeling, I simply let the headache that I am feeling go and it is gone. This feeling can be used to help guide you and your loved ones through perilous times. You might be in a group of people and get a bad feeling with this group and you may be with another group and receive a good feeling. This is spirit communicating with you. You may be dating someone and whenever you are together there is a good feeling, this you need to listen to. There may be someone else you are dating and everything looks good on paper, but the feeling you get when you are with this person is not a good feeling. Trust your feelings. You might be looking at new job opportunities. After looking and interviewing for different jobs, there is one job that you have a good feeling about.

THE HUMAN HEART

The human heart is the most amazing of God's creations. Not only is the physical heart a sight to behold but the human heart is connected to our spiritual heart which is the most wondrous of all. It is our spiritual heart that is a microcosm or hologram of God and the universe. It contains spiritual Babylon, but also the kingdom of heaven, the valley of decision (valley of Armageddon) and the Light of Christ. There is a vast wealth of knowledge, wisdom and power that the human heart can access.

As my heart began opening I was amazed at what things I knew and what information I could access. Not all information is pleasant information. I remember walking down the hall and greeting one of my colleagues. I greeted him cordially and he did the same. He had a smile on his face and so did I. I had a pain in my heart for my heart was open. This colleague of mine hated me and this caused me pain. There is a price to be paid for having an open heart and traveling the path of enlightenment. I could not handle the pain and had to close my heart, for the pain was great and saddened me. I eventually learned that although it was true that this colleague of mine hated me it usually is nothing personal. It is most often that I have reminded him of someone else he hated (projection), his own issues, something I represent or his issues with God. Once I toughened up and did not take things personally anymore, then I could open my heart again. The rewards far outweigh the pain.

The heart can access information, give you knowledge and wisdom. It can tell you where to move to, who to marry, which groups you should belong to. It is the clearest path and clearest connection to the higher power.

DREAMS

Dreams are fascinating tools that we can rely upon for communication with God. In our sleep our minds and spirits are set free and this is when communication from God has the least barriers to get through for communication. Dreams have a very important function in our day to day living. It is a time for our brains to process all our experiences. Our dreams can help us deal with an abusive boss, a problem with someone we work with and get us on the right track. Dreams are important for our mental health.

Dreams can also be a very powerful way to communicate with the higher power. Once you wake up it is important to write your dream down, or it will soon be forgotten. It is important to note that God usually does not usually communicate literally through our dreams, but often uses symbols for the communication. Therein lays the key to dream interpretation, to know the symbols. For this purpose, I recommend purchasing a copy of Betty Bethard's book The Dream Book. Although this book does not cover all the symbols that God uses, it is an enlightened book and very helpful for dream interpretation. This is one of my favorite ways of receiving communication from God, and found it to be very accurate. Not only for helping make life decisions but for bringing to my conscious awareness why I am the way I am. It is a very powerful way to unlock the mysteries within, and Sigmund Freud was wise to use dreams and dream interpretation on his patients.

Dreams can show the future. I was pleasantly surprised to see things in the future that had not yet happened. This was a gift to be used wisely and I usually used this gift to help my patients. This dream would typically occur on a Friday night and would show me something that was about to happen the next week. I would be shown the face of someone that I had never met and then be shown what was going to happen. As the week unfolded I would meet the patient I had never met before and his face would be exactly as it was shown in my dream. The event would unfold as it did in my dream. I was then shown that with this knowledge of future events could be used to change future events. I would be shown a patient and an injury that could occur then be shown corrective management to prevent the injury to the patient. I may have gotten a little prideful with this gift to help my patients and I developed an unhealthy attitude. My attitude became, "Well if God is watching over my patients then I can relax and let Him do all the work and all the driving." Bad attitude and wrong thinking, and I needed to be taught a lesson. Soon there was a patient who had a very loose tooth that he did not tell me about in preoperative evaluation. My anesthetic management did not change at all and it was work as usual. During establishment of a secure airway for the operation, I knocked out a tooth. As it turned out the tooth was very loose, would have eventually come out, but I was humbled. It even struck a note of fear in me. The knocking out of a tooth is a minor complication that can occur under anesthesia for an operation. The higher power was teaching me a lesson and I received it loud and clear. After all the dust had settled and things were back to normal, I received the final clarification of the lesson from the higher power. "YOU DO YOUR JOB AND WE WILL DO OURS!" the spirit firmly told me. I was grateful to not let pride enter my heart and once again be on the right path.

Seeing future events in my dreams has come to the point to where there is no doubt. It is just another way that God communicates with me as I watch over myself, my loved ones and my patients.

VISIONS

Visions are another way for God to communicate with us and they are linked to the same way we receive information in our dreams. Visions can occur in our dreams and this is usually how they start. It is much easier for a vision to occur in our dream state than the waking state of mind. This dream will be noticed by the quality of the dream. Usually dreams are like the cartoons that you would see in the 1950's on an antiquated television set. They are fuzzy and lacking in vivid detail. A vision in the dream state has very vivid quality. It is like seeing something with blue ray DVD on a very high definition television screen. More importantly is the spiritual impact of the vision in the dream. There will be an impact on your soul and spiritual being. This is how you will know it was a message from God and not your mind working out details of the day.

These same messages that occur in the dream state can occur during the waking state of mind. It takes time and awakening of the spirit but it is by the same mechanism as dreaming. There is what you might call mini-visions. These appear as an image about one and half feet in front of your eyes. The image is again usually symbolic, and then you need to ask God for the meaning of the vision. Sometimes He will tell you without having to ask. There are also visions, which are larger in height and width and greater clarity than what I call a mini-vision. They occur about one and half feet in front of your eyes, but it is the quality, vividness and spiritual impact on your soul and spiritual being that will leave no doubt the source of the vision, which is God.

STILL SMALL VOICE

This is a very important source of communication with your soul, the angels and God. It is usually just a thought and that does not downplay its importance or usefulness. This source of communication from God is basic as love is basic to our nature. Yes, there are lots of voices in our head which is very normal. "Sit up straight." "Put your best foot forward." "What makes you think you can do that?" We have these thoughts which can be very negative thoughts or very positive thoughts. It is important to sift through all this mind chatter and voices in the crowd, for the still inner small voice which can be your soul, the angels or God Himself speaking to His most precious child. This voice can come at any time, but often comes in the time of need. When your soul and angels are concerned for your health and welfare they will put through a Herculean effort on their part to get you the message that you need. In time of great need, will come forth great effort from the other side of the veil. This message may not be because of large spiritual strides on your part, but because the need is great. It is best not to wait until health and well-being and impending danger are lurking in the horizon to start listening to the still small voice within. With practice, you will be able to discern the still small voice and who is communicating with you.

This voice does not come from oscillation in airwaves, falling upon our eardrum creating the voice that we can physically hear. This is our spiritual hearing and it is just as real as our physical hearing. Rarely, does it become loud. I have a friend who lived in a foreign country and being around twenty years old played a lot with her friends. One day there was a voice she had not heard before. "Leave town now," the voice said. This was odd for she had not heard the voice before. Again, the voice said, "Leave town now." My friend did not know quite what to make of this, but she kept hearing the voice and it got louder and louder. "Leave town now!" The voice became so loud and forceful that she made the decision to leave town, if for no other reason, to see if the voice in her head would stop. My friend left town and then she received some bad news. Her friends were driving in a car, there was an accident and all her friends were killed. My friend would have been in that car with her friends and been killed if she had not listened to the voice within and followed the advice. Hopefully, we do not have to have Herculean efforts by the spirits on the other side of the veil for us to listen. Hopefully we will be more receptive to those that are trying to help us and watch over us.

I must add that there is a Lord of Darkness. He exists and so do the angels that serve him. Again, discernment is important. If a voice asks you to harm someone else, then tell that spirit to go away. Thereby you will know how to discern the voice that is speaking to you. If that voice is speaking for your welfare or that of your loved ones, then you know the source. If the voice is not speaking for your welfare, your loved ones or even someone you don't know, then you will know it came from a source you don't want to listen to.

REVELATION

God is God of revelation. Revelation was meant to be such a natural part of our daily living that when we receive it, it is nothing extraordinary but a normal part of our everyday lives. It is like miracles that were meant to be a natural phenomenon. God can give you the answer to any question, and can lead away from danger and into safety.

Revelation was meant to be a part of our everyday lives, as were miracles. The world will try and get you to believe that revelation, miracles, healing and communication with the One who watches over us all is impossible. As the veil drops revelation and communication with God and the angels will happen with greater and greater frequency.

PRICELESS

What is your greatest treasure? I ask this without judgment. Is it your beloved wife, your amazing child, a priceless jewel, your home, your friends or your land? These can be taken away when you least expect it. Your riches can be stolen, your reputation ruined, your health failing, your loved ones and friends betray you. All the things which you might hold on to for dear life can be taken away. Your relationship with the One who created you can never be taken away. No matter the fear instilled in you, intimidation or being in places where all love and hope fade. There is no one who can take away who you are. You are a child of the Most High God. We have only forgotten who we are and that we can have a one on one relationship with Him. **It is your birthright!** People have had this dream throughout the ages, to have a one on one communication with the greatest of them all. This gift exceeds all known wealth and it is yours for the asking. You do not have to go to your priest or Rabbi, have an intermediary who will relay your message to God. All that is needed is the desire to renew the relationship that you already have, but have forgotten about. God lives within your heart and all that is needed is the key to unlock the door. The key is the desire to know Him and have a one on one relationship with Him. This key will unlock the door. You will no longer search the cosmos, labor over ancient texts or need to find the Guru on the mountain in Tibet to find God. God has been patiently waiting for you to return home. You have the key to open the door and He will be your lifeline through perilous times. Man has dreamed of having this communication, and one on one relationship with God from the beginning of time. This relationship with God and communication with one who loves us without end is, priceless.

BIBLIOGRAPHY

QUOTES

1. The Bible; King James Version
2. The Book of Mormon
3. Doctrine and Covenants
4. *Pope Francis-* November 2015,
5. Koran
   a. *Book 37, Number 4281-Narrated Mu'adh ibn Jabal: (Translation of Sunan Abu-Dawud)*
   b. *"Az-Zalzalah"-*
   c. *Islam- Ahmad-*
   d. *- Tirmidhi*
6. Bhuddism
   a. Author Unknown- -Agharti
   b. *Prophecy of Shambala (Buddhist, BEF 700 CE):*
   c. *Digha Nikaya iii.71-72, Cakkavatti-Sihanada Suttanta*
   d. *Lotus Sutra 13-*
   e. *The following are excerpts from a number of prophecies and scriptures*
   f. *Padmasambhhava*
   g. *Prophecy of Shambala (Buddhist, BEF 700 CE)-*
   h. *Digha Nikaya iii.71-72, Cakkavatti-Sihanada Suttanta-*
7. Hinduism
   a. *summer of 1983, Guru Bhagwan Rajneesh Chandra*
   b. *"The Coming of the Great Avatar and the Return of the Golden Age"-*
   c. *Hindu Gurus*
8. Mother Mary
   a. Todd Dixon

    b. Gianna Sullivan

    c. *(Our Lady of Fatima) - Spoken to three children July 1917*

9. Higher Power- Todd Dixon

10. Written Prophecies in How God Will Save the World- Todd Dixon

11. Hopi Prophecy-from Writings of White Feather

12. Native American

    a. North American: Anishinaabe-Ojibwe- "The Seven Fires"

    b. *"Returning to Spirit and Sacred Law. The Fifth World of Peace is birthing"-Apache*

    c. *Cherokee- "The Rattlesnake Prophecy and the Time of the Beloved Woman".*

13. Mayan Priests

14. Kogi- South America

15. *Q'eros Inca- "Pachakuti*

16. *Australian Aborigine- "The End of the 40,000 year Dreamtime"*

17. *Dogon tribe in western Africa*

18. Nostradamus

19. Edgar Cayce

20. Benu

21. Ruth Montgomery

22. Herbert Benson MD, Harvard Cardiologist and author, article on fear.

BOOKS, ARTICLES AND WEB SITES

1. BBC- newton: the dark heretic

2. The shamanic times-http://theshamanictimes.com/buddhist-indigenous-prophecies-2012.html

3. Catholic Online- Our Lady of Guadalupe-http://www.catholic.org/about/guadalupe.php

4. Http://infallible-catholic.blogspot.com/2012/04/miraculous-image-of-our-lady-of.html

5. FULFILLED PROPHECIES OF THE HOLY QURAN
By Ansar Raza, Canada- https://www.alislam.org/library/articles/prophecies.html

6. CNN- Quake moved Japan coast 8 feet, shifted earth's axis- http://www.cnn.com/2011/WORLD/asiapcf/03/12/japan.earthquake.tsunami.earth/

7. Sir Isaac Newton, Dr. Robert A. Hatch- University of Florida.

8. Bhuddhist Prophecies and the Coming of the Maitraya- http://www.iawwai.com/buddhistprophecies.html

9. Wikipedia
    a. Isaac Newton
    b. Awanyu
    c. Permian-Triassic Extinction Event
    d. 1918 Flu Epidemic
    e. 1964 Alaska Earthquake

10. The Feathered serpent-http://www.atlantisquest.com/Quetzal.html

11. The Mayan Calendar- http://www.webexhibits.org/calendars/calendar-mayan.html

12. Ocean Acidification-http://www.pmel.noaa.gov/co2/story/What+is+Ocean+Acidification%3F

13. What is galactic alignment-http://www.alignment2012.com/whatisga.htm

14. Which modern day countries did the Roman Empire comprise of?-http://www.roman-empire.net/maps/empire/extent/rome-modern-day-nations.html

15. CDC- 2014 Ebola Outbreak West Africa and About Ebola Virus Disease- CDC.gov

16. Aftermath- google books-Solar Meridian crossing galactic equator-https://books.google.com/books?Id=Jf99l5uQqlMC&pg=PP1

4&dq=solar+meridian+crossing+galactic+equator+astronomer+ex
planation&hl=en&sa=X&ei=Jp2cVKejK5SgyASYk4KoAw&ved=
0ccsq6aewaa#v=onepage&q=solar%20meridian%20crossing%20
galactic%20equator%20astronomer%20explanation&f=false

17. History Channel- Black Death- http://www.history.com/
topics/black-death

18. Testimony of the Holy Quran by Hazrat Mirza, Signs of
Last Days- http://www.muslim.org/books/testi-hq/ch2a.htm

19. Edgarcayce.org- http://www.edgarcayce.org/are/blog.aspx?Id=
2863&blogid=445

20. Edgar Cayce on the Future- http://www.near-death.com/
paranormal/edgar-cayce/future.html

21. Nostradamus.org-

22. Earth Magnetic Field Reversal-http://www.pureenergysystems.
com/news/2005/02/27/6900064_Magnet_Pole_Shift/

23. Geodynamo-http://www.es.ucsc.edu/~glatz/geodynamo.html

24. Magnetic Storm- NOVA- http://www.pbs.org/wgbh/nova/mag-
netic/about.html

25. South Atlantic Anomaly- NASA.gov-http://heasarc.gsfc.nasa.gov/
docs/rosat/gallery/display/saa.html
   a. South Atlantic Anomaly-https://en.wikipedia.org/wiki/South_
   Atlantic_Anomaly

26. Babylonian Empire-Livius.org- http://www.livius.org/articles/
place/babylonian-empire/?

27. CLIMATE CHANGE
   a. EPA.gov- https://www3.epa.gov/climatechange/basics
   b. Methane Hydrate Stability and Anthropogenic Climate
   Change; Biosciences- http://www.biogeosciences.net/4/521/
   2007/bg-4-521-2007.html

    c. Global Warming Could Release Permafrost Carbon- Live Science-http://www.livescience.com/807-global-warming-release-permafrost-carbon.html

    d. Global Warming Fast Facts- National Geographic News, June 14, 2007- http://news.nationalgeographic.com/news/2004/12/1206_041206_global_warming.html

    e. Methane Clarate- Wikipedia.org- https://en.wikipedia.org/wiki/Methane_clathrate

    f. Permafrost Melting and Stability of Offshore Methane Hydrates Subject to Global Warming- International Journal of Offshore and Polar Engineering, Vol 4, No. 2, June 1994 (ISSN 1053-5381) Savvas G. Hatzikiriakos and Peter Englezos, University of British Columbia, Vancouver, Canada

    g. Ocean Temperatures Continue to Rise, Climate Researchers Say, by Staff Reports, Friday July 17, 2009, 12.51 PM- http://www.oregonlive.com/news/index.ssf/2009/07/ocean_temperatures_continue_to.html

    h. Scientists Find New Global Warming Threat from Melting Permafrost, USA Today, by Seth Borenstein, Associated Press, USA Today- 9/6/2006 - http://usatoday30.usatoday.com/tech/science/discoveries/2006-09-06-permafrost-warming_x.htm

    i. Thawing Permafrost Likely to Boost Global Warming, New Assessment Concludes, America Institute of Biological Sciences, Sept 2, 2008- https://www.sciencedaily.com/releases/2008/09/080901084854.htm

28. PANGEA- Wikipedia.org
29. EARTHQUAKES-

    a. The Great 1906 San Francisco Earthquake, USGS.gov- http://earthquake.usgs.gov/regional/nca/1906/18april/index.php

30. EDGAR CAYCE- On the Future- http://www.near-death.com/paranormal/edgar-cayce/future.html

31. ALBERT EINSTEIN- BIOGRAPHICAL- Nobelprize.org- http://www.nobelprize.org/nobel_prizes/physics/laureates/1921/einstein-bio.html

32. FALLING STARS-
   a. Asteroid- Wikipedia.org
   b. Dinosaur Killer Asteroid Crater Imaged for First Time, National Geographic News, Thursday, Oct 28, 2010-http://news.nationalgeographic.com/news/2003/03/0307_030307_impactcrater.html
   c. Meteor Explodes Over Canada- Astroengine.com- https://astroengine.com/2008/11/21/asteroid-explodes-over-canada/
   d. Star of Bethlehem- Wikipedia.com- https://en.wikipedia.org/wiki/Star_of_Bethlehem#cite_note-9
   e. Tunguska Event- Wikipedia.org- https://en.wikipedia.org/wiki/Tunguska_event
      1. Tunguska, June 30, 1908 "the sky split in two and fire appeared high and wide over forest."- https://unitedcats.wordpress.com/2008/06/30/tunguska-june-30-1908-the-sky-split-in-two-and-fire-appeared-high-and-wide-over-the-forest/

2. HOPI PROPHECY -
   a. The Hopi Prophecy came from White Feather (Hopi) who spoke to David Young (Minister). These words (prophecy) of White Feather became a published manuscript (Methodist and Presbyterian Churches), some of these prophecies later published by Frank Waters.

Date: December 31, 1993
Source: Book of The Hopi
By: Frank Waters

Source Material by: Oswald White Bear Fredericks
Copyright 1963, by Frank Waters
SBN 345-01717-X-125
Library of Congress Catalog No. 63-19606
Published by: Ballantine Books, Inc.
101 Fifth Ave, New York, N.Y. 10003 Paperback Edition: Page 408

34. ISAAC NEWTON

   a. BBC- Newton: The Dark Heretic; Saturday 1 March, BBC TWO-http://www.bbc.co.uk/pressoffice/pressreleases/stories/2003/02_february/22/newton_2060.shtml

   b. Wikipedia.org

   *c. Sir Isaac Newton, Dr. Robert Hatch- University of Florida-*http://users.clas.ufl.edu/ufhatch/pages/01-Courses/current-courses/08sr-newton.htm

   d. Isaac Newton's Life, Isaac Newton Institute for Mathematical Sciences- http://www.newton.ac.uk/about/isaac-newton/life

   *e. Wolfram Research-*http://scienceworld.wolfram.com/biography/Newton.html

   f. Reformation.org- http://www.reformation.org/newton.html

35. CREATION OF THE STATE OF ISRAEL

   a. Creation of State of Israel, ADL.org- http://archive.adl.org/israel/record/creation.html

   b. Formation of Israel-http://www.theocracywatch.org/christian_zionism_israel_forms.htm

36. PLAGUES

   a. CDC- CDC.gov

   b. Black Death, Wikipedia- https://en.wikipedia.org/wiki/Black_Death

   c. Malaria, CDC.gov

   d. Influenza Pandemic, Wikipedia; https://en.wikipedia.org/wiki/Influenza_pandemic

  e. Pandemic- Wikipedia
  f. Influenza- Flu.gov
  g. Plagues and Epidemics- http://theplumber.com/plagues-epidemics/
  h. Influenza Pandemic of 1918, Stanford.edu- http://virus.stanford.edu/uda/index.html
  i. The Black Death, 1348- Eyewitness to History.com- http://www.eyewitnesstohistory.com/plague.htm

37. POLLUTION
  a. Pollution Facts, Worstpolluted.org- http://www.worstpolluted.org/pollution-facts-2009.html

38. RAPTURE
  a. The Dispensational Origins of Moern Premillennialism and John Nelson Darby by Jack Van Deventer- http://www.sullivan-county.com/news/cathouse/darby.htm

39. VOLCANOES
  a. Mt. St. Helens- http://www.olywa.net/radu/valerie/sthelens.html
  b. Volcanic Ash Impacts and Mitigation- USGS.gov- https://volcanoes.usgs.gov/volcanic_ash/

Figures

1. "The State of Israel Is Born." *The Palestine Post* [Jerusalem] 14 May 1948: n. pag. Web.
2. *The Fall of the Berlin Wall, 1989.* 1989. Senate of Berlin, Berlin. *Wikipedia.* Web. <https://en.wikipedia.org/wiki/Berlin_Wall#/media/File:Thefalloftheberlinwall1989.JPG>.
3. Aleksandrowicz, Frank John. *Air Pollution.* 1973. National Archives, Washington, D.C. *New York Times Green Blog.* Web.

<Frank Aleksandrowicz/Documerica: view of Cleveland captured in 1973>.

4. Stöckli, Reto. *The Blue Marble*. 2002. Visible Earth, NASA Goddard Space Flight Center. *NASA Visible Earth*. Web. <http://visibleearth.nasa.gov/view.php?id=57723>.

5. DeLange, Audrey, and George DeLange. *Aztec Calendar Stone*. 2005. *Wikimedia Commons*. Web. <https://commons.wikimedia.org/wiki/File:Aztec_calendar_stone.jpg>.

6. Wobble of a Spinning Top

7. Wobble of Planet Earth- Todd Dixon MD 2016

8. Precession-Earth's Axis Rotation Through Thirteen Constellations- Todd Dixon MD 2016

9. Jurvetson, Steve. *Milky Way in the Night Sky*. 2007. Melno Park. *Wikimedia Commons*. Web. <https://commons.wikimedia.org/wiki/File:Milky_Way_Night_Sky_Black_Rock_Desert_Nevada.jpg>.

10. The Sacred Cross- Todd Dixon MD 2016

11. Eddo. *Quetzalcoatl, God of Wisdom*. Digital image. *Wikimedia Commons*. Wikipedia, 1 Jan. 2011. Web. <https://commons.wikimedia.org/wiki/File:Quetzalcoatl.svg>.

12. Los Alamos National Labratory. *Rock Art at Tsirege Depicting Awanyu*. Digital image. *Wikimedia Commons*. Wikipedia, 5 July 2009. Web. <https://commons.wikimedia.org/wiki/File:Tsirege_Petroglyph_depicting_Awanyu.jpg>.

13. *1918 Spanish Influenza Ward at Camp Funston, Kansas*. 1918. National Museum of Health and Medicine, Washington, D.C. *Wikimedia Commons*. Web. <https://commons.wikimedia.org/wiki/File:CampFunstonKS-InfluenzaHospital.jpg>.

14. "Mapa Del Confín Del Imperio Romano." *Wikimedia Commons*. N.p., n.d. Web. <https://commons.wikimedia.org/wiki/File:Mapa_del_Conf%C3%ADn_del_Imperio_Romano.gif>.

15. Awalt, Jesse B. *Muammar Al-Gaddafi at the 12th AU Summit.* Digital image. *Defense Imagery Management Operations Center.* United States Navy, 2 Feb. 2009. Web. <https://commons.wiki-media.org/wiki/File:Muammar_al-Gaddafi_at_the_AU_summit.jpg>.

16. "Indian Reservations in the Continental United States." *Bureau of Indian Affairs.* Print.

17. United States Geological Survey. "Plate Tectonics." *United States Geological Survey.* Web. <http://pubs.usgs.gov/gip/dynamic/slabs.html>.

18. Stoffer, Phil. "Physiographic Provinces Map of California (With Geology)." *Geology Cafe.* Web. <http://geologycafe.com/california/maps/provinces1.htm>.

19. Genthe, Arnold. *San Francisco Earthquake of 1906.* Digital image. *Wikimedia Commons.* Wikipedia, 21 Jan. 2010. Web. <https://commons.wikimedia.org/wiki/File:San_Francisco_Fire_Sacramento_Street_1906-04-18.jpg>.

20. Shaman Vision of the Remaining Golden Gate Bridge after San Francisco Sinks into the Ocean from a Major Earthquake- Todd Dixon MD 2016

21. United States Geological Survey. "Cascadia Earthquake Sources." *Western Region Geologic Information Server.* Web. <http://wrgis.wr.usgs.gov/wgmt/pacnw/pacnweq/casceq.html>.

22. Reinhardt, John. *Mt. Vesuvius Eruption, 1944.* Digital image. *Wikimedia Commons.* Wikipedia, 13 Oct. 2007. Web. <https://en.wikipedia.org/wiki/Mount_Vesuvius#/media/File:Mt_Vesuvius_Erupting_1944.jpg>.

23. Lancevortex. *Pompeii Garden of the Fugitives.* Digital image. *Wikimedia Commons.* Wikipedia, 30 Jan. 2000. Web. <https://en.wikipedia.org/wiki/Pompeii#/media/File:Pompeii_Garden_of_the_Fugitives_02.jpg>.

24. United States Geological Survey. *Mount St. Helens Eruption.* Digital image. *PBS Newshour.* NewsHour Productions LLC, 17 May 2015. Web. <http://www.pbs.org/newshour/rundown/lessons-learned-35-years-since-1980-eruption-mount-st-helens/>.

25. Ernst, Michael. "Antarctic Temperatures vs. CO2 Concentrations Over 400,000 Years." *UT News.* Web. <http://news.utexas.edu/2010/11/17/humans-now-steer-climate-bus>.

26. Yellowstone Caldera- A Super Volcano (Image courtesy US Geological Survey)

27. The Kuiper Belt (from NASA.gov) http://www.space.com/16144-kuiper-belt-objects.html

28. Mdf. "Inner Solar System." *Wikimedia Commons.*Web.
    a. <https://en.wikipedia.org/wiki/Asteroid_belt#/media/File:InnerSolarSystem-en.png>.

29. Revera, Gregory H. *Full Moon.* Digital image. *Wikimedia Commons.* Wikipedia, 22 Oct. 2010. Web. <https://en.wikipedia.org/wiki/Moon#/media/File:FullMoon2010.jpg>.

30. Cburnett. *Panoramic Image of Meteor Crater.* Digital image. *Wikimedia Commons.* Wikipedia, 26 May 2007. Web. <https://en.wikipedia.org/wiki/Meteor_Crater#/media/File:Barringer_Crater_panoramic.jpg>.

31. Weaver, H., and E. Smith. *Comet Schumacher-Levy 9 Breaks into 21 Fragments.* Digital image. *Wikimedia Commons.* Wikipedia, 24 May 2005. Web. <https://en.wikipedia.org/wiki/Comet_Shoemaker%E2%80%93Levy_9#/media/File:Shoemaker-Levy_9_on_1994-05-17.png>.

32. Comet Schumacher Levy 9 Collides with Jupiter (Image ifa.hawaii.edu)
    a. http://www.ifa.hawaii.edu/images/sl9/jup0613.gif
    b. http://www.ifa.hawaii.edu/images/sl9/

33. di Bondone, Giotto. *Adoration of the Magi.* ~1300s. Fresco. Scrovegni Chapel, Padua, Veneto, Italy.

34. "World Population: 1950-2050." *U.S. Census Bureau.* 27 Sept 2016. Web. <http://www.census.gov/population/international/data/idb/worldpopgraph.php>.

35. "Locations of Geomagnetic Poles and Magnetic Poles." *Data Analysis Center for Geomagnetism and Space Magnetism.* Web. <http://wdc.kugi.kyoto-u.ac.jp/poles/polesexp.html>.

36. Cavit. "Magnetic North Pole Positions of the Earth." *Wikimedia Commons.* Web. <https://commons.wikimedia.org/wiki/File:Magnetic_North_Pole_Positions_2015.svg>.

37. Earth's Surface Magnetic Field- Image by Todd Dixon MD 2016

38. Earth's Core Magnetic Field- Image by Todd Dixon MD 2016

39. Layers of the Earth- Asthenosphere is Flowing Molten Rock and Not Rigid (Image from Wikipedia.com)
    a. https://en.wikipedia.org/wiki/Asthenosphere#/media/File:Earth-cutaway-schematic-english.svg

40. A drawing of Ezekiel's Temple by Henry Sulley (Wikipedia.com)
    a. https://en.wikipedia.org/wiki/Henry_Sulley

41. Shiva, Andrew. *The Dome of the Rock.* Digital image. *Wikimedia Commons.* Wikipedia, 13 Nov. 2013. Web. <https://en.wikipedia.org/wiki/Dome_of_the_Rock#/media/File:Israel-2013(2)-Jerusalem-View_of_the_Dome_of_the_Rock_%26_Temple_Mount_02.jpg>.

42. Clothes Fall Off as Synthetic Materials Fall Apart- Todd Dixon MD 2016

43. Zatko, Jan. *Our Lady of Guadalupe, Mexico City.* Digital image. *Wikimedia Commons.* Wikipedia, 16 Mar. 2005. Web. <https://commons.wikimedia.org/wiki/File:Our_Lady_of_Guadalupe.JPG>.

44. Close up Image Our Lady of Guadalupe (Photo by Lyricmac)

a. https://en.wikipedia.org/wiki/Our_Lady_of_Guadalupe#/media/File:El_Rostro_de_la_Virgen.jpg

45. Bramley, Barrington. *Portrait of Isaac Newton*. 1992. Oil on canvas. Institute for Mathematical Sciences, University of Cambridge.

46. Mahatma Gandhi (Public Domain)

a. https://en.wikipedia.org/wiki/Mahatma_Gandhi#/media/File:Portrait_Gandhi.jpg

TABLES

1. "Fear vs. Love Chart" Todd Dixon MD

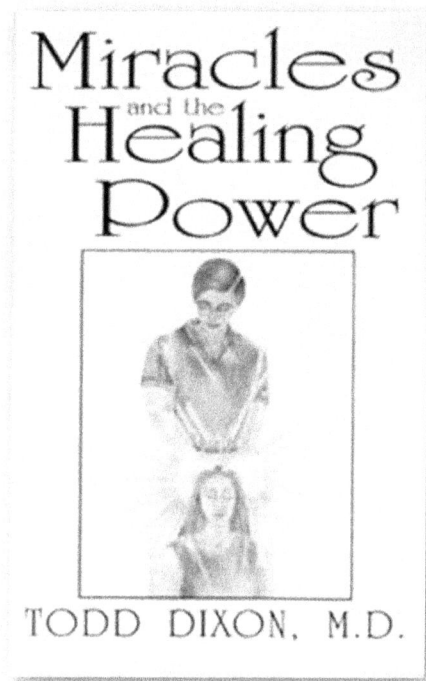

Miracles and the Healing Power

TODD DIXON, M.D.

IN A QUIET residential neighborhood outside a major metropolitan city lives a woman with an extraordinary gift. She is performing miracles. She has cured cancer, hepatitis, infertility and hundreds of other diseases. I verified many of these miracles. This book is about her, the people she has healed and the force behind her miracles.

This book will introduce you to a power that you may tap into for your own health and well-being. I believe the most powerful tool to cure disease is modern day medical technology combined with the healing power. With this combination, there is no disease that cannot be cured, no illness cannot be overcome. This power can be harnessed for the benefit of all mankind. I believe it is time.

Todd Dixon MD

This book can be purchased on Amazon.com

345

www.ingramcontent.com/pod-product-compliance
Lightning Source LLC
LaVergne TN
LVHW051450080426
835509LV00017B/1723